DREAMS
OF THE
RAREBIT
FIEND

WINSOR McCAY

DOVER PUBLICATIONS, INC., NEW YORK

This Dover edition, first published in 1973, is a republication of the work originally published by the Frederick A. Stokes Company, New York, in 1905. The final page has been omitted here. The present edition contains a new Publisher's Note and additional illustrations. For further bibliographical information see the Publisher's Note, especially page xiii.

The publisher is grateful to the Library of the University of Illinois (Franklin J. Meine American Humor and Folklore Collection) for making its copy of the book available for reproduction.

International Standard Book Number: 0-486-21347-1
Library of Congress Catalog Card Number: 73-75868

Manufactured in the United States of America
Dover Publications, Inc.
31 East 2nd Street, Mineola, N.Y. 11501

PUBLISHER'S NOTE

Winsor McCay

The outstanding American graphic artist Winsor Zenic McCay was born in Spring Lake, Michigan, on September 26, 1869 (1871 has also been given as his birth year). Spring Lake was in a heavily forested area; McCay's father was a lumber mill worker. As a boy McCay was already constantly drawing. He received some rudimentary art instruction from a teacher in Ypsilanti named Goodeson, who placed great stress on the rendering of perspective—a most important element in McCay's mature art. Another lasting stimulus to his imagination was his circus experience: at the age of 17 he traveled to Chicago with a circus and designed advertisements for the company. In Chicago he had some more art lessons and earned his living by drawing signs and posters. He was about 19 when he made the first of the two decisive moves in his life—to Cincinnati.

There McCay settled down, marrying a debutante in 1891; there his son Winsor, Jr., and his daughter were born. He was employed by the business-man Philip Morton as a "scenic artist." Apparently his chief duty was to design posters for the sideshow attractions in Morton's Dime Museum; his small studio was located over that establishment. When Morton received contracts for grandiose temporary constructions to celebrate American victories in the 1898 war, McCay designed the huge street arches and reconstituted the battle of Santiago harbor on the Ohio River.

By the end of the century McCay had begun his journalistic career. After illustrating news stories for the *Times-Star* and doing a number of success-ful pro-Republican cartoons for the *Commercial Gazette*, he was hired by the larger *Enquirer* to draw pro-Democrat cartoons. (Throughout his life, it was hard to pin down McCay's political affiliations, though in his later years he was pretty clearly a conservative and isolationist.) Once on the staff of the *Enquirer*, McCay contributed many sorts of drawings, finally becoming art director and supplying the art for a strip, *Jungle Imps* (also influential in his later work), which was written by the paper's Sunday editor, George Randolph Chester. The *Imps* appeared from January through November of 1903.

During these years McCay also had cartoons published in magazines. Some of his work that appeared in the humor magazine *Life* in 1902 caught

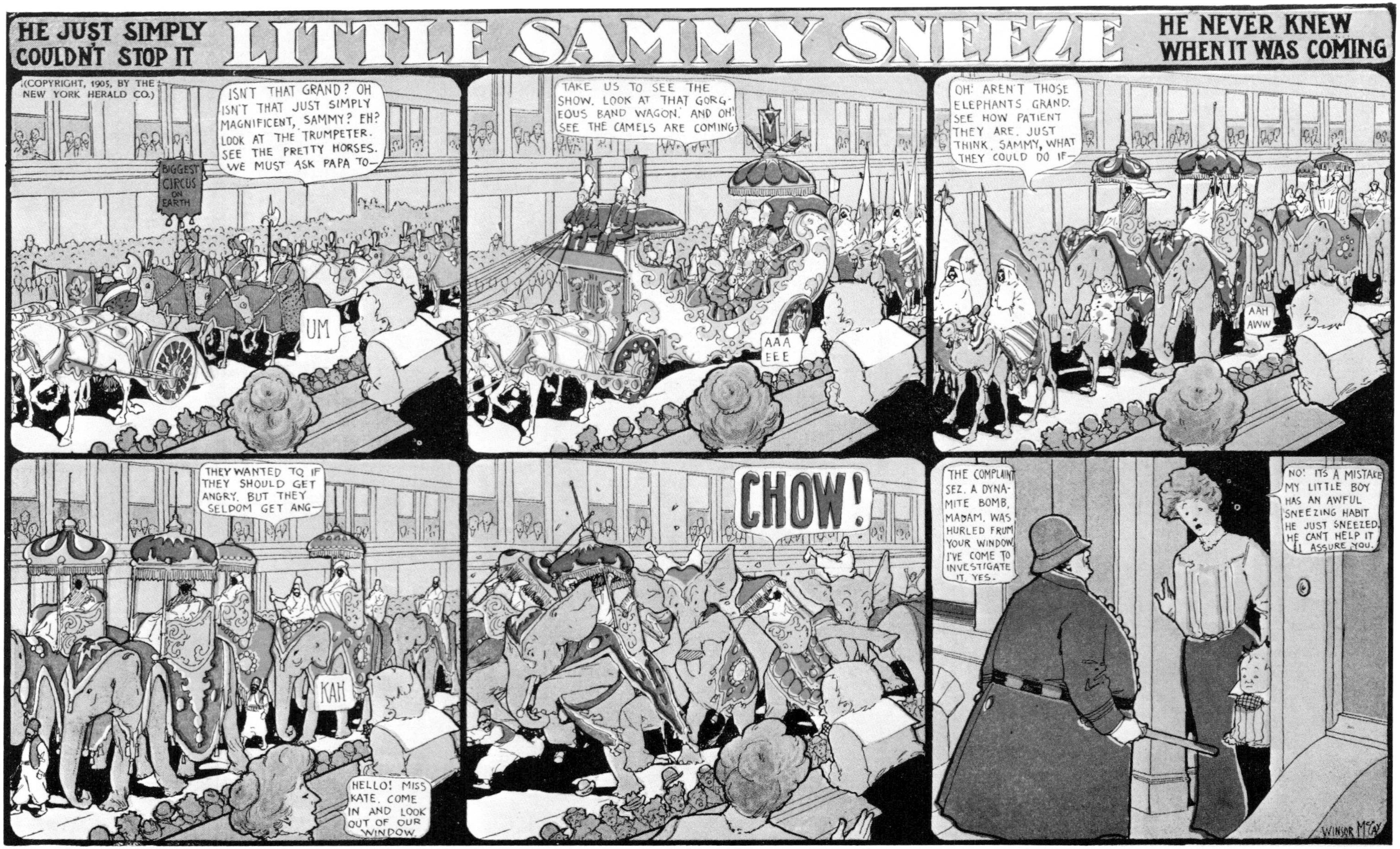
HE JUST SIMPLY COULDN'T STOP IT
LITTLE SAMMY SNEEZE
HE NEVER KNEW WHEN IT WAS COMING
(COPYRIGHT, 1905, BY THE NEW YORK HERALD CO.)
ISN'T THAT GRAND? OH ISN'T THAT JUST SIMPLY MAGNIFICENT, SAMMY? EH? LOOK AT THE TRUMPETER. SEE THE PRETTY HORSES. WE MUST ASK PAPA TO—
BIGGEST CIRCUS ON EARTH
UM
TAKE US TO SEE THE SHOW. LOOK AT THAT GORGEOUS BAND WAGON! AND OH! SEE THE CAMELS ARE COMING.
AAA EEE
OH! AREN'T THOSE ELEPHANTS GRAND. SEE HOW PATIENT THEY ARE. JUST THINK, SAMMY, WHAT THEY COULD DO IF—
AAH AWW
THEY WANTED TO IF THEY SHOULD GET ANGRY. BUT THEY SELDOM GET ANG—
KAH
HELLO! MISS KATE. COME IN AND LOOK OUT OF OUR WINDOW.
CHOW!
THE COMPLAINT SEZ, A DYNAMITE BOMB, MADAM, WAS HURLED FRUM YOUR WINDOW. I'VE COME TO INVESTIGATE IT, YES.
NO! ITS A MISTAKE MY LITTLE BOY HAS AN AWFUL SNEEZING HABIT HE JUST SNEEZED. HE CANT HELP IT I ASSURE YOU.
WINSOR McCAY

Fig. 1: A sequence from McCay's *Little Sammy Sneeze* (1905).

the eye of James Gordon Bennett, publisher of the *New York Herald*, who invited McCay to work for him in New York. Though sorry to leave Cincinnati, which he considered his home and which he was always glad to revisit in later years, McCay could hardly turn down the salary and prestige Bennett was offering.

In New York, where he arrived at the end of 1903, he became a staff illustrator on Bennett's *Evening Telegram*, soon graduating to comic strips for that paper and eventually for the glorious morning *Herald* itself. Among the many strips and series McCay worked on during his eight years with Bennett were *Dull Care, Poor Jake, The Man from Montclair, The Faithful Employee, Mr. Bosh, A Pilgrim's Progress, Midsummer Day Dreams* and *It's Nice To Be Married*. Two strips that were more important were based on the foibles of unusual children. *Little Sammy Sneeze* made his first appearance in the *Herald* in September 1904, before McCay had been in New York a year. In each sequence this little boy's cataclysmic sternutations brought some proceedings to a sudden halt (see Figure 1, which features the recurring McCay theme of the circus parade). *Hungry Henrietta*, heroine of a strip that ran for the first few months of 1905, was a ravenous infant.

That year, 1905, was to be a magical one for McCay. It saw the beginning of *Dreams of the Rarebit Fiend,* the subject of the present volume, in the *Evening Telegram*, and—in the October 15 issue of the Sunday *Herald*—the birth of *Little Nemo in Slumberland*, McCay's masterpiece and, in the opinion of many judges, the supreme all-time masterpiece of the comic strip considered as graphic art. This is not the place for an extended appreciation of *Little Nemo*, which has frequently been reprinted in larger or smaller selections and even more frequently discussed in books and magazines. *Little Nemo*, though based directly on the oneiric atmosphere of the *Rarebit Fiend*, developed into a continuous story (whereas each *Fiend* sequence is self-contained) and made much more use of architectural and other settings in the artwork (whereas the *Fiend* has minimal settings).

The extreme popularity of the *Rarebit Fiend* and *Little Nemo* (information on stage and film tie-ins is given below) led the artist on to further activities. In 1907 he toured major cities east of the Mississippi on a vaudeville circuit, doing two 20-minute acts of chalk talks and lightning sketches daily and continuing to draw his various newspaper strips in his hotel rooms. In New York he shared a vaudeville bill with Houdini and W. C. Fields.

By 1909 McCay was already at work on animated cartoons, beginning with a version of *Little Nemo*. Though J. Stuart Blackton in America and Emile Cohl in France had preceded him in this line, McCay's *Gertie the Dinosaur* was the first widely popular animated cartoon in history (see Figure 2). He toured with *Gertie,* accompanying its projection in theaters with his live commentary. Between 1910 and 1917 he drew several more films of 4,000 to 10,000 frames each, all humorous. In 1918, he did one of 25,000 frames—apparently the first anywhere of such length—*The Sinking of the Lusitania.* His last animation, *The Flying House,* was produced in 1920. He continued to show his cartoons in personal vaudeville appearances in the 20's.

Meanwhile he had left Bennett for Hearst in 1911. He continued the adventures of Little Nemo for three or four more years (as *In the Land of Wonderful Dreams*), but for Hearst he chiefly did editorial cartoons. In 1924 he switched to the *Herald-Tribune,* where he revived *Little Nemo* for a little while. Returning to Hearst, he reverted to daily political cartoons and large Sunday drawings to accompany the conservative editorials of Arthur Brisbane. These drawings were all too often bloodless allegories, conspicuously labeled, but the draftsmanship was consistently fine.

McCay also did some advertising art anonymously in the 20's and 30's. He kept on working steadily until his sudden death on July 26, 1934.*

* The publisher is grateful to Mr. Gary Silver of San Francisco for his permission to make free use in the present note of information he has collected on the life of Winsor McCay.

Fig. 2: Winsor McCay showing his creation Gertie the Dinosaur to the cartoonist George McManus and others at a dinner party. (Courtesy The Museum of Modern Art/Film Stills Archive)

Dreams of the Rarebit Fiend

In the comparative study of comics in general and McCay's work in particular, the *Rarebit Fiend* is perhaps chiefly significant as a "dry run" for *Little Nemo;* it already has the dream (or nightmare) situation, the awakening at the end of each sequence, the distortion of sizes, shapes and ages, the airship, the cannibals (descendants of the Cincinnati *Jungle Imps*), the large figures bestriding and damaging cities (precursors of King Kong) and even such specific pre-echoes of *Nemo* as the Santa Claus icicle. But the *Fiend* fully deserves attention in its own right; it is highly amusing in itself, and it has unique features that do not recur in *Nemo*.

How did the strip originate? As usual in such matters, there are conflicting reports. Gary Silver states that the *Fiend* was suggested to McCay "in a little café off Herald Square by a rotund gentleman who had indulged too freely of Welsh rabbits." McCay himself, in a 1907 newspaper interview (which also clears up the mystery of his signature "Silas"), gave the following story:

> "The Dream of the Rarebit Fiend" is an evolution of a drawing I made for the New York Telegram two years ago. . . . You know how a cigaret fiend is when he gets up in the morning and can't find a dope stick? Well, I drew a picture once showing a fiend at the north pole without a cigaret and about ready to die. I introduced some other characters who happened to have paper and tobacco and a match, but the only match went out before they got a light. Then I had to frame up a finish and I made it a dream. My employer suggested that I make him a series of pictures and make them as rarebit dreams and you know the result. . . . You will notice that I sign . . . my rarebit pictures "Silas." Well, my contract would not allow me to sign my real name when I started to draw those pictures for the New York papers and I had to make a name. An old fellow who drives a garbage cart by the New York Herald office every day is my namesake. He is a quaint character and known as Silas. I just borrowed his name. . . . As for "Little Nemo," that is an idea I got from the "Rarebit Fiend" to please the little folk.

The last sentence in this quotation points up the basic difference in content between *Nemo* and the *Fiend*. The latter is mainly for grown-ups. Not only does the emphasis on death and disfigurement make the *Fiend* an early monument of "cruel" or "sick" humor; the dream fantasies that McCay taps so unerringly are those of little boys in *Nemo* (giants, masquerades, fantastic travel adventures, "dreams of glory" in the Steig sense—wishes, fears and frustrations tailored to a child's size), but generally those of adults in the *Fiend* (embarrassment through nudity, transvestism, inability to perform occupational duties or having a peccadillo discovered; loss of identity; fear of dying, going mad or disappointing a sex partner).

Figure 3

Figure 4

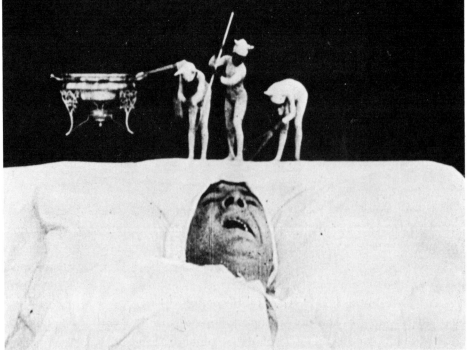

Figs. 3–6: Stills from Porter's film *The Dream of a Rarebit Fiend* (1906), based on McCay's strip. (Courtesy The Museum of Modern Art/Film Stills Archive)

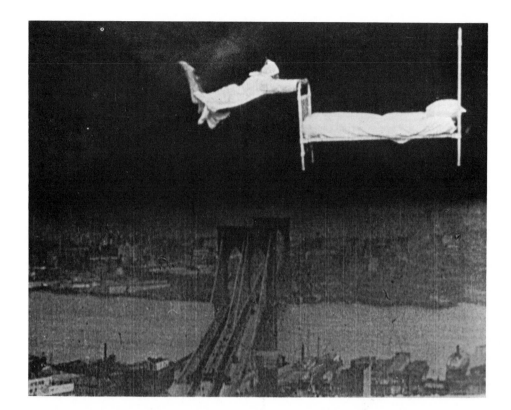

Figure 5

Figure 6

Naturally the *Fiend* also includes the anxiety dreams and wish-fulfillment fantasies that children and adults share. Curiously, in some of the sequences the dreamer is merely the sympathetic spectator of embarrassment suffered by someone near and dear. In a couple of other instances McCay seems to be making free use of the general dream theme of his strip, abandoning the nightmares imputed to the welsh rabbit (and the whole midnight supper) for grandiose success dreams more closely associated with opium.

The series contains several amusing references to current events in New York and elsewhere. The *Fiend* cityscape includes two then-new buildings, the 1902 Flatiron and the 1904 St. Regis Hotel (masquerading as the "St. Ragis"). The Russo-Japanese war of 1904/05 and the revolutionary turmoil in Russia in 1905 are both alluded to, as are the American elections of 1904, in which Theodore Roosevelt defeated Alton Brooks Parker.

As for the sources of the *Fiend* (other than the earlier work of McCay himself already mentioned), they are numerous and varied. In his admirable introduction to the French edition of the largest book publication of *Little Nemo* (published by Pierre Horay in association with Garzanti, 1969), Claude Moliterni mentions numerous publications of the period, ephemeral and otherwise, that concerned humorous dreams, all of which were likely to be familiar to McCay. It might be added that the flood of perspiration in one *Fiend* sequence is closely related to the pool of tears in *Alice in Wonderland*. Moreover, an important possible influence on McCay that has never yet been emphasized is that of Gelett Burgess. The Boston humorist's verbal and visual whimsies collected in *The Burgess Nonsense Book* in 1901 included people stuck in glue, a giant horse wrecking the roofs of houses, a man walking on people's heads and other motifs that recur in the *Fiend*.

The years around the turn of the century witnessed a lively interplay of the various arts of entertainment, and the comics were not neglected. By 1900 Blackton had already made live-action films based on Frederick Burr Opper's strip *Happy Hooligan*. There was a musical comedy based on Schultze's *Foxy Grandpa* in 1902, and one celebrating Richard Outcault's *Buster Brown* in 1905. Then in 1908 Master Gabriel, the midget who portrayed Buster Brown, created the title role in the musical *Little Nemo*, which boasted a Victor Herbert score. We have already noted McCay's animation of *Little Nemo* in 1909; he was to animate the *Fiend* (as *The Adventures of a Rarebit Eater*) in 1916/17. But it was another film that was to help immortalize the *Fiend* strip.

In 1906 the outstanding American pioneer filmmaker Edwin S. Porter, who worked for the Edison Company, created a seven-minute live-action trick film that remains a classic of the early cinema: *The Dream of a Rarebit Fiend*, based directly on McCay's strip. The role of the fiend was played by John P. Brawn. The stills in Figures 3–6 illustrate various moments of the plot: the reeling world of the homeward bound carouser, the chafing-dish imps tormenting him in his bed, the giddy flight of the bed through the night sky, and his landing on a steeple. The resemblance to the McCay sequence on page 13 is unmistakable. (In *Les Pionniers du cinéma 1897–1909,* the second volume of his monumental *Histoire générale du cinéma,* Georges Sadoul mentions some cinematic antecedents of this film, including the British director Cecil Hepworth's *The Glutton's Nightmare* of 1901.)

In 1907 another related Edison product was issued: a cylinder recording (Edison 9585) of the Edison Military Band playing a piece called "Dream of the Rarebit Fiend" (available on LP in Folkways' *Phono-Cylinders,* Vol. I, 1961, FS 3886). It is highly probable that this music was written in conjunction with the Edison film, perhaps to be performed along with the projection in first-run theaters. The main theme of the witty, burlesque-sinister march is:

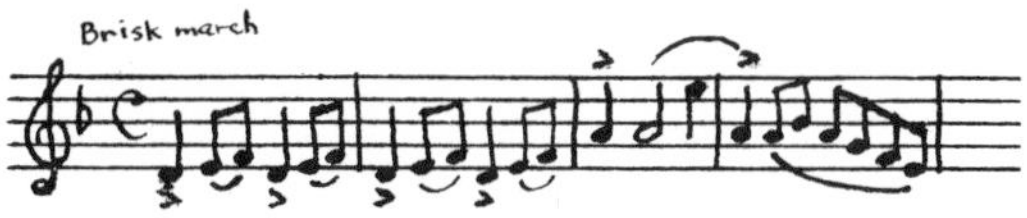
Brisk march

Sixty-one sequences of the *Fiend* were issued in book form by Frederick A. Stokes (a publisher who served the cause of humorous art well) as early as 1905, the year in which the strip first appeared. It is this book publication that is here reprinted. The final sequence (self-contained and involving no other part of the book) has been omitted in the present edition, since it was felt that its minority-group humor, though innocent and acceptable in its own age of "rugged individualism," was unpalatable today. All the rest is here for your enjoyment—in a ten-percent enlargement for greater legibility.

DREAMS
OF THE
RAREBIT
FIEND

DREAMS OF THE

RAREBIT FIEND

THE HAPPY CREATIONS WHICH APPEAR INSIDE ARE THE REPRODUCTIONS OF A COMIC SERIES NOW RUNNING IN *THE NEW YORK EVENING TELEGRAM*. THEY HAVE CAUSED MANY PEOPLE TO LAUGH AND SOME, PERCHANCE, TO WEEP; FOR IT FREQUENTLY HAPPENS THAT IS ONE MAN'S FOOD IS ANOTHER'S POISON. NEVERTHELESS, THE POPULARITY OF THIS SERIES HAS SO GROWN AND THE MANIFESTATIONS OF APPROVAL HAVE BECOME SO NUMEROUS, ALONG WITH A SUGGESTION THAT THE CREATIONS BE GIVEN SOME PERMANENT FORM THAT, *THE NEW YORK EVENING TELEGRAM* HAS GENEROUSLY PERMITTED THE AUTHOR AND PUBLISHER TO MAKE THE BOOK POSSIBLE. THE VERY VITALITY OF THE SERIES LIES IN THE PUBLIC'S APPRECIATION, AND, GROUNDED ON THIS FACT, THE PRESENT VOLUME IS SUBMITTED FOR FURTHER APPROVAL.

WINSOR McCAY "SILAS"

RAREBIT SYMBOLISM

IT IS NO HUMORIST'S FANCY THAT THE RAREBIT IS A THING OF DREAMS. CLOTHED IN GOLD AND BREATHING A FRAGRANCE THAT FILLS THE NOSTRILS WITH A CHARM MORE BEWITCHING THAN WOODLAND ODERS, IT IS, TO A SOUL ATTUNED TO IT'S BEAUTIES, A THING OF GLORIOUS REVERIE BY DAY AND MATCHLESS DREAMS BY NIGHT. MELLOWED BY THE SOUL OF GOOD OLD ALE, EMBODYING THE SUN-HUED PRODUCT OF GENEROUS DARIES, IT SYMBOLIZES AT ONCE BOTH THE CITY AND THE COUNTRY. IT IS THE TOKEN OF GENEROSITY, OF FRIENDSHIP, AND CLUB-SHIP. AND WHEREVER MEN HAVE GATHERED TO EAT AND DRINK AND ENJOY THAT BROADENING AND GENTLE INTERCOURSE THAT GOES WITH DINNING, THE RAREBIT IS A SYMBOL WITH WHICH TO CONJURE.

IT IS THE INSPIRATION OF THE POET AND MEN ARE BETTER BECAUSE IT HAS BEEN CREATED. NO BARD CAN ADEQUATELY SING ITS SONG FOR IT IS DEEP AS HUMAN NATURE AND AS BROAD AS THE WORLD. AS IT'S INGREDIENTS BLEND INTO A HARMONIOUS WHOLE, WITH CREAMY RYTHM AND CULINARY CADENCE, LIKE AN EXQUISITE POEM, IT EXEMPLIFIES IT'S MISSION ON EARTH.

IF IT TRAIL IT'S GOLDEN GARMENTS INTO DREAMS AND OPENS UP A WONDERLAND IN THE SPACE THAT LIES BETWEEN SLEEPING AND WAKING, THEN INDEED SHOULD WE FEEL BLESSED. AND YET, WHO SHALL MURMUR IF, LIKE THE LEGENDARY SUCCUBUS, IT COME TO US IN THE MYSTERIOUS GLOOM OF SLEEP TO ENFOLD US WITH IT'S CLINGING ARMS, BREATHING IT'S ODERS ON OUR LIPS, AND, KISSING US, MAKE US FEEL HOW FUTILE ARE ALL OTHER THINGS IN LIFE!

IT'S GLORY WILL NEVER FADE. IT'S CHARM WILL GROW AS THE HEART OF MAN HAS GROWN IN HUMANITY AND FELLOWSHIP, AND WHO KNOWS BUT IN TIME THE RAREBIT MAY STAND AS A SYMBOL OF THE VERY FELLOWSHIP OF MAN?

RANDOLPH C. LEWIS.

ON THE HISTORY OF THE WELSH RABBIT

At the outset of a treatise which has for it's purpose a historical inquiry into this important subject, it should be made plain, that we are to treat of the WELSH RABBIT,[1] not of the Welsh "rarebit" or the rara bit or the rare-a-bit[2] or anything else that has more than one "r" to it's name. "Rabbit" it was when first it attained it's place in history and "rabbit" it continued until a cabal, sometime supposed to have been the same that made it "keramics" and "Vogner" and "one's s-self" foisted the anaemic title on an unwitting world.

The origin of the Welsh rabbit is so ancient that in tracing it we cross the boundary of authentic history into the territory of legend. By some it is asserted that it was an ancient Druidical conception, members of this faction going so far as to say they have in spirit participated at sacrifices in the ceremonies of which it played an important part[3] Others trace it to a fire in a cheese factory near the village of Swythyfllyn in the Fourth Century, where a fireman found in what was thought to be a menace to his life a delectable incident of the conflagration[4]

It is believed by many that Gambricus, the Roman historian who accompanied the Roman invasion of Great Britain, 68 A.D. referred to the Welsh Rabbit in one incident since republished.* Then did the Romas uttering a great shout dash upon the walls and ramparts at the evening hour. So quickly did they attack, that the Walesmen either threw away their arms in flight or suffered themselves to be made hostages. When the Romans had entered the city they found the Wales to have abandoned their evening meal which they had been about to eat. Then the Romans singing songs of victory sat themselves down to this evening meal which consisted of one dish of the consistency of thickened megathlem, of the color of gold, of which one strand did suffer itself to be lengthened as a bow string, easily twined into the long hair of the heavy fighting men.

"When it had come the middle watch of the night, there arose from all parts of the Roman camp a great outcry, many calling for a libation to Jupiter, declared the gods had brought to them a vision their mothers-in-law; their creditors or else had put them to the performance of strange labors and tortures."[5] It was known to the ancient Welsh bards. The manuscript verses of Morgan ap-Swylswlysen preserved in the Bodelain liabary at Oxford, contain one metrical reference to it beginning; "Yspyluw-Slanthu ystv." It was known to Shakespeare[6] It was a staple artical of diet at the old Mermaid Tavern, the Mitre and the Cheshire Cheese. Poets and men of letters of the Victorian era flourished on it[7] and today its use[8] has become almost universal[9]

REFERENCES FOR THIS TREATISE.
1 - "Wild Animals I have met."
2 - Journal of the Massachusetts Historical Society. 1871 - pp 9 - 1456
3 - "Gimblentz's "Ancient Interior Decorating." Fox's Book of Martyrs"
4 - Annals of the Welsh Underwriters Association.
5 - Gibbon's - "Rise and Fall of the Roman Empire."
6 - Clarence in the Tower: Oh I have spent a miserable night.
7 - The Dream of Eugene Aram
8 - Report Allied Boards of Foreign Missions.
9 - See any bill of fare.

T. B. HANLY

CONCERNING THE SYMPTOMS

Careful investigation of the physiological effects of rarebits points to the conclusion that their power in producing dreams is in direct proportion to their tensile strength. The symtoms of rarebit eating may be seen in traveling about a great city at the after theatre supper hour. Many of the victims show a ruddy countenance. a confused method of locomotion and a feverish condition of their vocabularies. Others develope a dull and sodden lethargy and boast that the rubber like substance which they have eaten will hurt no one.

Study of one thousand and one cases made under the supervision of a staff of physicians connected with the Physchopathic Ward of Bellevue Hospital developed astonishing scientific results. All of the victims upon their arrival at the institution were put in strait jackets and manacles and tightly strapped to their beds. Smitherson's patent Revograph was applied in each case and the pictures of the dreams experienced by each patient were magnified and thrown upon large white sheets, placed at the end of the beds in the thoroughly darkened ward. In the interests of science, as well as in corroboration of the explorations made by Mr. M^CAy it must be said that in all but three cases, the rarebit eaters were troubled by visions of a distressing nature. Armadilloes, red serpents, green street cars, and innumerable objects were portrayed upon the screens as they passed through the disordered faculties of the dreamers. Casein poisoning is a recognized scientific fact.

In the three cases which showed immunity from the effects of the deadly agglomeration of cheese and ale, postmortem examinations of the pasts of the patients were made. It would, of course hardly agree with professional ethics to give the names of the sufferers. I may, however, mention the case of Mr. D, a person of methodical habits who at precisely the hour of twelve thirty P.M, each day went to a certain chop house for Luncheon. He was in constant contemplation of sundry bills representing the annual purchase of cheese made by the proprietor, and within reach of the place. where the golden ingots of molten gastritis were run into the delft molds. Although Mr. D was not habitually addicted to the practice of rarebit eating he had obtained the mental concept by daily reading of the bills that the substance was good for him and the fumes of the cooking had year after year thoroughly permeated his system. He ate sparingly of a rarebit on one accasion and showed no acute symtoms. The dream chart revealed him with one foot on a blue lead pencil and the other on a pair of shears while he was shouting that he was a Roman rider at the Hippodrome.

Mr. X was found to be a celebrated glass eater which accounted for the expression of contentment and professional pride upon his face. Another who shall be known here as Z had a mild attack and from the confused state of the chart and the picture it developed that he was suffering originally from the delusion that he was an elephant. He turned from side to side with the motion peculiar to a pachyderm, calling loudly "More Hay." It was ascertained that the unfortunate man was addicted to the eating of dried grass to such an extent that he could not be induced to eat even table d'hote dinners unless they were baled.

From these few facts it may be seen that the rarebit dream is almost a reality and that for a materializing seance nothing is better adapted than melted cheese tempered with brown October ale.

JOHN W. HARRINGTON.

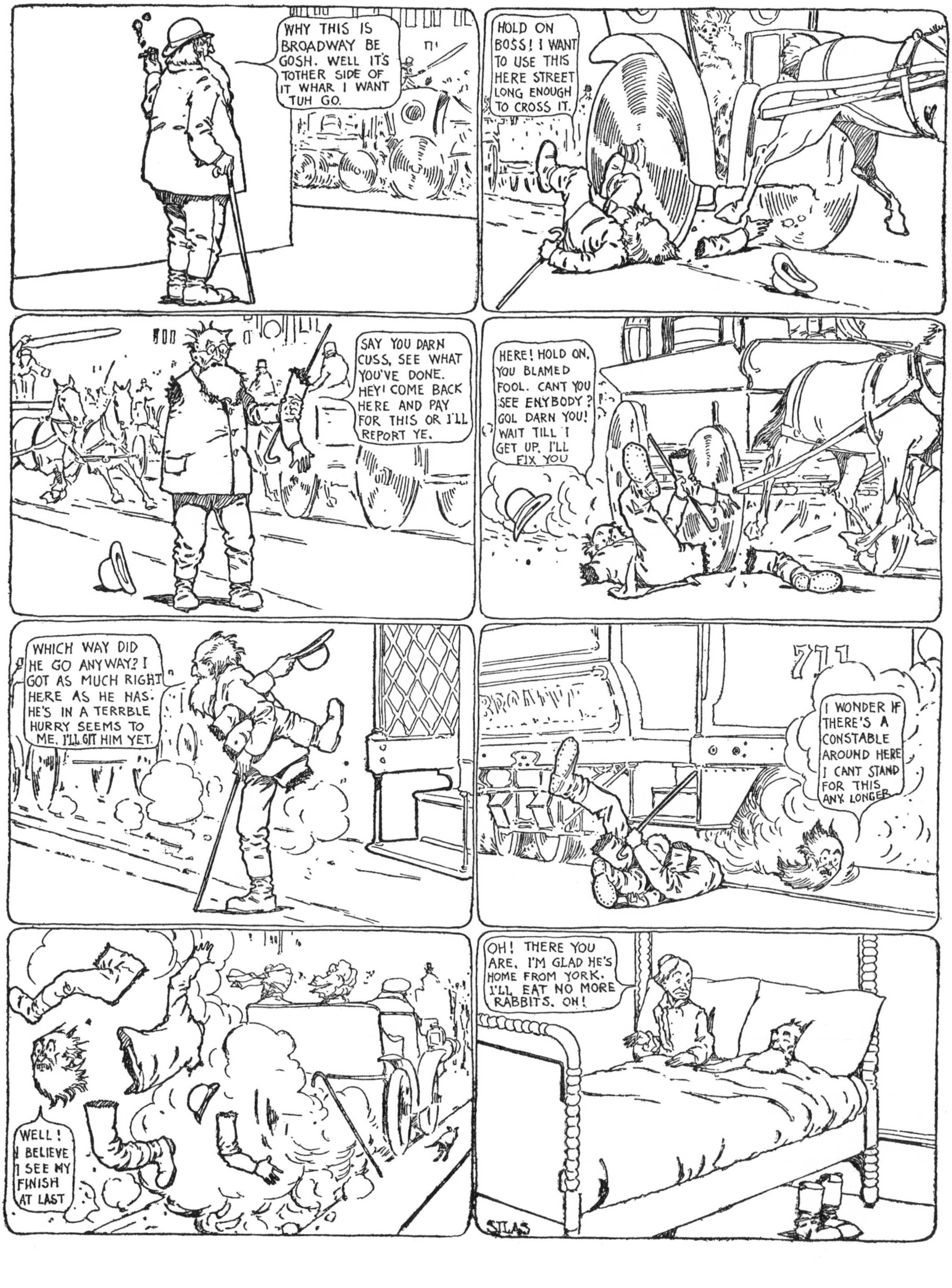
WHY THIS IS BROADWAY BE GOSH. WELL IT'S TOTHER SIDE OF IT WHAR I WANT TUH GO.
HOLD ON BOSS! I WANT TO USE THIS HERE STREET LONG ENOUGH TO CROSS IT.
SAY YOU DARN CUSS, SEE WHAT YOU'VE DONE. HEY! COME BACK HERE AND PAY FOR THIS OR I'LL REPORT YE.
HERE! HOLD ON. YOU BLAMED FOOL. CANT YOU SEE ENYBODY? GOL DARN YOU! WAIT TILL I GET UP. I'LL FIX YOU
WHICH WAY DID HE GO ANYWAY? I GOT AS MUCH RIGHT HERE AS HE HAS. HE'S IN A TERRBLE HURRY SEEMS TO ME. I'LL GIT HIM YET.
I WONDER IF THERE'S A CONSTABLE AROUND HERE I CANT STAND FOR THIS ANY LONGER
WELL! I BELIEVE I SEE MY FINISH AT LAST
OH! THERE YOU ARE. I'M GLAD HE'S HOME FROM YORK. I'LL EAT NO MORE RABBITS. OH!
SILAS

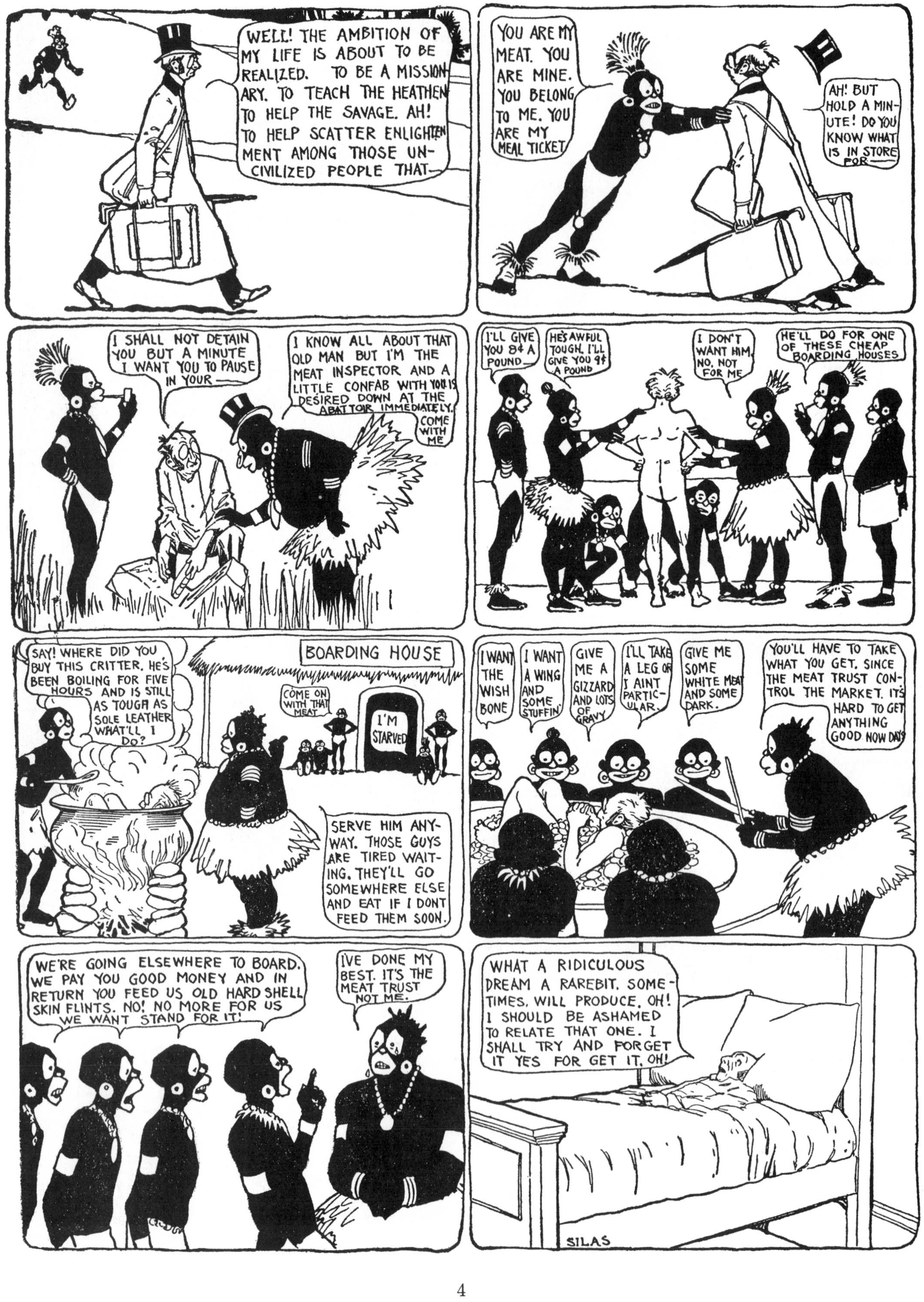

WELL! THE AMBITION OF MY LIFE IS ABOUT TO BE REALIZED. TO BE A MISSIONARY. TO TEACH THE HEATHEN TO HELP THE SAVAGE. AH! TO HELP SCATTER ENLIGHTENMENT AMONG THOSE UNCIVILIZED PEOPLE THAT—
YOU ARE MY MEAT. YOU ARE MINE. YOU BELONG TO ME. YOU ARE MY MEAL TICKET
AH! BUT HOLD A MINUTE! DO YOU KNOW WHAT IS IN STORE FOR—
I SHALL NOT DETAIN YOU BUT A MINUTE I WANT YOU TO PAUSE IN YOUR—
I KNOW ALL ABOUT THAT OLD MAN BUT I'M THE MEAT INSPECTOR AND A LITTLE CONFAB WITH YOU IS DESIRED DOWN AT THE ABATTOIR IMMEDIATELY. COME WITH ME
I'LL GIVE YOU 8¢ A POUND
HE'S AWFUL TOUGH. I'LL GIVE YOU 9¢ A POUND
I DON'T WANT HIM, NO, NOT FOR ME
HE'LL DO FOR ONE OF THESE CHEAP BOARDING HOUSES
SAY! WHERE DID YOU BUY THIS CRITTER. HE'S BEEN BOILING FOR FIVE HOURS AND IS STILL AS TOUGH AS SOLE LEATHER WHAT'LL I DO?
BOARDING HOUSE
COME ON WITH THAT MEAT
I'M STARVED
SERVE HIM ANYWAY. THOSE GUYS ARE TIRED WAITING. THEY'LL GO SOMEWHERE ELSE AND EAT IF I DONT FEED THEM SOON.
I WANT THE WISH BONE
I WANT A WING AND SOME STUFFIN'
GIVE ME A GIZZARD AND LOTS OF GRAVY
I'LL TAKE A LEG OR I AINT PARTICULAR.
GIVE ME SOME WHITE MEAT AND SOME DARK.
YOU'LL HAVE TO TAKE WHAT YOU GET. SINCE THE MEAT TRUST CONTROL THE MARKET. IT'S HARD TO GET ANYTHING GOOD NOW DAYS
WE'RE GOING ELSEWHERE TO BOARD. WE PAY YOU GOOD MONEY AND IN RETURN YOU FEED US OLD HARD SHELL SKIN FLINTS. NO! NO MORE FOR US WE WANT STAND FOR IT!
I'VE DONE MY BEST. IT'S THE MEAT TRUST NOT ME.
WHAT A RIDICULOUS DREAM A RAREBIT, SOMETIMES, WILL PRODUCE. OH! I SHOULD BE ASHAMED TO RELATE THAT ONE. I SHALL TRY AND FORGET IT YES FOR GET IT, OH!
SILAS

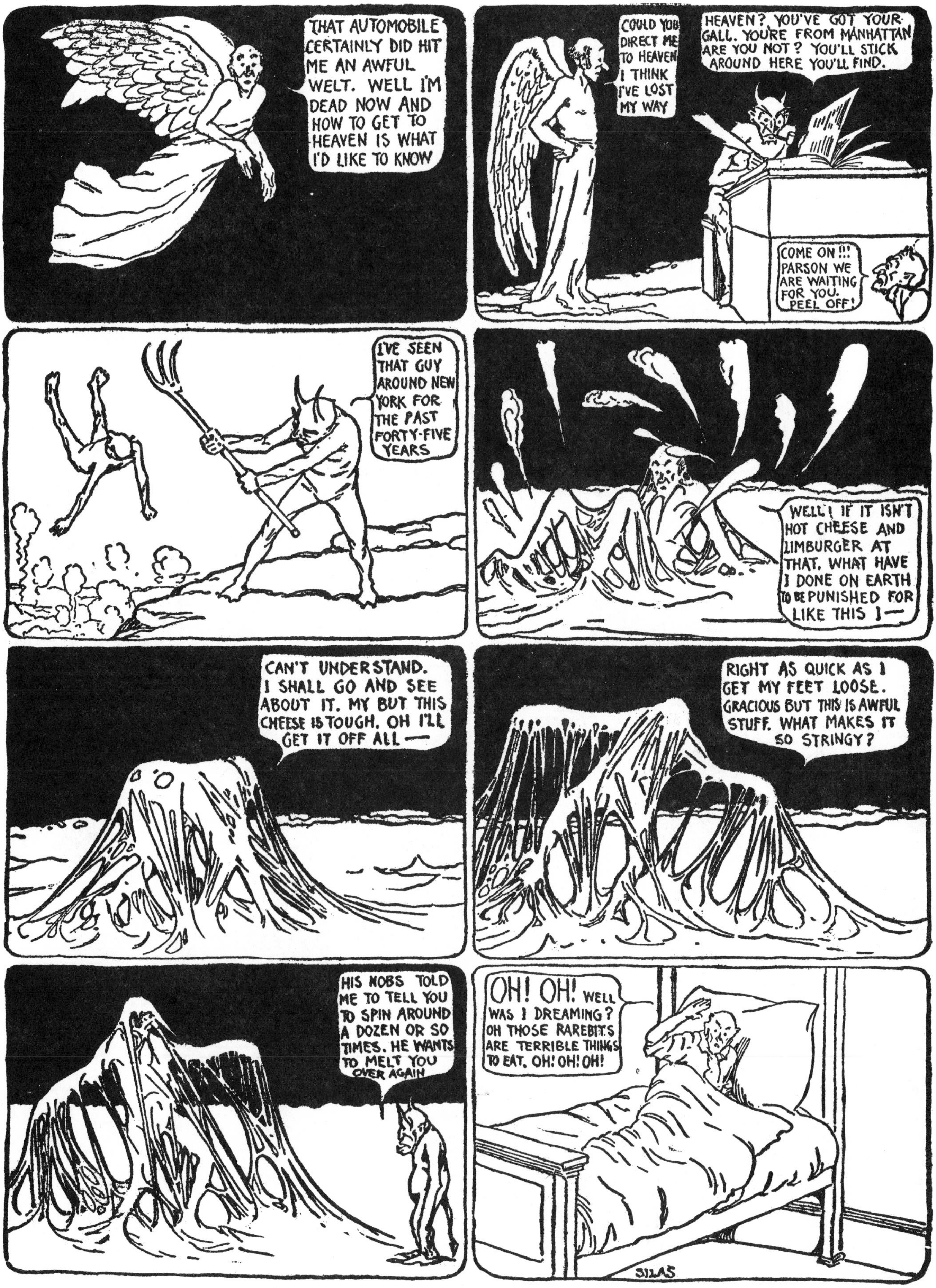
THAT AUTOMOBILE CERTAINLY DID HIT ME AN AWFUL WELT. WELL I'M DEAD NOW AND HOW TO GET TO HEAVEN IS WHAT I'D LIKE TO KNOW
COULD YOU DIRECT ME TO HEAVEN I THINK I'VE LOST MY WAY
HEAVEN? YOU'VE GOT YOUR GALL. YOU'RE FROM MANHATTAN ARE YOU NOT? YOU'LL STICK AROUND HERE YOU'LL FIND.
COME ON!!! PARSON WE ARE WAITING FOR YOU. PEEL OFF!
I'VE SEEN THAT GUY AROUND NEW YORK FOR THE PAST FORTY-FIVE YEARS
WELL! IF IT ISN'T HOT CHEESE AND LIMBURGER AT THAT. WHAT HAVE I DONE ON EARTH TO BE PUNISHED FOR LIKE THIS I—
CAN'T UNDERSTAND. I SHALL GO AND SEE ABOUT IT. MY BUT THIS CHEESE IS TOUGH. OH I'LL GET IT OFF ALL—
RIGHT AS QUICK AS I GET MY FEET LOOSE. GRACIOUS BUT THIS IS AWFUL STUFF. WHAT MAKES IT SO STRINGY?
HIS NOBS TOLD ME TO TELL YOU TO SPIN AROUND A DOZEN OR SO TIMES. HE WANTS TO MELT YOU OVER AGAIN
OH! OH! WELL WAS I DREAMING? OH THOSE RAREBITS ARE TERRIBLE THINGS TO EAT. OH! OH! OH!
SILAS

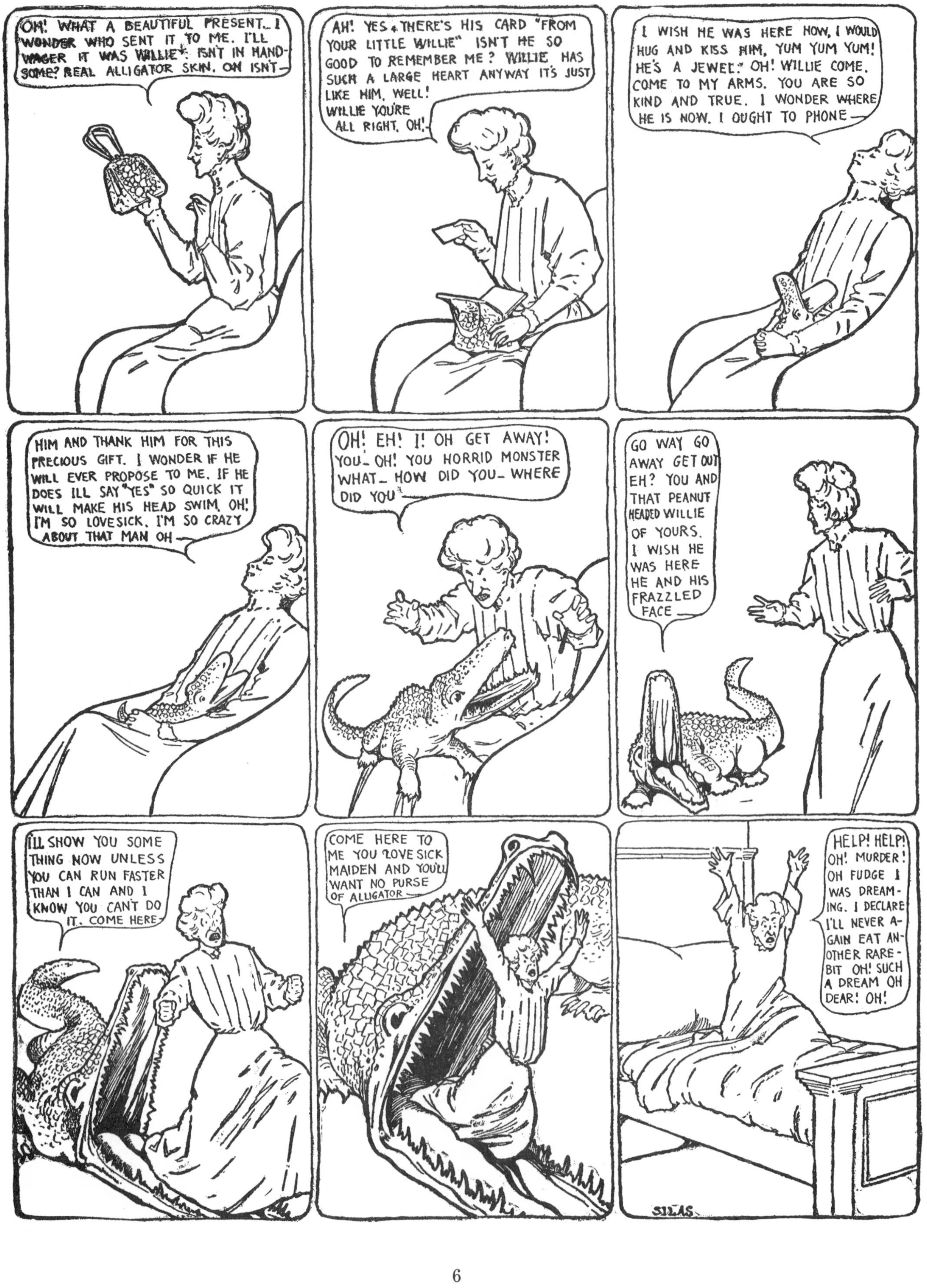
OH! WHAT A BEAUTIFUL PRESENT. I WONDER WHO SENT IT TO ME. I'LL WAGER IT WAS WILLIE. ISN'T IN HANDSOME? REAL ALLIGATOR SKIN. OH ISN'T—
AH! YES & THERE'S HIS CARD "FROM YOUR LITTLE WILLIE" ISN'T HE SO GOOD TO REMEMBER ME? WILLIE HAS SUCH A LARGE HEART ANYWAY IT'S JUST LIKE HIM. WELL! WILLIE YOU'RE ALL RIGHT. OH!
I WISH HE WAS HERE NOW, I WOULD HUG AND KISS HIM, YUM YUM YUM! HE'S A JEWEL. OH! WILLIE COME. COME TO MY ARMS. YOU ARE SO KIND AND TRUE. I WONDER WHERE HE IS NOW. I OUGHT TO PHONE—
HIM AND THANK HIM FOR THIS PRECIOUS GIFT. I WONDER IF HE WILL EVER PROPOSE TO ME. IF HE DOES ILL SAY "YES" SO QUICK IT WILL MAKE HIS HEAD SWIM. OH! I'M SO LOVESICK. I'M SO CRAZY ABOUT THAT MAN OH—
OH! EH! I! OH GET AWAY! YOU_ OH! YOU HORRID MONSTER WHAT_ HOW DID YOU_ WHERE DID YOU—
GO WAY GO AWAY GET OUT EH? YOU AND THAT PEANUT HEADED WILLIE OF YOURS. I WISH HE WAS HERE HE AND HIS FRAZZLED FACE—
I'LL SHOW YOU SOME THING NOW UNLESS YOU CAN RUN FASTER THAN I CAN AND I KNOW YOU CAN'T DO IT. COME HERE—
COME HERE TO ME YOU LOVE SICK MAIDEN AND YOU'LL WANT NO PURSE OF ALLIGATOR—
HELP! HELP! OH! MURDER! OH FUDGE I WAS DREAMING. I DECLARE I'LL NEVER AGAIN EAT ANOTHER RAREBIT OH! SUCH A DREAM OH DEAR! OH!
SILAS.

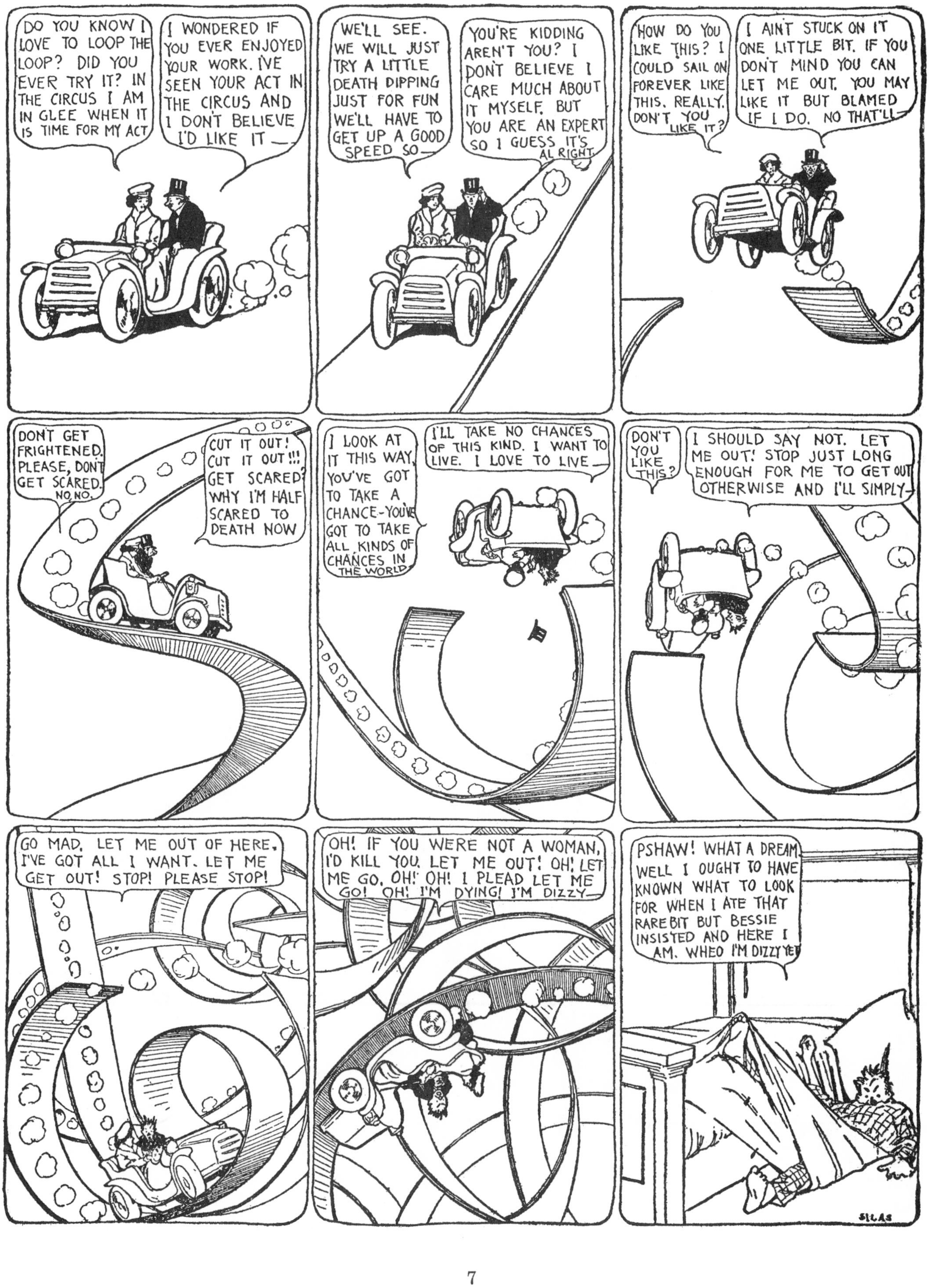
DO YOU KNOW I LOVE TO LOOP THE LOOP? DID YOU EVER TRY IT? IN THE CIRCUS I AM IN GLEE WHEN IT IS TIME FOR MY ACT
I WONDERED IF YOU EVER ENJOYED YOUR WORK. I'VE SEEN YOUR ACT IN THE CIRCUS AND I DON'T BELIEVE I'D LIKE IT —
WE'LL SEE. WE WILL JUST TRY A LITTLE DEATH DIPPING JUST FOR FUN WE'LL HAVE TO GET UP A GOOD SPEED SO—
YOU'RE KIDDING AREN'T YOU? I DON'T BELIEVE I CARE MUCH ABOUT IT MYSELF. BUT YOU ARE AN EXPERT SO I GUESS IT'S AL RIGHT.
HOW DO YOU LIKE THIS? I COULD SAIL ON FOREVER LIKE THIS. REALLY. DON'T YOU LIKE IT?
I AINT STUCK ON IT ONE LITTLE BIT. IF YOU DON'T MIND YOU CAN LET ME OUT. YOU MAY LIKE IT BUT BLAMED IF I DO. NO THAT'LL—
DON'T GET FRIGHTENED. PLEASE, DON'T GET SCARED. NO, NO.
CUT IT OUT! CUT IT OUT!!! GET SCARED? WHY I'M HALF SCARED TO DEATH NOW
I LOOK AT IT THIS WAY, YOU'VE GOT TO TAKE A CHANCE-YOU'VE GOT TO TAKE ALL KINDS OF CHANCES IN THE WORLD
I'LL TAKE NO CHANCES OF THIS KIND. I WANT TO LIVE. I LOVE TO LIVE —
DON'T YOU LIKE THIS?
I SHOULD SAY NOT. LET ME OUT! STOP JUST LONG ENOUGH FOR ME TO GET OUT OTHERWISE AND I'LL SIMPLY—
GO MAD. LET ME OUT OF HERE. I'VE GOT ALL I WANT. LET ME GET OUT! STOP! PLEASE STOP!
OH! IF YOU WERE NOT A WOMAN, I'D KILL YOU. LET ME OUT! OH! LET ME GO. OH! OH! I PLEAD LET ME GO! OH! I'M DYING! I'M DIZZY—
PSHAW! WHAT A DREAM. WELL I OUGHT TO HAVE KNOWN WHAT TO LOOK FOR WHEN I ATE THAT RAREBIT BUT BESSIE INSISTED AND HERE I AM. WHEO I'M DIZZY YET
SILAS

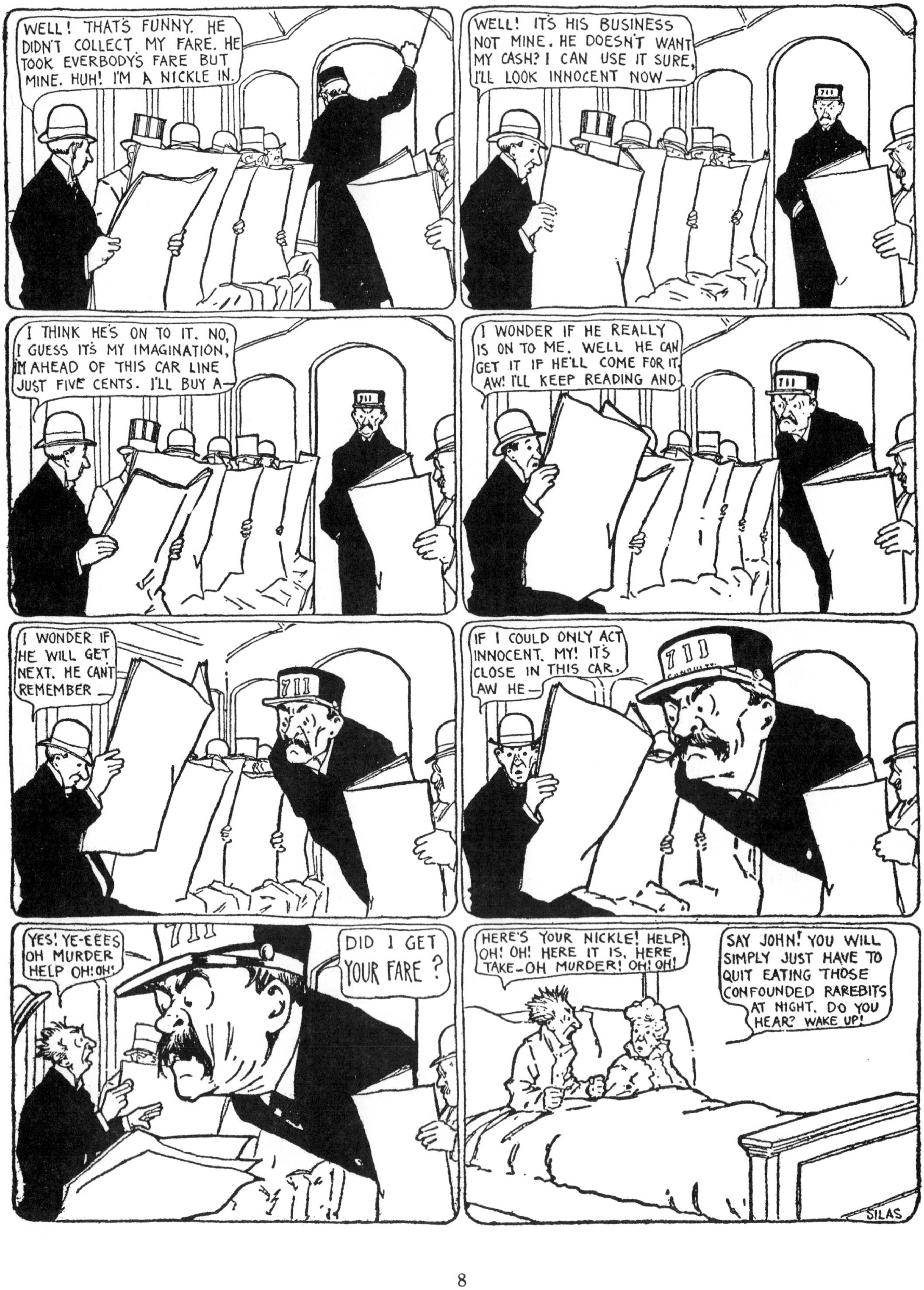
WELL! THAT'S FUNNY. HE DIDN'T COLLECT MY FARE. HE TOOK EVERBODY'S FARE BUT MINE. HUH! I'M A NICKLE IN.
WELL! IT'S HIS BUSINESS NOT MINE. HE DOESN'T WANT MY CASH? I CAN USE IT SURE, I'LL LOOK INNOCENT NOW—
I THINK HE'S ON TO IT. NO, I GUESS IT'S MY IMAGINATION, I'M AHEAD OF THIS CAR LINE JUST FIVE CENTS. I'LL BUY A—
I WONDER IF HE REALLY IS ON TO ME. WELL HE CAN GET IT IF HE'LL COME FOR IT. AW! I'LL KEEP READING AND—
I WONDER IF HE WILL GET NEXT. HE CAN'T REMEMBER—
IF I COULD ONLY ACT INNOCENT. MY! IT'S CLOSE IN THIS CAR. AW HE—
YES! YE-EEES OH MURDER HELP OH! OH!
DID I GET YOUR FARE ?
HERE'S YOUR NICKLE! HELP! OH! OH! HERE IT IS. HERE TAKE-OH MURDER! OH! OH!
SAY JOHN! YOU WILL SIMPLY JUST HAVE TO QUIT EATING THOSE CONFOUNDED RAREBITS AT NIGHT. DO YOU HEAR? WAKE UP!
SILAS

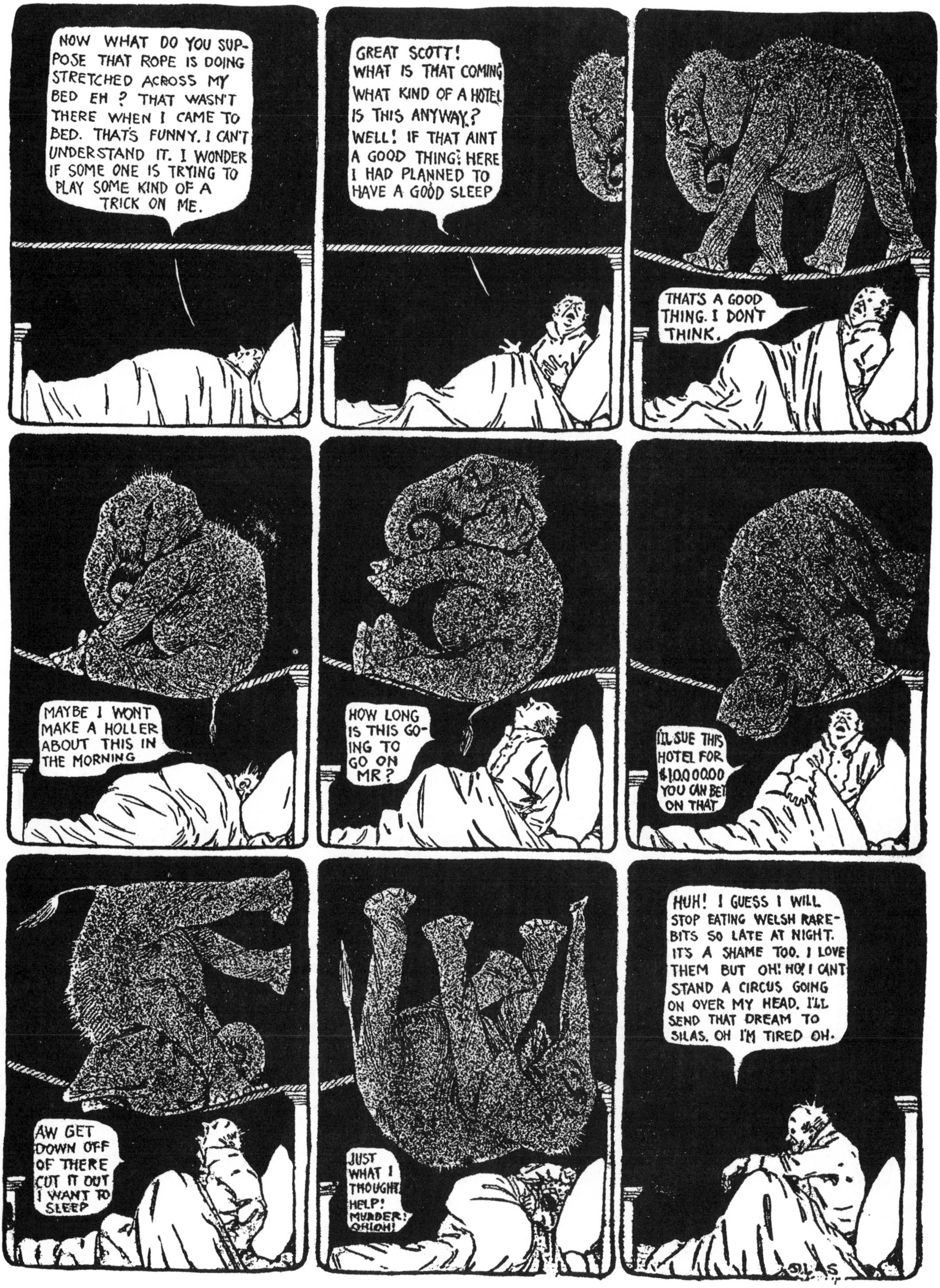
NOW WHAT DO YOU SUPPOSE THAT ROPE IS DOING STRETCHED ACROSS MY BED EH ? THAT WASN'T THERE WHEN I CAME TO BED. THAT'S FUNNY. I CAN'T UNDERSTAND IT. I WONDER IF SOME ONE IS TRYING TO PLAY SOME KIND OF A TRICK ON ME.
GREAT SCOTT! WHAT IS THAT COMING WHAT KIND OF A HOTEL IS THIS ANYWAY? WELL! IF THAT AINT A GOOD THING! HERE I HAD PLANNED TO HAVE A GOOD SLEEP
THAT'S A GOOD THING. I DON'T THINK.
MAYBE I WONT MAKE A HOLLER ABOUT THIS IN THE MORNING
HOW LONG IS THIS GOING TO GO ON MR?
I'LL SUE THIS HOTEL FOR $10,000.00 YOU CAN BET ON THAT
AW GET DOWN OFF OF THERE CUT IT OUT I WANT TO SLEEP
JUST WHAT I THOUGHT HELP! MURDER! OH! OH!
HUH! I GUESS I WILL STOP EATING WELSH RAREBITS SO LATE AT NIGHT. IT'S A SHAME TOO. I LOVE THEM BUT OH! HO! I CANT STAND A CIRCUS GOING ON OVER MY HEAD. I'LL SEND THAT DREAM TO SILAS. OH I'M TIRED OH.
SILAS

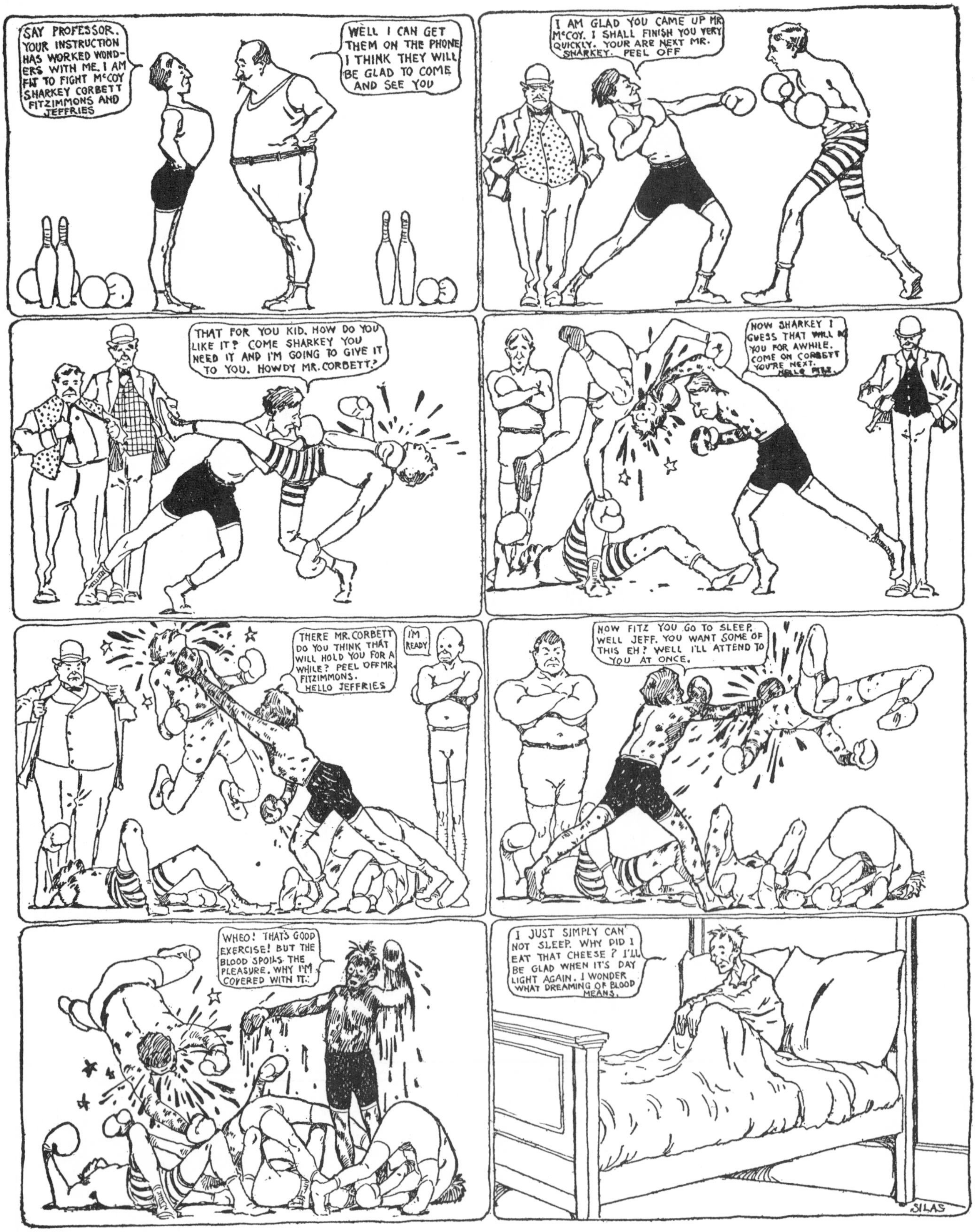
SAY PROFESSOR. YOUR INSTRUCTION HAS WORKED WONDERS WITH ME. I AM FIT TO FIGHT McCOY SHARKEY CORBETT FITZIMMONS AND JEFFRIES
WELL I CAN GET THEM ON THE PHONE I THINK THEY WILL BE GLAD TO COME AND SEE YOU
I AM GLAD YOU CAME UP MR McCOY. I SHALL FINISH YOU VERY QUICKLY. YOUR ARE NEXT MR. SHARKEY. PEEL OFF
THAT FOR YOU KID. HOW DO YOU LIKE IT? COME SHARKEY YOU NEED IT AND I'M GOING TO GIVE IT TO YOU. HOWDY MR. CORBETT?
NOW SHARKEY I GUESS THAT WILL
YOU FOR AWHILE. COME ON CORBETT YOU'RE NEXT.
THERE MR. CORBETT DO YOU THINK THAT WILL HOLD YOU FOR A WHILE? PEEL OFF MR. FITZIMMONS. HELLO JEFFRIES
I'M READY
NOW FITZ YOU GO TO SLEEP. WELL JEFF. YOU WANT SOME OF THIS EH? WELL I'LL ATTEND TO YOU AT ONCE.
WHEO! THAT'S GOOD EXERCISE! BUT THE BLOOD SPOILS THE PLEASURE. WHY I'M COVERED WITH IT.
I JUST SIMPLY CAN NOT SLEEP. WHY DID I EAT THAT CHEESE? I'LL BE GLAD WHEN IT'S DAY LIGHT AGAIN. I WONDER WHAT DREAMING OF BLOOD MEANS.
SILAS

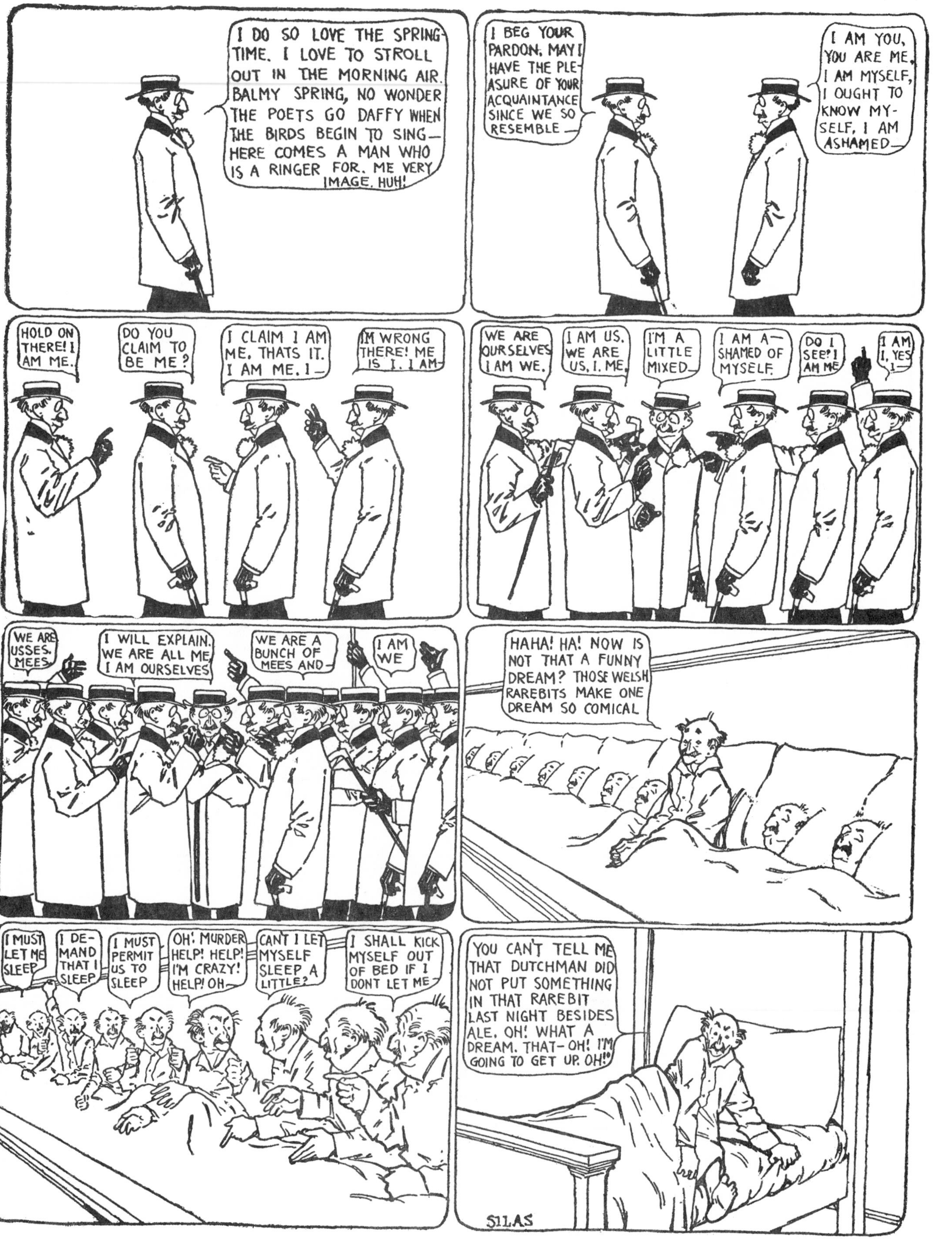
I DO SO LOVE THE SPRING-TIME. I LOVE TO STROLL OUT IN THE MORNING AIR. BALMY SPRING, NO WONDER THE POETS GO DAFFY WHEN THE BIRDS BEGIN TO SING— HERE COMES A MAN WHO IS A RINGER FOR. ME VERY IMAGE. HUH!
I BEG YOUR PARDON, MAY I HAVE THE PLE-ASURE OF YOUR ACQUAINTANCE SINCE WE SO RESEMBLE—
I AM YOU, YOU ARE ME, I AM MYSELF, I OUGHT TO KNOW MY-SELF, I AM ASHAMED—
HOLD ON THERE! I AM ME.
DO YOU CLAIM TO BE ME?
I CLAIM I AM ME. THATS IT. I AM ME. I—
I'M WRONG THERE! ME IS I. I AM—
WE ARE OURSELVES I AM WE.
I AM US. WE ARE US, I. ME.
I'M A LITTLE MIXED—
I AM A-SHAMED OF MYSELF.
DO I SEE? I AM ME
I AM I, YES I—
WE ARE USSES. MEES.
I WILL EXPLAIN. WE ARE ALL ME I AM OURSELVES
WE ARE A BUNCH OF MEES AND—
I AM WE
HAHA! HA! NOW IS NOT THAT A FUNNY DREAM? THOSE WELSH RAREBITS MAKE ONE DREAM SO COMICAL
I MUST LET ME SLEEP
I DE-MAND THAT I SLEEP
I MUST PERMIT US TO SLEEP
OH! MURDER HELP! HELP! I'M CRAZY! HELP! OH—
CANT I LET MYSELF SLEEP A LITTLE?
I SHALL KICK MYSELF OUT OF BED IF I DONT LET ME—
YOU CAN'T TELL ME THAT DUTCHMAN DID NOT PUT SOMETHING IN THAT RAREBIT LAST NIGHT BESIDES ALE. OH! WHAT A DREAM. THAT—OH! I'M GOING TO GET UP. OH!!
SILAS

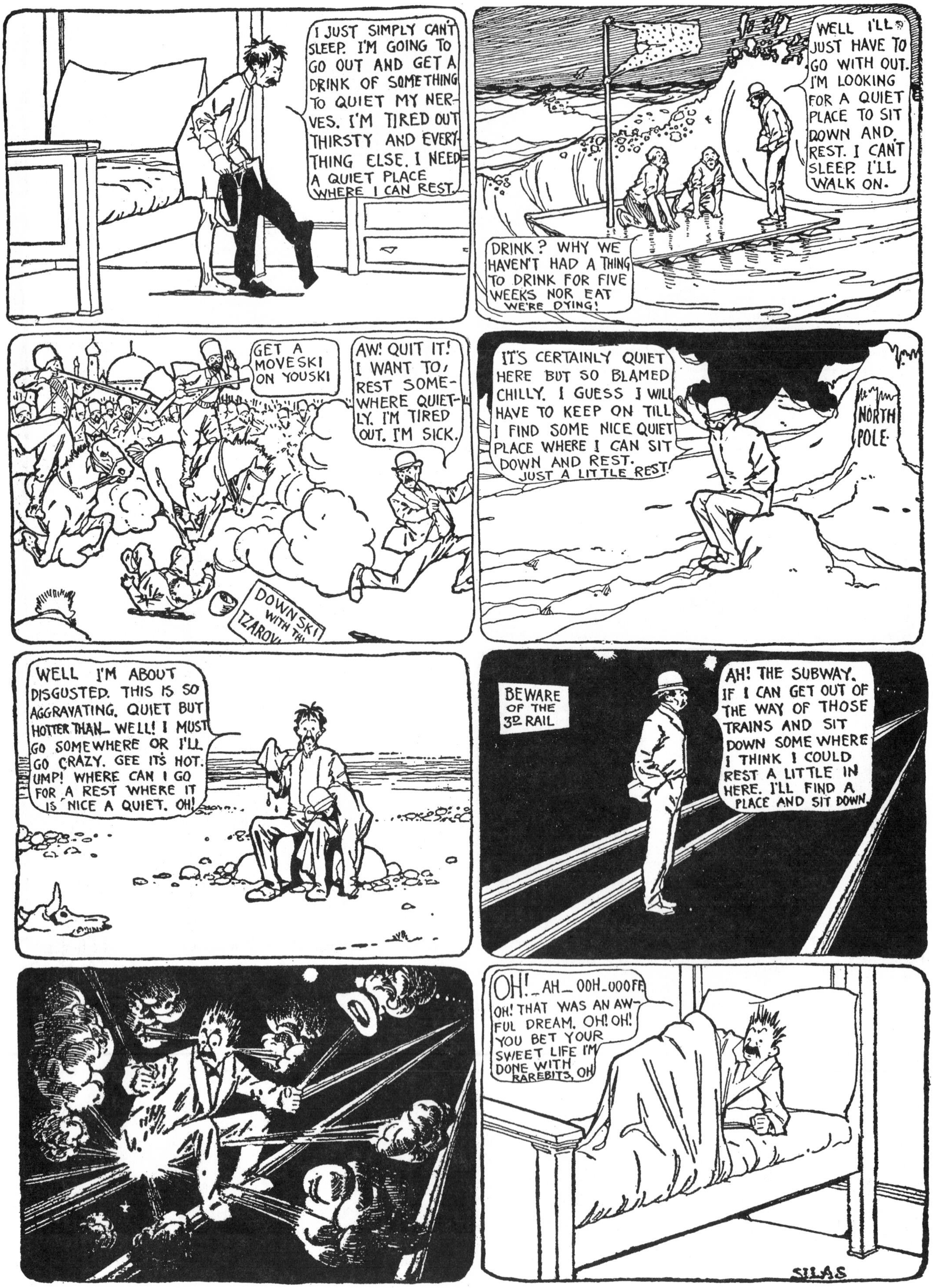
I JUST SIMPLY CAN'T SLEEP. I'M GOING TO GO OUT AND GET A DRINK OF SOMETHING TO QUIET MY NERVES. I'M TIRED OUT THIRSTY AND EVERYTHING ELSE. I NEED A QUIET PLACE WHERE I CAN REST.
WELL I'LL JUST HAVE TO GO WITH OUT. I'M LOOKING FOR A QUIET PLACE TO SIT DOWN AND REST. I CAN'T SLEEP. I'LL WALK ON.
DRINK? WHY WE HAVEN'T HAD A THING TO DRINK FOR FIVE WEEKS NOR EAT WE'RE DYING!
GET A MOVESKI ON YOUSKI
AW! QUIT IT! I WANT TO, REST SOMEWHERE QUIETLY. I'M TIRED OUT. I'M SICK.
DOWNSKI WITH THE TZAROV
IT'S CERTAINLY QUIET HERE BUT SO BLAMED CHILLY. I GUESS I WILL HAVE TO KEEP ON TILL I FIND SOME NICE QUIET PLACE WHERE I CAN SIT DOWN AND REST. JUST A LITTLE REST.
NORTH POLE
WELL I'M ABOUT DISGUSTED. THIS IS SO AGGRAVATING. QUIET BUT HOTTER THAN— WELL! I MUST GO SOMEWHERE OR I'LL GO CRAZY. GEE IT'S HOT. UMP! WHERE CAN I GO FOR A REST WHERE IT IS NICE A QUIET. OH!
BEWARE OF THE 3D RAIL
AH! THE SUBWAY. IF I CAN GET OUT OF THE WAY OF THOSE TRAINS AND SIT DOWN SOME WHERE I THINK I COULD REST A LITTLE IN HERE. I'LL FIND A PLACE AND SIT DOWN.
OH!_AH_OOH_OOOFF. OH! THAT WAS AN AWFUL DREAM. OH! OH! YOU BET YOUR SWEET LIFE I'M DONE WITH RAREBITS, OH
SILAS

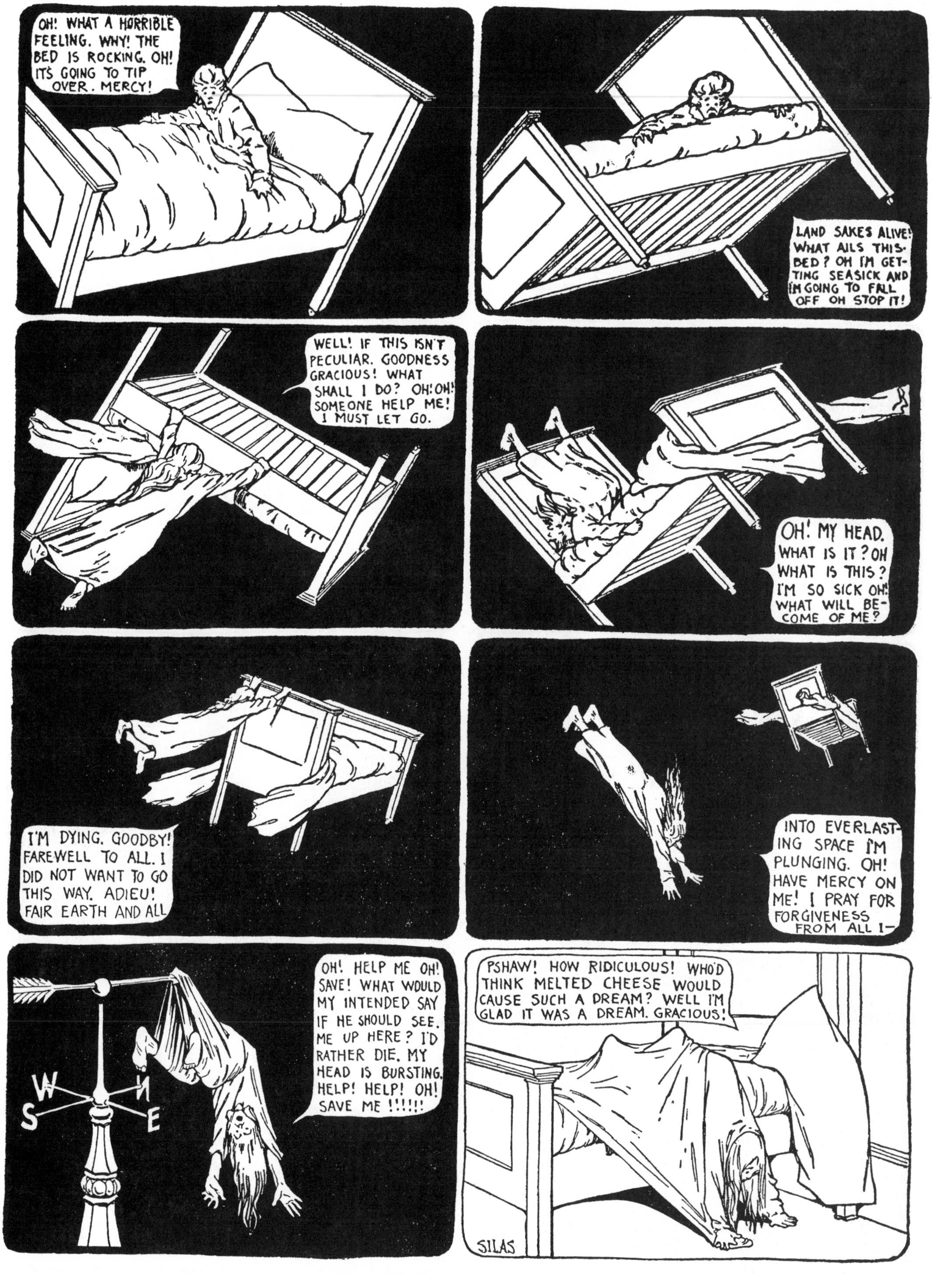
OH! WHAT A HORRIBLE FEELING. WHY! THE BED IS ROCKING. OH! ITS GOING TO TIP OVER. MERCY!
LAND SAKES ALIVE! WHAT AILS THIS-BED? OH I'M GET-TING SEASICK AND I'M GOING TO FALL OFF OH STOP IT!
WELL! IF THIS ISN'T PECULIAR. GOODNESS GRACIOUS! WHAT SHALL I DO? OH! OH! SOMEONE HELP ME! I MUST LET GO.
OH! MY HEAD. WHAT IS IT? OH WHAT IS THIS? I'M SO SICK OH! WHAT WILL BE-COME OF ME?
I'M DYING. GOODBY! FAREWELL TO ALL. I DID NOT WANT TO GO THIS WAY. ADIEU! FAIR EARTH AND ALL
INTO EVERLAST-ING SPACE I'M PLUNGING. OH! HAVE MERCY ON ME! I PRAY FOR FORGIVENESS FROM ALL I—
OH! HELP ME OH! SAVE! WHAT WOULD MY INTENDED SAY IF HE SHOULD SEE. ME UP HERE? I'D RATHER DIE. MY HEAD IS BURSTING. HELP! HELP! OH! SAVE ME !!!!!!
W
N
S
E
PSHAW! HOW RIDICULOUS! WHO'D THINK MELTED CHEESE WOULD CAUSE SUCH A DREAM? WELL I'M GLAD IT WAS A DREAM. GRACIOUS!
SILAS

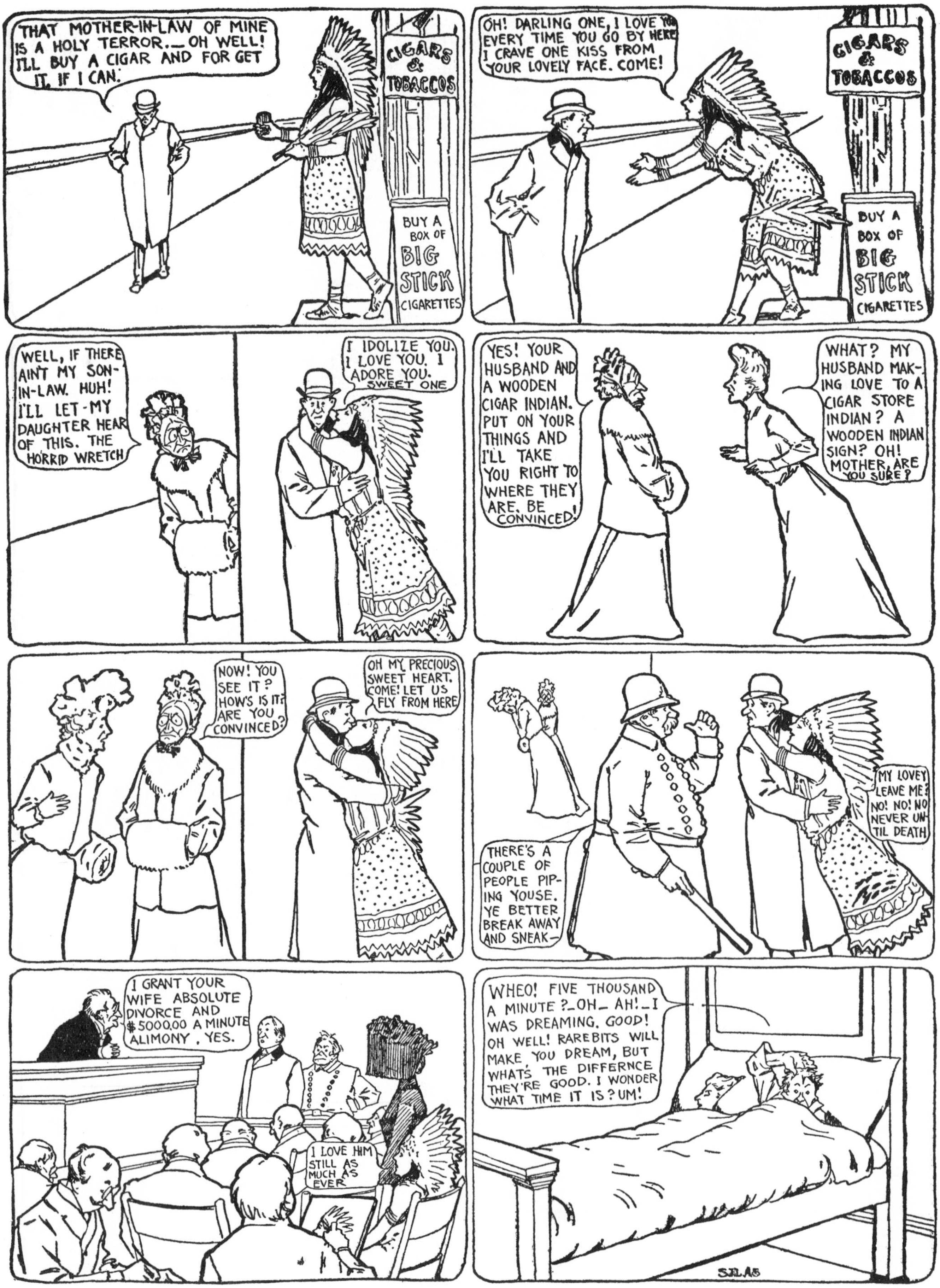
THAT MOTHER-IN-LAW OF MINE IS A HOLY TERROR._ OH WELL! I'LL BUY A CIGAR AND FOR GET IT, IF I CAN.
CIGARS & TOBACCOS
BUY A BOX OF BIG STICK CIGARETTES
OH! DARLING ONE, I LOVE YOU EVERY TIME YOU GO BY HERE I CRAVE ONE KISS FROM YOUR LOVELY FACE. COME!
CIGARS & TOBACCOS
BUY A BOX OF BIG STICK CIGARETTES
WELL, IF THERE AIN'T MY SON-IN-LAW. HUH! I'LL LET MY DAUGHTER HEAR OF THIS. THE HORRID WRETCH
I IDOLIZE YOU. I LOVE YOU. I ADORE YOU. SWEET ONE
YES! YOUR HUSBAND AND A WOODEN CIGAR INDIAN. PUT ON YOUR THINGS AND I'LL TAKE YOU RIGHT TO WHERE THEY ARE. BE CONVINCED!
WHAT? MY HUSBAND MAKING LOVE TO A CIGAR STORE INDIAN? A WOODEN INDIAN SIGN? OH! MOTHER, ARE YOU SURE?
NOW! YOU SEE IT? HOW'S IS IT? ARE YOU CONVINCED?
OH MY PRECIOUS SWEET HEART. COME! LET US FLY FROM HERE
MY LOVEY LEAVE ME? NO! NO! NO NEVER UNTIL DEATH
THERE'S A COUPLE OF PEOPLE PIPING YOUSE. YE BETTER BREAK AWAY AND SNEAK—
I GRANT YOUR WIFE ABSOLUTE DIVORCE AND $5000.00 A MINUTE ALIMONY, YES.
I LOVE HIM STILL AS MUCH AS EVER
WHEO! FIVE THOUSAND A MINUTE?_OH_ AH!_I WAS DREAMING. GOOD! OH WELL! RAREBITS WILL MAKE YOU DREAM, BUT WHAT'S THE DIFFERNCE THEY'RE GOOD. I WONDER WHAT TIME IT IS? UM!
SILAS

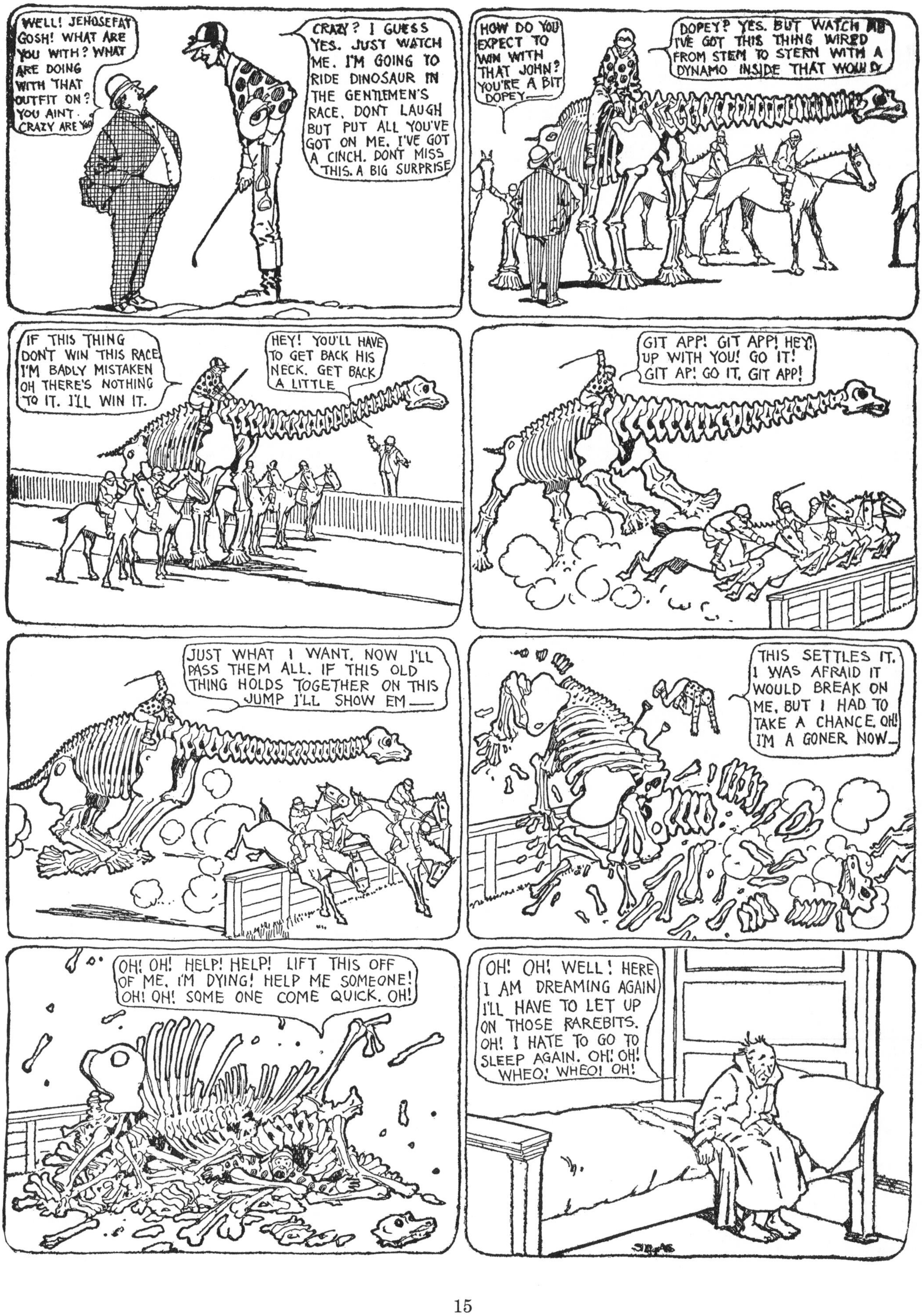
WELL! JEHOSEFAT GOSH! WHAT ARE YOU WITH? WHAT ARE DOING WITH THAT OUTFIT ON? YOU AINT CRAZY ARE YOU
CRAZY? I GUESS YES. JUST WATCH ME. I'M GOING TO RIDE DINOSAUR IN THE GENTLEMEN'S RACE. DONT LAUGH BUT PUT ALL YOU'VE GOT ON ME. I'VE GOT A CINCH. DONT MISS THIS. A BIG SURPRISE
HOW DO YOU EXPECT TO WIN WITH THAT JOHN? YOU'RE A BIT DOPEY
DOPEY? YES. BUT WATCH I'VE GOT THIS THING WIRED FROM STEM TO STERN WITH A DYNAMO INSIDE THAT WOULD
IF THIS THING DON'T WIN THIS RACE I'M BADLY MISTAKEN OH THERE'S NOTHING TO IT. I'LL WIN IT.
HEY! YOU'LL HAVE TO GET BACK HIS NECK. GET BACK A LITTLE
GIT APP! GIT APP! HEY! UP WITH YOU! GO IT! GIT AP! GO IT, GIT APP!
JUST WHAT I WANT. NOW I'LL PASS THEM ALL. IF THIS OLD THING HOLDS TOGETHER ON THIS JUMP I'LL SHOW EM
THIS SETTLES IT. I WAS AFRAID IT WOULD BREAK ON ME, BUT I HAD TO TAKE A CHANCE. OH! I'M A GONER NOW
OH! OH! HELP! HELP! LIFT THIS OFF OF ME, I'M DYING! HELP ME SOMEONE! OH! OH! SOME ONE COME QUICK. OH!
OH! OH! WELL! HERE I AM DREAMING AGAIN I'LL HAVE TO LET UP ON THOSE RAREBITS. OH! I HATE TO GO TO SLEEP AGAIN. OH! OH! WHEO! WHEO! OH!
SILAS

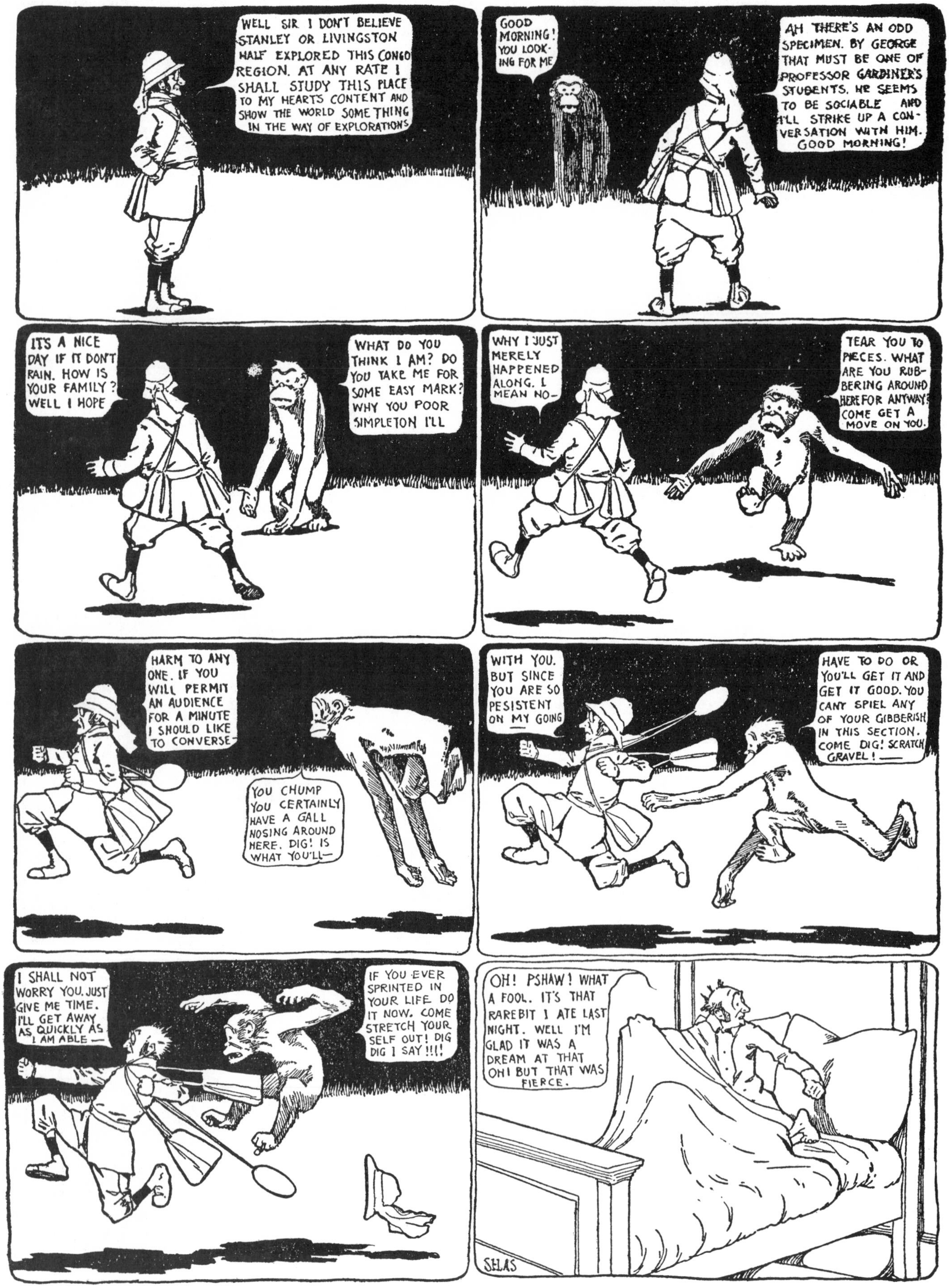
WELL SIR I DON'T BELIEVE STANLEY OR LIVINGSTON HALF EXPLORED THIS CONGO REGION. AT ANY RATE I SHALL STUDY THIS PLACE TO MY HEARTS CONTENT AND SHOW THE WORLD SOME THING IN THE WAY OF EXPLORATIONS
GOOD MORNING! YOU LOOKING FOR ME
AH THERE'S AN ODD SPECIMEN. BY GEORGE THAT MUST BE ONE OF PROFESSOR GARDINER'S STUDENTS. HE SEEMS TO BE SOCIABLE AND I'LL STRIKE UP A CONVERSATION WITH HIM. GOOD MORNING!
IT'S A NICE DAY IF IT DON'T RAIN. HOW IS YOUR FAMILY? WELL I HOPE
WHAT DO YOU THINK I AM? DO YOU TAKE ME FOR SOME EASY MARK? WHY YOU POOR SIMPLETON I'LL
WHY I JUST MERELY HAPPENED ALONG. I MEAN NO-
TEAR YOU TO PIECES. WHAT ARE YOU RUBBERING AROUND HERE FOR ANYWAY? COME GET A MOVE ON YOU.
HARM TO ANY ONE. IF YOU WILL PERMIT AN AUDIENCE FOR A MINUTE I SHOULD LIKE TO CONVERSE
YOU CHUMP YOU CERTAINLY HAVE A GALL NOSING AROUND HERE. DIG! IS WHAT YOU'LL—
WITH YOU. BUT SINCE YOU ARE SO PESISTENT ON MY GOING
HAVE TO DO OR YOU'LL GET IT AND GET IT GOOD. YOU CANT SPIEL ANY OF YOUR GIBBERISH IN THIS SECTION. COME DIG! SCRATCH GRAVEL! —
I SHALL NOT WORRY YOU. JUST GIVE ME TIME. I'LL GET AWAY AS QUICKLY AS I AM ABLE —
IF YOU EVER SPRINTED IN YOUR LIFE DO IT NOW. COME STRETCH YOUR SELF OUT! DIG DIG I SAY!!!
OH! PSHAW! WHAT A FOOL. IT'S THAT RAREBIT I ATE LAST NIGHT. WELL I'M GLAD IT WAS A DREAM AT THAT OH! BUT THAT WAS FIERCE.
SILAS

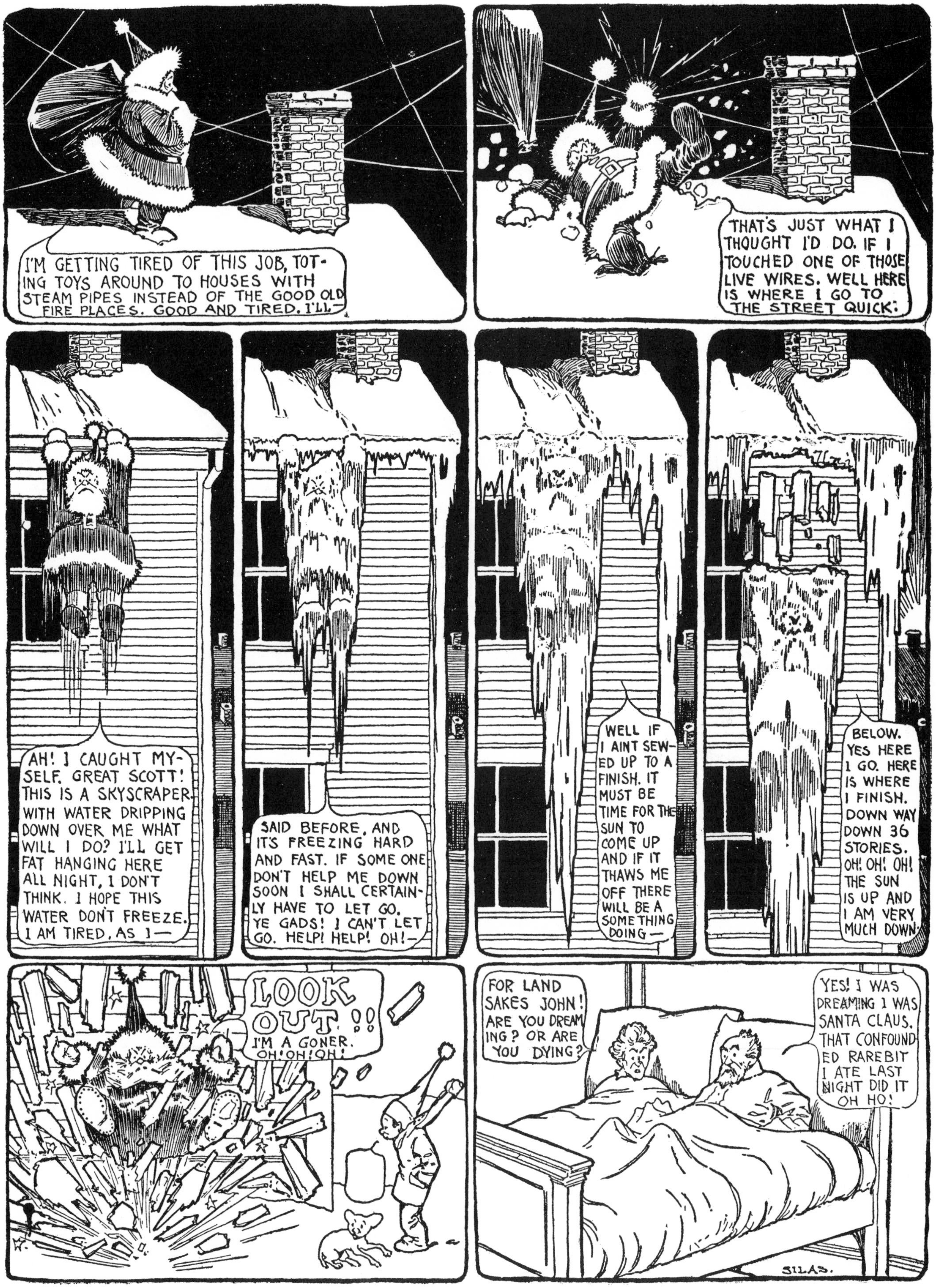

I'M GETTING TIRED OF THIS JOB, TOTING TOYS AROUND TO HOUSES WITH STEAM PIPES INSTEAD OF THE GOOD OLD FIRE PLACES. GOOD AND TIRED. I'LL
THAT'S JUST WHAT I THOUGHT I'D DO. IF I TOUCHED ONE OF THOSE LIVE WIRES. WELL HERE IS WHERE I GO TO THE STREET QUICK.
AH! I CAUGHT MYSELF. GREAT SCOTT! THIS IS A SKYSCRAPER WITH WATER DRIPPING DOWN OVER ME WHAT WILL I DO? I'LL GET FAT HANGING HERE ALL NIGHT, I DON'T THINK. I HOPE THIS WATER DON'T FREEZE. I AM TIRED, AS I—
SAID BEFORE, AND IT'S FREEZING HARD AND FAST. IF SOME ONE DON'T HELP ME DOWN SOON I SHALL CERTAINLY HAVE TO LET GO. YE GADS! I CAN'T LET GO. HELP! HELP! OH!—
WELL IF I AINT SEWED UP TO A FINISH. IT MUST BE TIME FOR THE SUN TO COME UP AND IF IT THAWS ME OFF THERE WILL BE A SOME THING DOING—
BELOW. YES HERE I GO. HERE IS WHERE I FINISH. DOWN WAY DOWN 36 STORIES. OH! OH! OH! THE SUN IS UP AND I AM VERY MUCH DOWN.
LOOK OUT!!
I'M A GONER. OH! OH! OH!
FOR LAND SAKES JOHN! ARE YOU DREAMING? OR ARE YOU DYING?
YES! I WAS DREAMING I WAS SANTA CLAUS. THAT CONFOUNDED RAREBIT I ATE LAST NIGHT DID IT OH HO!
SILAS.

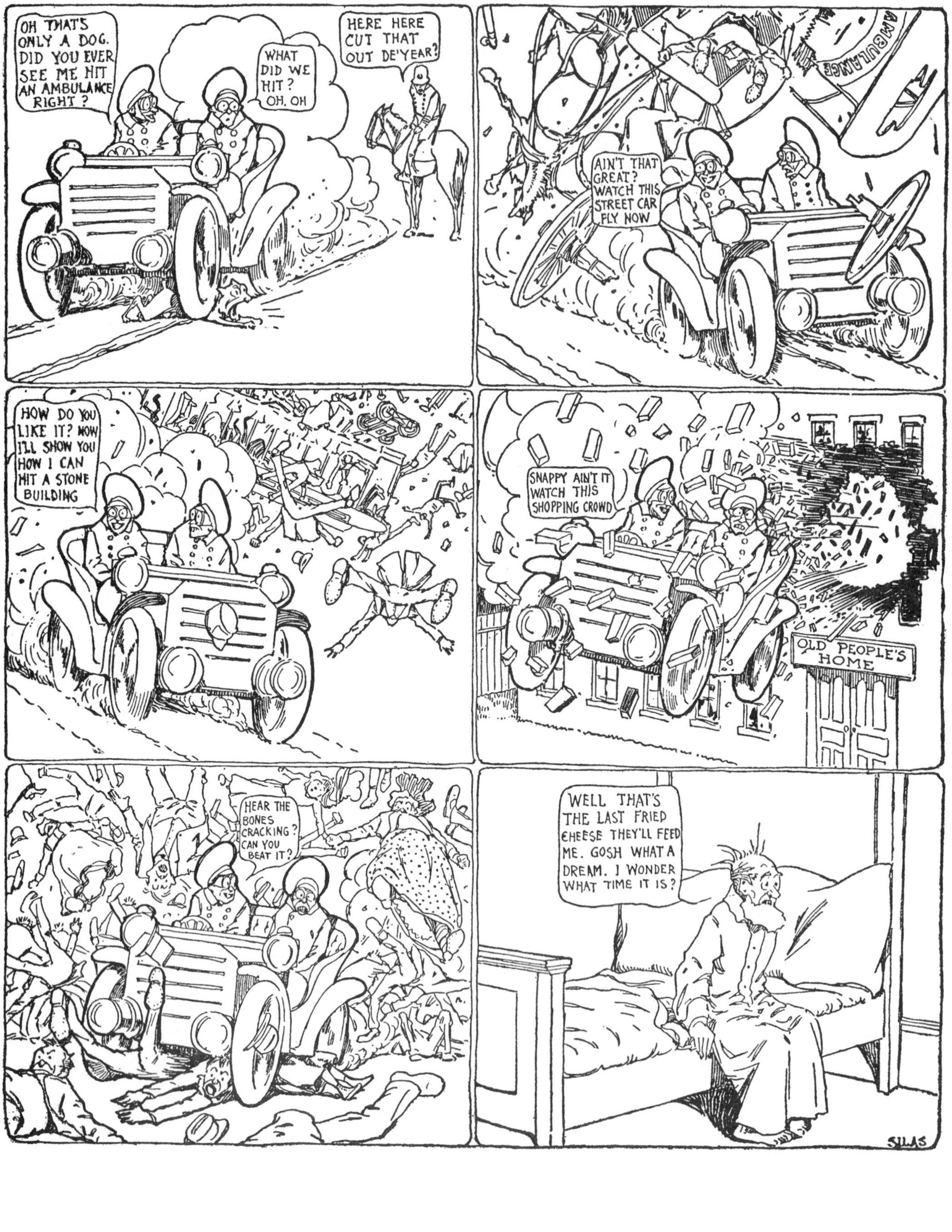

OH THAT'S ONLY A DOG. DID YOU EVER SEE ME HIT AN AMBULANCE RIGHT?
WHAT DID WE HIT? OH. OH
HERE HERE CUT THAT OUT DE'YEAR?
AMBULANCE
AIN'T THAT GREAT? WATCH THIS STREET CAR FLY NOW
HOW DO YOU LIKE IT? NOW I'LL SHOW YOU HOW I CAN HIT A STONE BUILDING
SNAPPY AIN'T IT WATCH THIS SHOPPING CROWD
OLD PEOPLE'S HOME
HEAR THE BONES CRACKING? CAN YOU BEAT IT?
WELL THAT'S THE LAST FRIED CHEESE THEY'LL FEED ME. GOSH WHAT A DREAM. I WONDER WHAT TIME IT IS?
SILAS

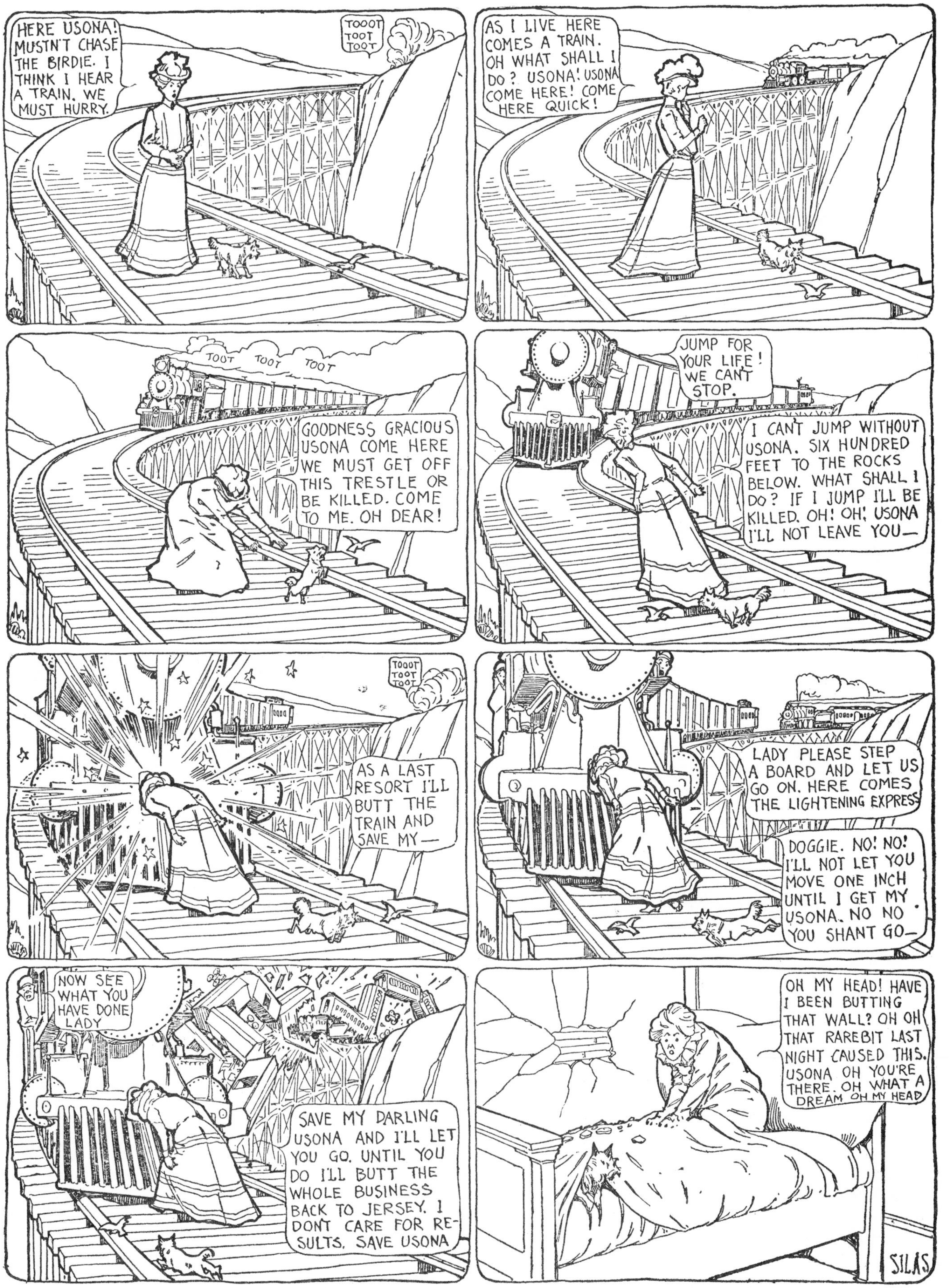
HERE USONA! MUSTN'T CHASE THE BIRDIE. I THINK I HEAR A TRAIN. WE MUST HURRY.
TOOOT TOOT TOOT
AS I LIVE HERE COMES A TRAIN. OH WHAT SHALL I DO? USONA! USONA COME HERE! COME HERE QUICK!
TOOT TOOT TOOT
GOODNESS GRACIOUS USONA COME HERE WE MUST GET OFF THIS TRESTLE OR BE KILLED. COME TO ME. OH DEAR!
JUMP FOR YOUR LIFE! WE CAN'T STOP.
I CAN'T JUMP WITHOUT USONA. SIX HUNDRED FEET TO THE ROCKS BELOW. WHAT SHALL I DO? IF I JUMP I'LL BE KILLED. OH! OH! USONA I'LL NOT LEAVE YOU—
TOOOT TOOT TOOT
AS A LAST RESORT I'LL BUTT THE TRAIN AND SAVE MY—
LADY PLEASE STEP A BOARD AND LET US GO ON. HERE COMES THE LIGHTENING EXPRESS
DOGGIE. NO! NO! I'LL NOT LET YOU MOVE ONE INCH UNTIL I GET MY USONA. NO NO YOU SHANT GO—
NOW SEE WHAT YOU HAVE DONE LADY
SAVE MY DARLING USONA AND I'LL LET YOU GO. UNTIL YOU DO I'LL BUTT THE WHOLE BUSINESS BACK TO JERSEY. I DON'T CARE FOR RESULTS. SAVE USONA
OH MY HEAD! HAVE I BEEN BUTTING THAT WALL? OH OH THAT RAREBIT LAST NIGHT CAUSED THIS. USONA OH YOU'RE THERE. OH WHAT A DREAM OH MY HEAD
SILAS

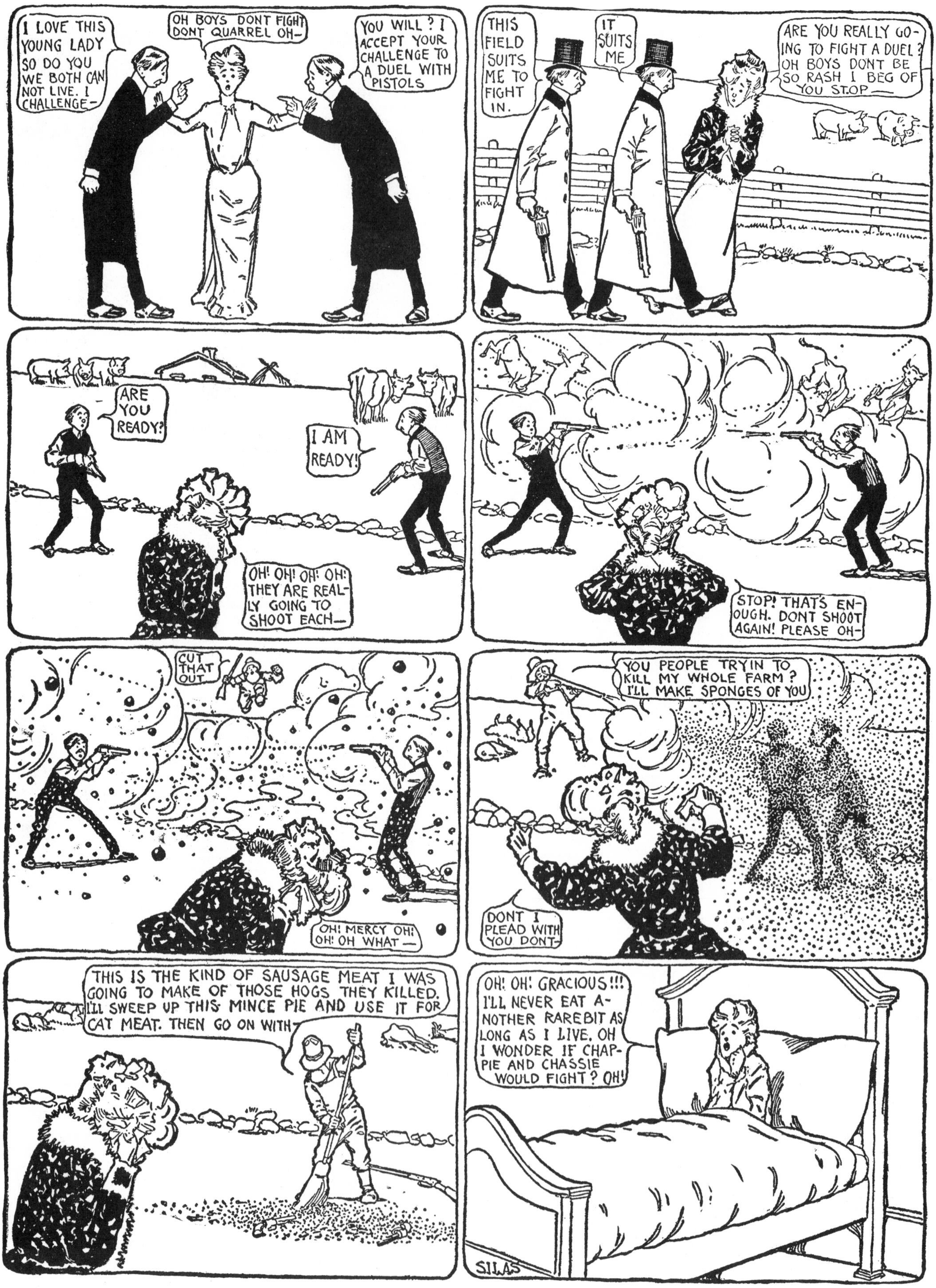
I LOVE THIS YOUNG LADY SO DO YOU WE BOTH CAN NOT LIVE. I CHALLENGE-
OH BOYS DONT FIGHT DONT QUARREL OH-
YOU WILL? I ACCEPT YOUR CHALLENGE TO A DUEL WITH PISTOLS
THIS FIELD SUITS ME TO FIGHT IN.
IT SUITS ME
ARE YOU REALLY GOING TO FIGHT A DUEL? OH BOYS DONT BE SO RASH I BEG OF YOU STOP—
ARE YOU READY?
I AM READY!
OH! OH! OH! OH! THEY ARE REALLY GOING TO SHOOT EACH—
STOP! THATS ENOUGH. DONT SHOOT AGAIN! PLEASE OH-
CUT THAT OUT
OH! MERCY OH! OH! OH WHAT—
YOU PEOPLE TRYIN TO KILL MY WHOLE FARM? I'LL MAKE SPONGES OF YOU
DONT I PLEAD WITH YOU DONT-
THIS IS THE KIND OF SAUSAGE MEAT I WAS GOING TO MAKE OF THOSE HOGS THEY KILLED. I'LL SWEEP UP THIS MINCE PIE AND USE IT FOR CAT MEAT. THEN GO ON WITH-
OH! OH! GRACIOUS!!! I'LL NEVER EAT ANOTHER RAREBIT AS LONG AS I LIVE. OH I WONDER IF CHAPPIE AND CHASSIE WOULD FIGHT? OH!
SILAS

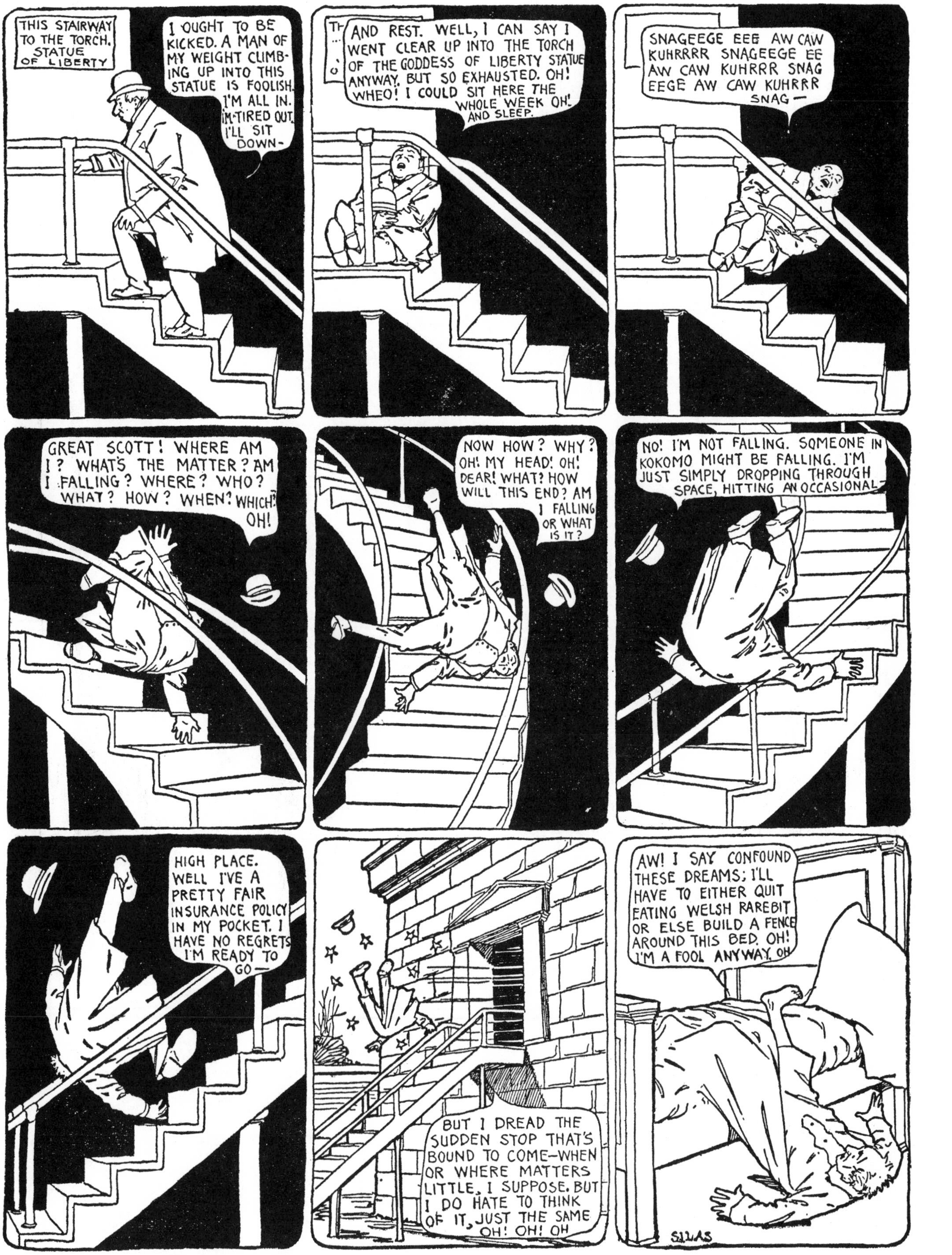
THIS STAIRWAY TO THE TORCH. STATUE OF LIBERTY
I OUGHT TO BE KICKED. A MAN OF MY WEIGHT CLIMBING UP INTO THIS STATUE IS FOOLISH. I'M ALL IN. I'M TIRED OUT. I'LL SIT DOWN-
AND REST. WELL, I CAN SAY I WENT CLEAR UP INTO THE TORCH OF THE GODDESS OF LIBERTY STATUE ANYWAY. BUT SO EXHAUSTED. OH! WHEO! I COULD SIT HERE THE WHOLE WEEK OH! AND SLEEP.
SNAGEEGE EEE AW CAW KUHRRRR SNAGEEGE EE AW CAW KUHRRR SNAG EEGE AW CAW KUHRRR SNAG—
GREAT SCOTT! WHERE AM I? WHAT'S THE MATTER? AM I FALLING? WHERE? WHO? WHAT? HOW? WHEN? WHICH? OH!
NOW HOW? WHY? OH! MY HEAD! OH! DEAR! WHAT? HOW WILL THIS END? AM I FALLING OR WHAT IS IT?
NO! I'M NOT FALLING. SOMEONE IN KOKOMO MIGHT BE FALLING. I'M JUST SIMPLY DROPPING THROUGH SPACE, HITTING AN OCCASIONAL-
HIGH PLACE. WELL I'VE A PRETTY FAIR INSURANCE POLICY IN MY POCKET. I HAVE NO REGRETS I'M READY TO GO—
BUT I DREAD THE SUDDEN STOP THAT'S BOUND TO COME—WHEN OR WHERE MATTERS LITTLE, I SUPPOSE. BUT I DO HATE TO THINK OF IT, JUST THE SAME OH! OH! OH
AW! I SAY CONFOUND THESE DREAMS; I'LL HAVE TO EITHER QUIT EATING WELSH RAREBIT OR ELSE BUILD A FENCE AROUND THIS BED. OH! I'M A FOOL ANYWAY. OH
SILAS

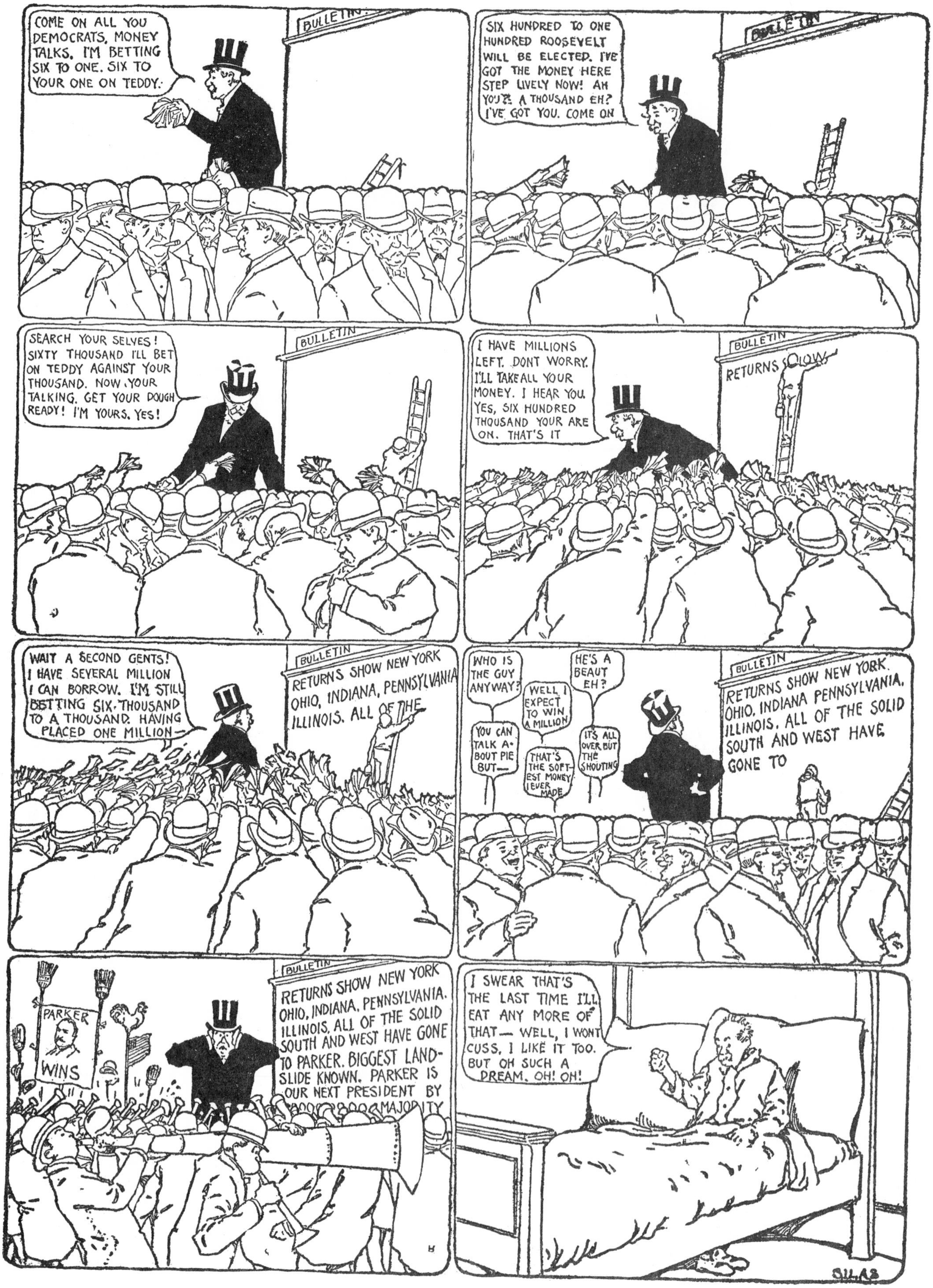
COME ON ALL YOU DEMOCRATS, MONEY TALKS. I'M BETTING SIX TO ONE. SIX TO YOUR ONE ON TEDDY.
BULLETIN
SIX HUNDRED TO ONE HUNDRED ROOSEVELT WILL BE ELECTED. I'VE GOT THE MONEY HERE STEP LIVELY NOW! AH YOU?? A THOUSAND EH? I'VE GOT YOU. COME ON
BULLETIN
SEARCH YOUR SELVES! SIXTY THOUSAND I'LL BET ON TEDDY AGAINST YOUR THOUSAND. NOW, YOUR TALKING. GET YOUR DOUGH READY! I'M YOURS. YES!
BULLETIN
I HAVE MILLIONS LEFT. DONT WORRY. I'LL TAKE ALL YOUR MONEY. I HEAR YOU. YES, SIX HUNDRED THOUSAND YOUR ARE ON. THAT'S IT
BULLETIN
RETURNS SHOW
WAIT A SECOND GENTS! I HAVE SEVERAL MILLION I CAN BORROW. I'M STILL BETTING SIX THOUSAND TO A THOUSAND. HAVING PLACED ONE MILLION—
BULLETIN
RETURNS SHOW NEW YORK OHIO, INDIANA, PENNSYLVANIA ILLINOIS. ALL OF THE
WHO IS THE GUY ANYWAY?
YOU CAN TALK ABOUT PIE BUT—
WELL I EXPECT TO WIN A MILLION
THAT'S THE SOFTEST MONEY I EVER MADE
HE'S A BEAUT EH?
IT'S ALL OVER BUT THE SHOUTING
BULLETIN
RETURNS SHOW NEW YORK. OHIO, INDIANA PENNSYLVANIA. ILLINOIS. ALL OF THE SOLID SOUTH AND WEST HAVE GONE TO
PARKER
WINS
BULLETIN
RETURNS SHOW NEW YORK OHIO, INDIANA, PENNSYLVANIA. ILLINOIS, ALL OF THE SOLID SOUTH AND WEST HAVE GONE TO PARKER. BIGGEST LANDSLIDE KNOWN. PARKER IS OUR NEXT PRESIDENT BY
MAJORITY
I SWEAR THAT'S THE LAST TIME I'LL EAT ANY MORE OF THAT— WELL, I WONT CUSS. I LIKE IT TOO. BUT OH SUCH A DREAM. OH! OH!
SILAS

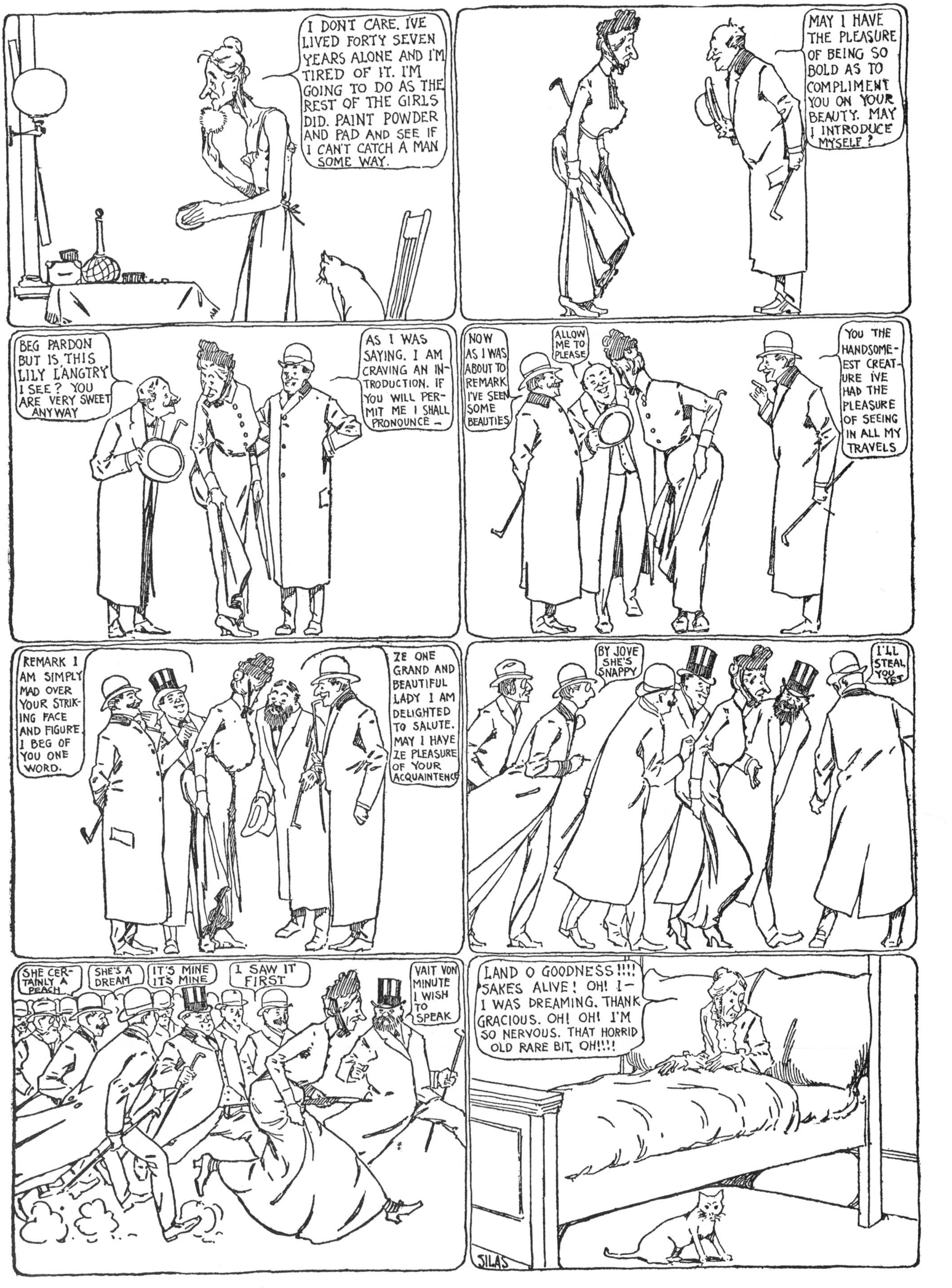

I DONT CARE. IVE LIVED FORTY SEVEN YEARS ALONE AND I'M TIRED OF IT. I'M GOING TO DO AS THE REST OF THE GIRLS DID. PAINT POWDER AND PAD AND SEE IF I CAN'T CATCH A MAN SOME WAY.
MAY I HAVE THE PLEASURE OF BEING SO BOLD AS TO COMPLIMENT YOU ON YOUR BEAUTY. MAY I INTRODUCE MYSELF?
BEG PARDON BUT IS THIS LILY LANGTRY I SEE? YOU ARE VERY SWEET ANYWAY
AS I WAS SAYING. I AM CRAVING AN INTRODUCTION. IF YOU WILL PERMIT ME I SHALL PRONOUNCE—
NOW AS I WAS ABOUT TO REMARK I'VE SEEN SOME BEAUTIES
ALLOW ME TO PLEASE
YOU THE HANDSOMEST CREATURE IVE HAD THE PLEASURE OF SEEING IN ALL MY TRAVELS
REMARK I AM SIMPLY MAD OVER YOUR STRIKING FACE AND FIGURE. I BEG OF YOU ONE WORD.
ZE ONE GRAND AND BEAUTIFUL LADY I AM DELIGHTED TO SALUTE. MAY I HAVE ZE PLEASURE OF YOUR ACQUAINTENCE
BY JOVE SHE'S SNAPPY
I'LL STEAL YOU YET
SHE CERTAINLY A PEACH
SHE'S A DREAM
IT'S MINE ITS MINE
I SAW IT FIRST
VAIT VON MINUTE I WISH TO SPEAK
LAND O GOODNESS!!!! SAKES ALIVE! OH! I— I WAS DREAMING. THANK GRACIOUS. OH! OH! I'M SO NERVOUS. THAT HORRID OLD RARE BIT. OH!!!!
SILAS

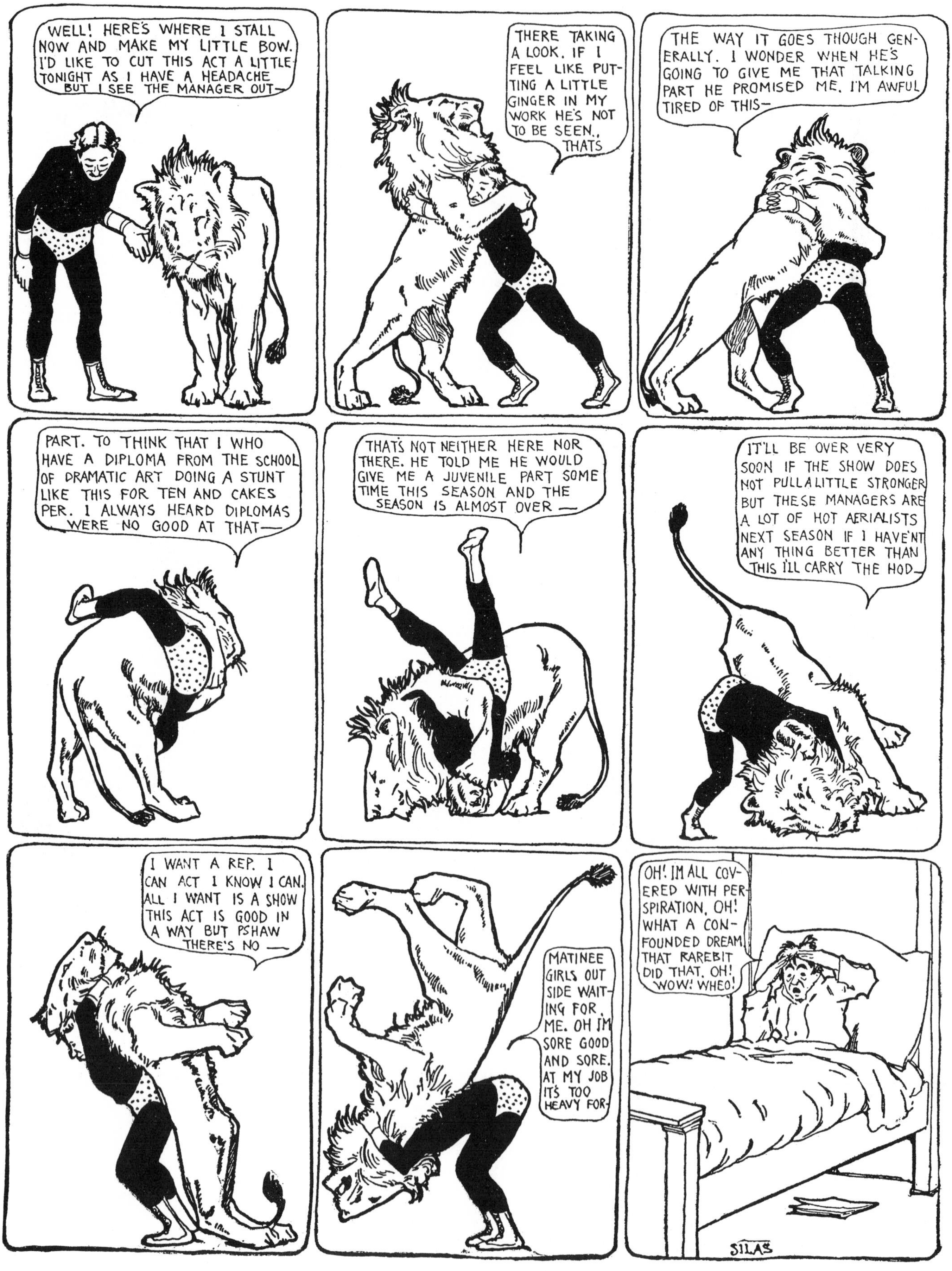
WELL! HERE'S WHERE I STALL NOW AND MAKE MY LITTLE BOW. I'D LIKE TO CUT THIS ACT A LITTLE TONIGHT AS I HAVE A HEADACHE BUT I SEE THE MANAGER OUT—
THERE TAKING A LOOK. IF I FEEL LIKE PUTTING A LITTLE GINGER IN MY WORK HE'S NOT TO BE SEEN., THATS
THE WAY IT GOES THOUGH GENERALLY. I WONDER WHEN HE'S GOING TO GIVE ME THAT TALKING PART HE PROMISED ME. I'M AWFUL TIRED OF THIS—
PART. TO THINK THAT I WHO HAVE A DIPLOMA FROM THE SCHOOL OF DRAMATIC ART DOING A STUNT LIKE THIS FOR TEN AND CAKES PER. I ALWAYS HEARD DIPLOMAS WERE NO GOOD AT THAT—
THAT'S NOT NEITHER HERE NOR THERE. HE TOLD ME HE WOULD GIVE ME A JUVENILE PART SOME TIME THIS SEASON AND THE SEASON IS ALMOST OVER —
IT'LL BE OVER VERY SOON IF THE SHOW DOES NOT PULL A LITTLE STRONGER BUT THESE MANAGERS ARE A LOT OF HOT AERIALISTS NEXT SEASON IF I HAVEN'T ANY THING BETTER THAN THIS I'LL CARRY THE HOD—
I WANT A REP. I CAN ACT I KNOW I CAN. ALL I WANT IS A SHOW THIS ACT IS GOOD IN A WAY BUT PSHAW THERE'S NO —
MATINEE GIRLS OUT SIDE WAITING FOR ME. OH I'M SORE GOOD AND SORE. AT MY JOB IT'S TOO HEAVY FOR—
OH! I'M ALL COVERED WITH PERSPIRATION. OH! WHAT A CONFOUNDED DREAM. THAT RAREBIT DID THAT. OH! WOW! WHEO!
SILAS

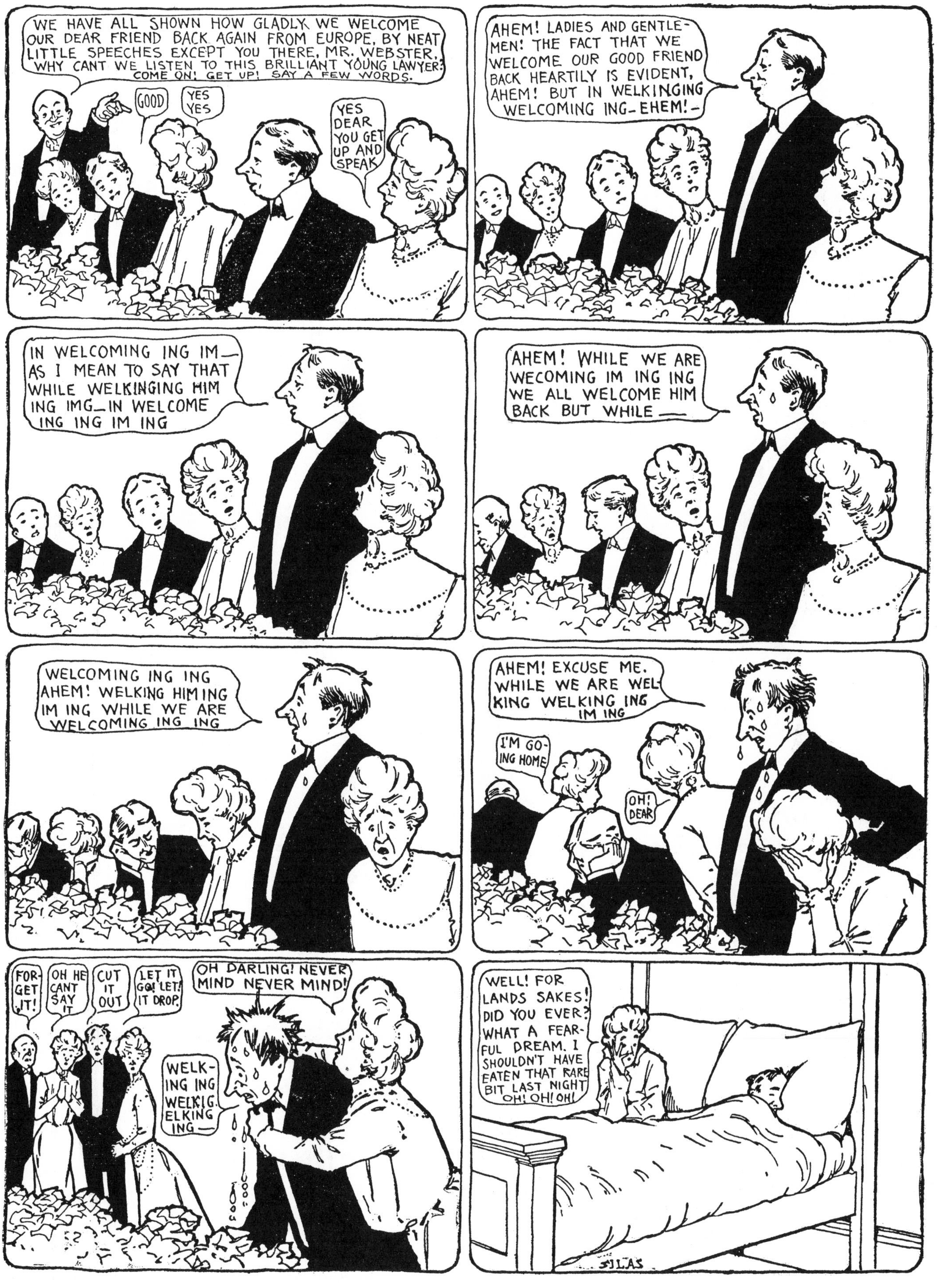
WE HAVE ALL SHOWN HOW GLADLY WE WELCOME OUR DEAR FRIEND BACK AGAIN FROM EUROPE, BY NEAT LITTLE SPEECHES EXCEPT YOU THERE, MR. WEBSTER. WHY CANT WE LISTEN TO THIS BRILLIANT YOUNG LAWYER? COME ON! GET UP! SAY A FEW WORDS.
GOOD
YES YES
YES DEAR YOU GET UP AND SPEAK
AHEM! LADIES AND GENTLEMEN! THE FACT THAT WE WELCOME OUR GOOD FRIEND BACK HEARTILY IS EVIDENT, AHEM! BUT IN WELKINGING WELCOMING ING-EHEM!-
IN WELCOMING ING IM— AS I MEAN TO SAY THAT WHILE WELKINGING HIM ING IMG—IN WELCOME ING ING IM ING
AHEM! WHILE WE ARE WECOMING IM ING ING WE ALL WELCOME HIM BACK BUT WHILE —
WELCOMING ING ING AHEM! WELKING HIMING IM ING WHILE WE ARE WELCOMING ING ING
AHEM! EXCUSE ME. WHILE WE ARE WELKING WELKING ING IM ING
I'M GOING HOME
OH! DEAR
FORGET IT!
OH HE CANT SAY IT
CUT IT OUT
LET IT GO! LET IT DROP.
OH DARLING! NEVER MIND NEVER MIND!
WELKING ING WELKIG. ELKING ING—
WELL! FOR LANDS SAKES! DID YOU EVER? WHAT A FEARFUL DREAM. I SHOULDN'T HAVE EATEN THAT RARE BIT LAST NIGHT OH! OH! OH!
SILAS

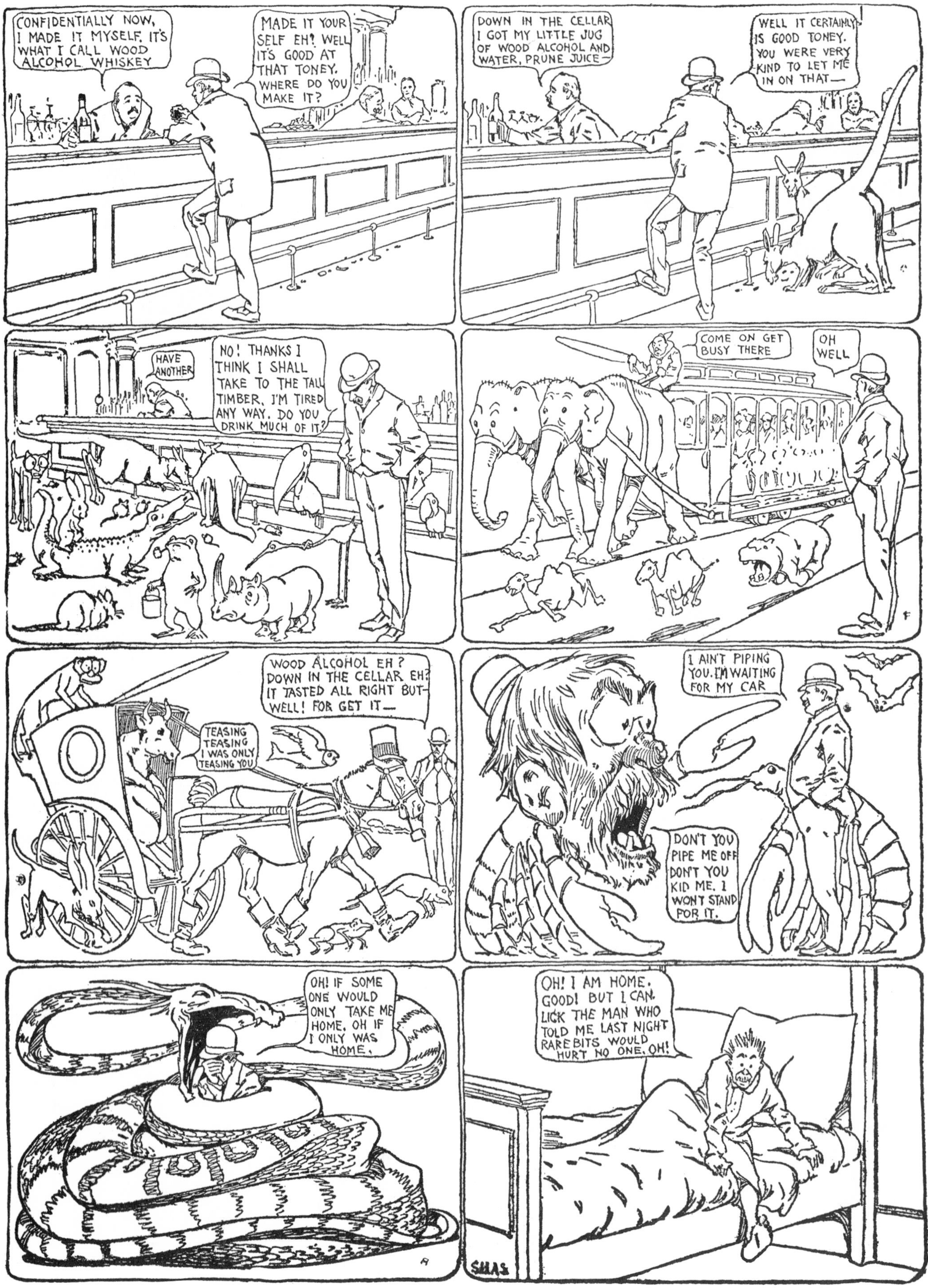
CONFIDENTIALLY NOW, I MADE IT MYSELF. IT'S WHAT I CALL WOOD ALCOHOL WHISKEY
MADE IT YOUR SELF EH? WELL IT'S GOOD AT THAT TONEY. WHERE DO YOU MAKE IT?
DOWN IN THE CELLAR I GOT MY LITTLE JUG OF WOOD ALCOHOL AND WATER, PRUNE JUICE—
WELL IT CERTAINLY IS GOOD TONEY. YOU WERE VERY KIND TO LET ME IN ON THAT—
HAVE ANOTHER
NO! THANKS I THINK I SHALL TAKE TO THE TALL TIMBER. I'M TIRED ANY WAY. DO YOU DRINK MUCH OF IT?
COME ON GET BUSY THERE
OH WELL
WOOD ALCOHOL EH? DOWN IN THE CELLAR EH? IT TASTED ALL RIGHT BUT- WELL! FOR GET IT—
TEASING TEASING I WAS ONLY TEASING YOU
I AIN'T PIPING YOU. I'M WAITING FOR MY CAR
DON'T YOU PIPE ME OFF DON'T YOU KID ME. I WON'T STAND FOR IT.
OH! IF SOME ONE WOULD ONLY TAKE ME HOME. OH IF I ONLY WAS HOME.
OH! I AM HOME. GOOD! BUT I CAN LICK THE MAN WHO TOLD ME LAST NIGHT RAREBITS WOULD HURT NO ONE. OH!
SILAS

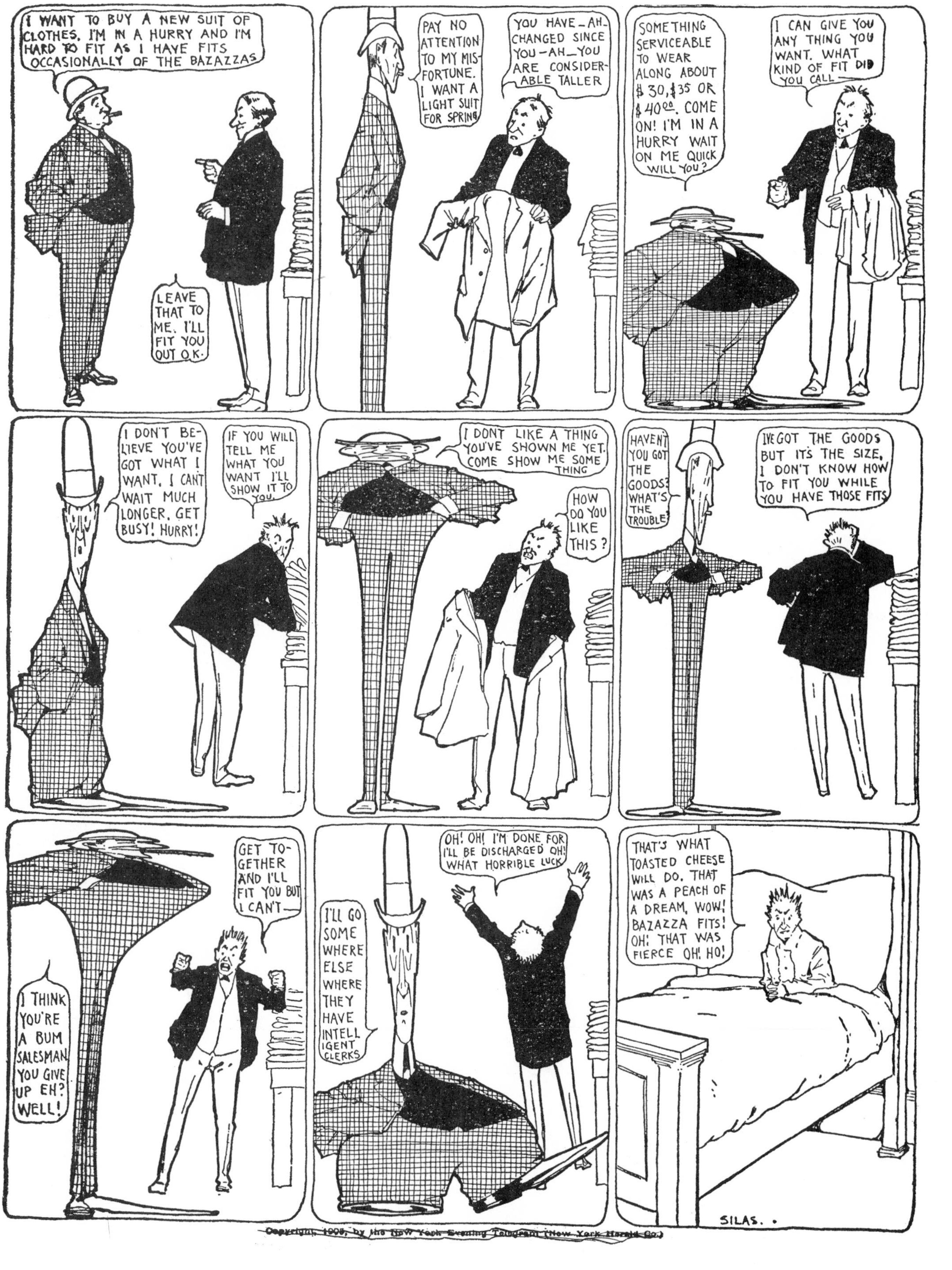
I WANT TO BUY A NEW SUIT OF CLOTHES. I'M IN A HURRY AND I'M HARD TO FIT AS I HAVE FITS OCCASIONALLY OF THE BAZAZZAS
LEAVE THAT TO ME. I'LL FIT YOU OUT O.K.
PAY NO ATTENTION TO MY MISFORTUNE. I WANT A LIGHT SUIT FOR SPRING
YOU HAVE_AH_CHANGED SINCE YOU-AH_YOU ARE CONSIDERABLE TALLER
SOMETHING SERVICEABLE TO WEAR ALONG ABOUT $30, $35 OR $40.00 COME ON! I'M IN A HURRY WAIT ON ME QUICK WILL YOU?
I CAN GIVE YOU ANY THING YOU WANT. WHAT KIND OF FIT DID YOU CALL_
I DON'T BELIEVE YOU'VE GOT WHAT I WANT. I CAN'T WAIT MUCH LONGER. GET BUSY! HURRY!
IF YOU WILL TELL ME WHAT YOU WANT I'LL SHOW IT TO YOU.
I DONT LIKE A THING YOU'VE SHOWN ME YET. COME SHOW ME SOME THING
HOW DO YOU LIKE THIS?
HAVEN'T YOU GOT THE GOODS? WHAT'S THE TROUBLE?
IVE GOT THE GOODS BUT ITS THE SIZE. I DON'T KNOW HOW TO FIT YOU WHILE YOU HAVE THOSE FITS
GET TOGETHER AND I'LL FIT YOU BUT I CAN'T_
I THINK YOU'RE A BUM SALESMAN YOU GIVE UP EH? WELL!
OH! OH! I'M DONE FOR I'LL BE DISCHARGED OH! WHAT HORRIBLE LUCK
I'LL GO SOME WHERE ELSE WHERE THEY HAVE INTELLIGENT CLERKS
THAT'S WHAT TOASTED CHEESE WILL DO. THAT WAS A PEACH OF A DREAM, WOW! BAZAZZA FITS! OH! THAT WAS FIERCE OH! HO!
SILAS.

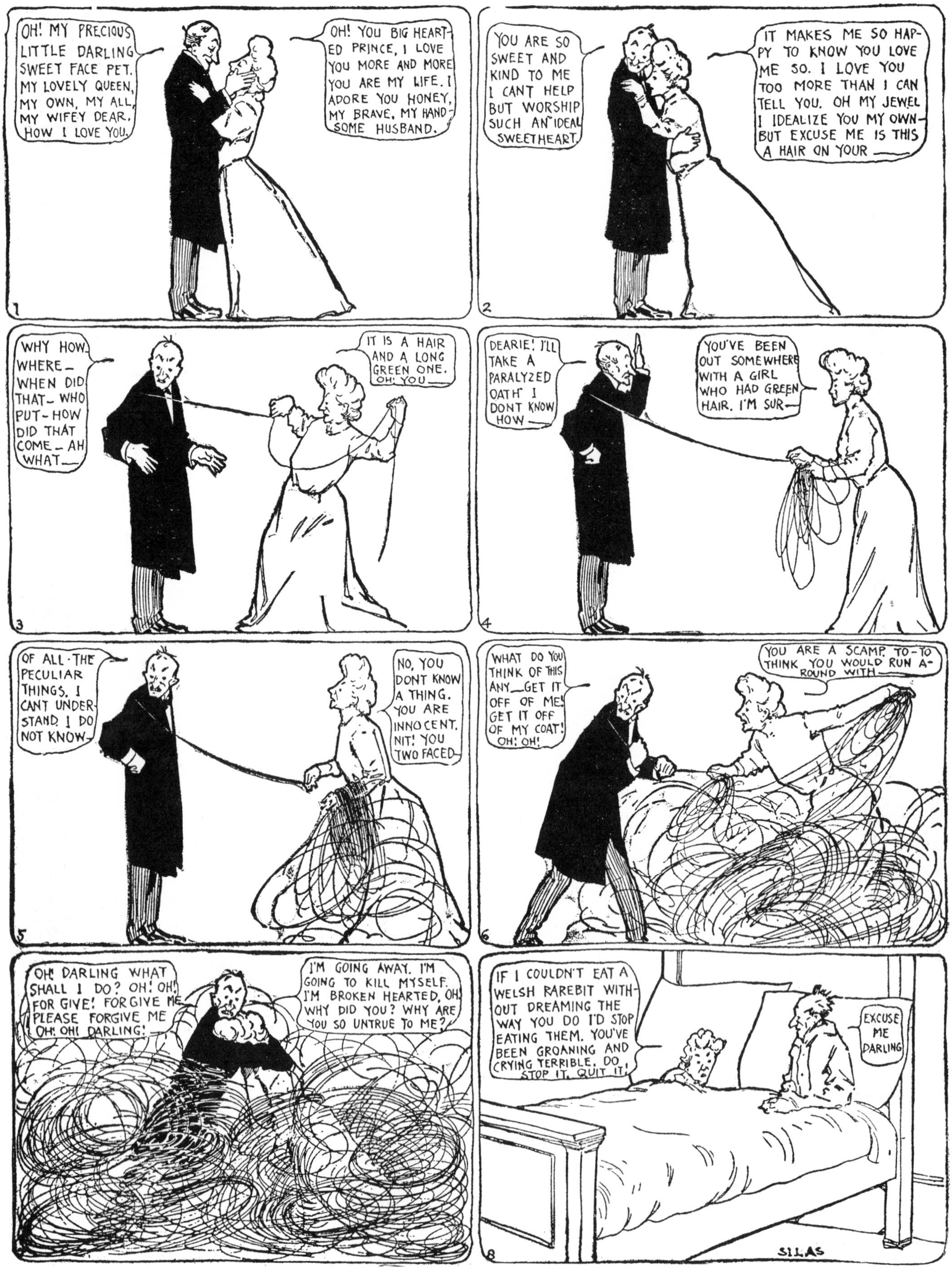
OH! MY PRECIOUS LITTLE DARLING SWEET FACE PET. MY LOVELY QUEEN, MY OWN, MY ALL, MY WIFEY DEAR. HOW I LOVE YOU.
OH! YOU BIG HEARTED PRINCE, I LOVE YOU MORE AND MORE YOU ARE MY LIFE. I ADORE YOU HONEY, MY BRAVE, MY HANDSOME HUSBAND.
YOU ARE SO SWEET AND KIND TO ME I CANT HELP BUT WORSHIP SUCH AN IDEAL SWEETHEART.
IT MAKES ME SO HAPPY TO KNOW YOU LOVE ME SO. I LOVE YOU TOO MORE THAN I CAN TELL YOU. OH MY JEWEL I IDEALIZE YOU MY OWN BUT EXCUSE ME IS THIS A HAIR ON YOUR —
WHY HOW WHERE — WHEN DID THAT — WHO PUT — HOW DID THAT COME — AH WHAT —
IT IS A HAIR AND A LONG GREEN ONE. OH! YOU —
DEARIE! I'LL TAKE A PARALYZED OATH I DONT KNOW HOW —
YOU'VE BEEN OUT SOMEWHERE WITH A GIRL WHO HAD GREEN HAIR. I'M SUR —
OF ALL THE PECULIAR THINGS. I CANT UNDERSTAND. I DO NOT KNOW —
NO, YOU DONT KNOW A THING. YOU ARE INNOCENT. NIT! YOU TWO FACED —
WHAT DO YOU THINK OF THIS ANY — GET IT OFF OF ME! GET IT OFF OF MY COAT! OH! OH!
YOU ARE A SCAMP. TO — TO THINK YOU WOULD RUN AROUND WITH —
OH! DARLING WHAT SHALL I DO? OH! OH! FORGIVE! FORGIVE ME PLEASE FORGIVE ME OH! OH! DARLING!
I'M GOING AWAY. I'M GOING TO KILL MYSELF. I'M BROKEN HEARTED, OH! WHY DID YOU? WHY ARE YOU SO UNTRUE TO ME?
IF I COULDN'T EAT A WELSH RAREBIT WITHOUT DREAMING THE WAY YOU DO I'D STOP EATING THEM. YOU'VE BEEN GROANING AND CRYING TERRIBLE. DO STOP IT. QUIT IT!
EXCUSE ME DARLING
SILAS

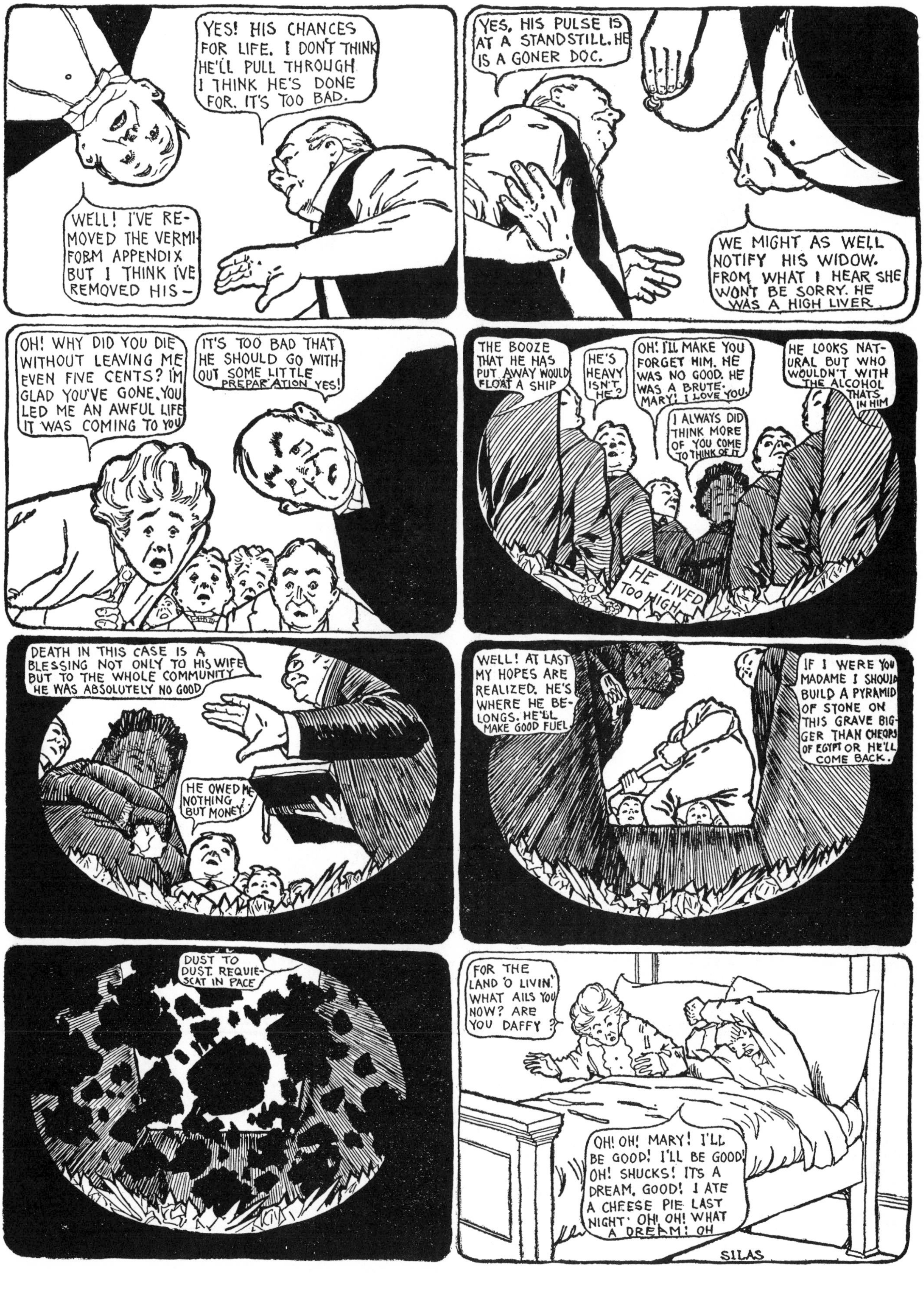
WELL! I'VE RE-MOVED THE VERMI-FORM APPENDIX BUT I THINK I'VE REMOVED HIS—
YES! HIS CHANCES FOR LIFE. I DON'T THINK HE'LL PULL THROUGH I THINK HE'S DONE FOR. IT'S TOO BAD.
YES, HIS PULSE IS AT A STANDSTILL. HE IS A GONER DOC.
WE MIGHT AS WELL NOTIFY HIS WIDOW. FROM WHAT I HEAR SHE WON'T BE SORRY. HE WAS A HIGH LIVER.
OH! WHY DID YOU DIE WITHOUT LEAVING ME EVEN FIVE CENTS? I'M GLAD YOU'VE GONE. YOU LED ME AN AWFUL LIFE IT WAS COMING TO YOU
IT'S TOO BAD THAT HE SHOULD GO WITH-OUT SOME LITTLE PREPARATION YES!
THE BOOZE THAT HE HAS PUT AWAY WOULD FLOAT A SHIP
HE'S HEAVY ISN'T HE?
OH! I'LL MAKE YOU FORGET HIM. HE WAS NO GOOD. HE WAS A BRUTE. MARY! I LOVE YOU.
I ALWAYS DID THINK MORE OF YOU COME TO THINK OF IT
HE LOOKS NAT-URAL BUT WHO WOULDN'T WITH THE ALCOHOL THATS IN HIM
HE LIVED TOO HIGH
DEATH IN THIS CASE IS A BLESSING NOT ONLY TO HIS WIFE BUT TO THE WHOLE COMMUNITY HE WAS ABSOLUTELY NO GOOD
HE OWED ME NOTHING BUT MONEY!
WELL! AT LAST MY HOPES ARE REALIZED. HE'S WHERE HE BE-LONGS. HE'LL MAKE GOOD FUEL
IF I WERE YOU MADAME I SHOULD BUILD A PYRAMID OF STONE ON THIS GRAVE BIG-GER THAN CHEOPS OF EGYPT OR HE'LL COME BACK.
DUST TO DUST. REQUIE-SCAT IN PACE
FOR THE LAND 'O LIVIN' WHAT AILS YOU NOW? ARE YOU DAFFY?
OH! OH! MARY! I'LL BE GOOD! I'LL BE GOOD! OH! SHUCKS! ITS A DREAM. GOOD! I ATE A CHEESE PIE LAST NIGHT. OH! OH! WHAT A DREAM! OH
SILAS

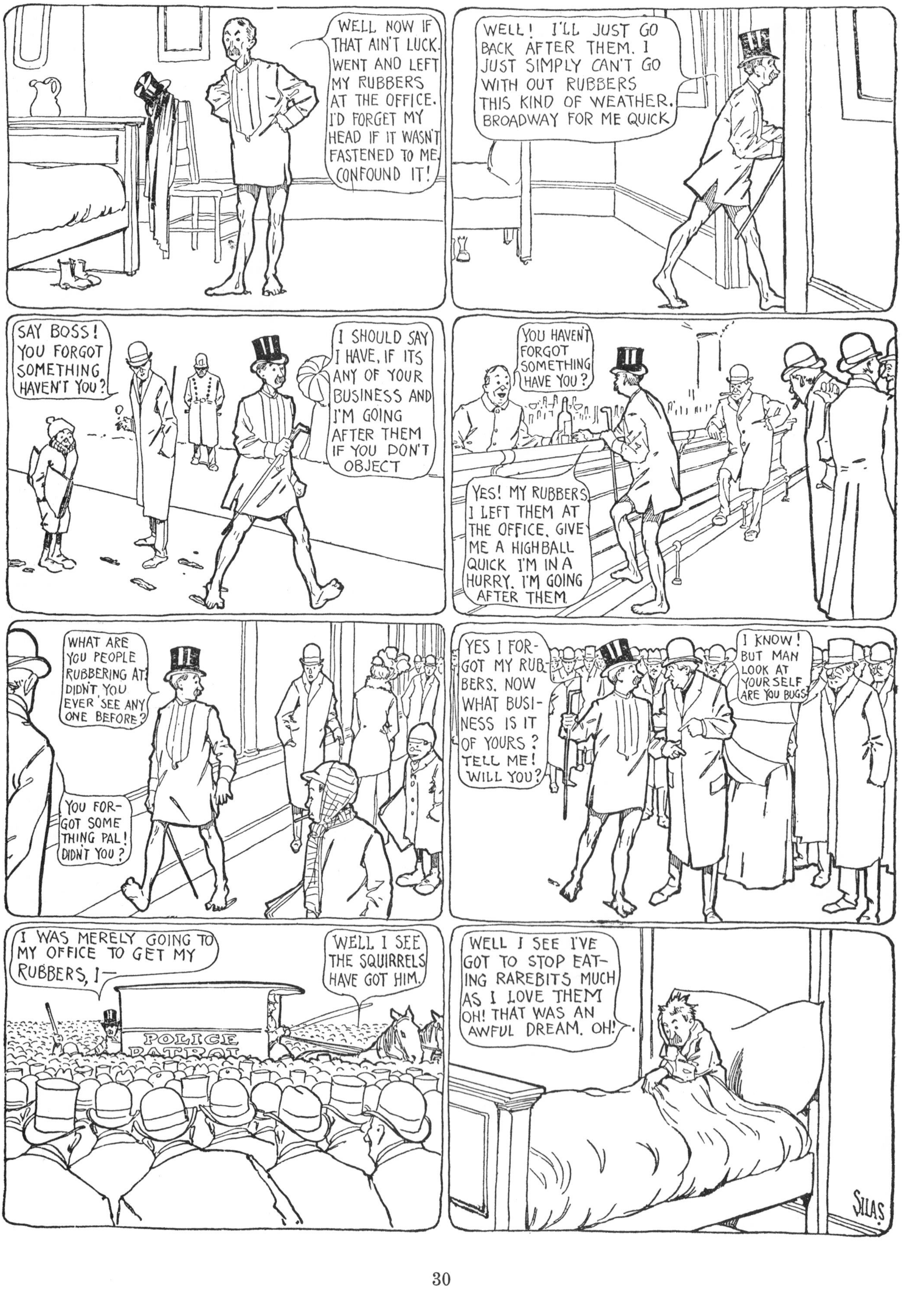
WELL NOW IF THAT AIN'T LUCK. WENT AND LEFT MY RUBBERS AT THE OFFICE. I'D FORGET MY HEAD IF IT WASN'T FASTENED TO ME. CONFOUND IT!
WELL! I'LL JUST GO BACK AFTER THEM. I JUST SIMPLY CAN'T GO WITH OUT RUBBERS THIS KIND OF WEATHER. BROADWAY FOR ME QUICK
SAY BOSS! YOU FORGOT SOMETHING HAVEN'T YOU?
I SHOULD SAY I HAVE, IF ITS ANY OF YOUR BUSINESS AND I'M GOING AFTER THEM IF YOU DON'T OBJECT
YOU HAVEN'T FORGOT SOMETHING HAVE YOU?
YES! MY RUBBERS. I LEFT THEM AT THE OFFICE. GIVE ME A HIGHBALL QUICK I'M IN A HURRY. I'M GOING AFTER THEM.
WHAT ARE YOU PEOPLE RUBBERING AT! DIDN'T YOU EVER SEE ANY ONE BEFORE?
YOU FOR-GOT SOME THING PAL! DIDN'T YOU?
YES I FOR-GOT MY RUB-BERS. NOW WHAT BUSI-NESS IS IT OF YOURS? TELL ME! WILL YOU?
I KNOW! BUT MAN LOOK AT YOURSELF ARE YOU BUGS?
I WAS MERELY GOING TO MY OFFICE TO GET MY RUBBERS, I—
WELL I SEE THE SQUIRRELS HAVE GOT HIM.
POLICE PATROL
WELL I SEE I'VE GOT TO STOP EAT-ING RAREBITS MUCH AS I LOVE THEM OH! THAT WAS AN AWFUL DREAM. OH!
SILAS

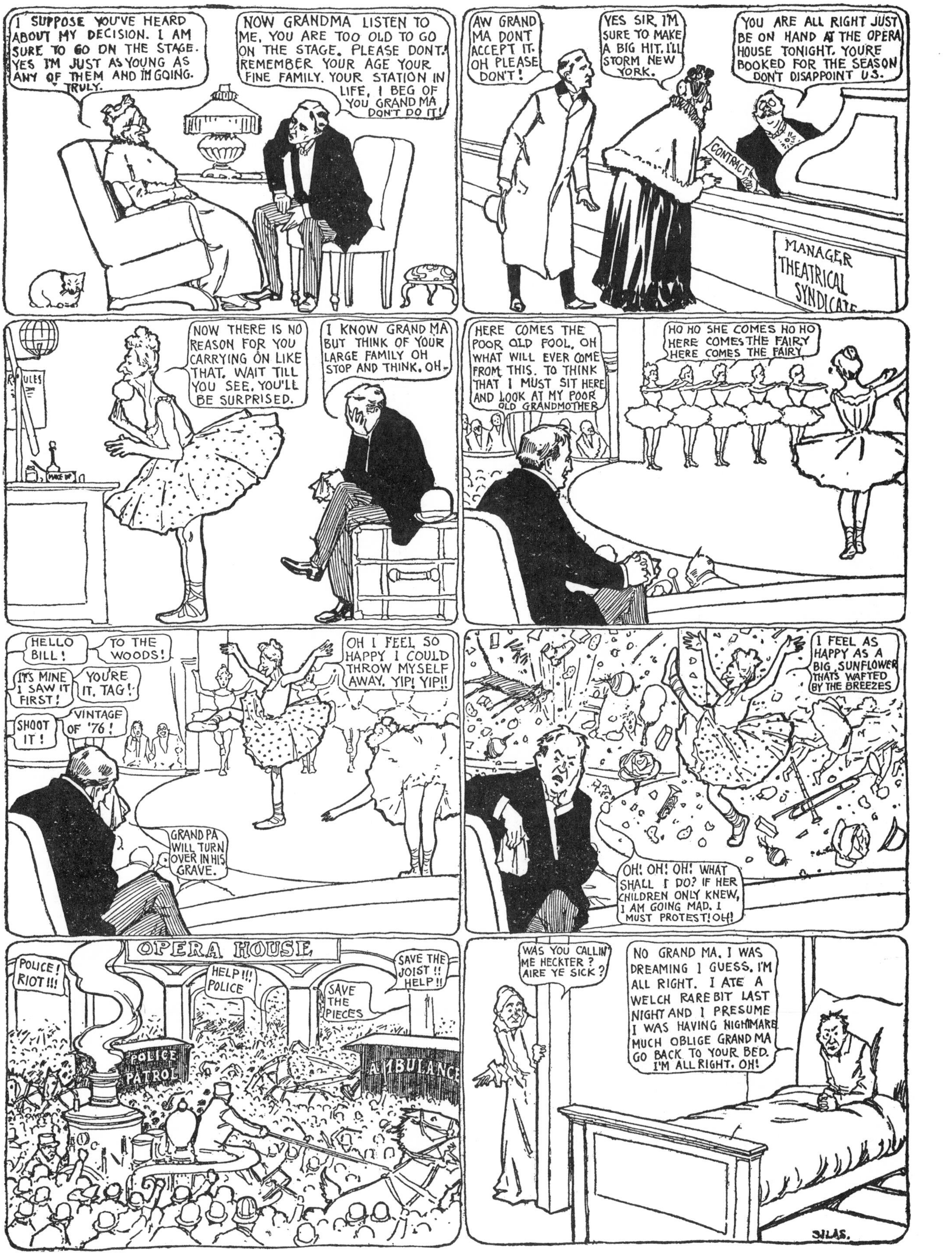
I SUPPOSE YOU'VE HEARD ABOUT MY DECISION. I AM SURE TO GO ON THE STAGE. YES I'M JUST AS YOUNG AS ANY OF THEM AND I'M GOING. TRULY.
NOW GRANDMA LISTEN TO ME, YOU ARE TOO OLD TO GO ON THE STAGE. PLEASE DONT! REMEMBER YOUR AGE YOUR FINE FAMILY. YOUR STATION IN LIFE, I BEG OF YOU GRAND MA DON'T DO IT!
AW GRAND MA DONT ACCEPT IT. OH PLEASE DON'T!
YES SIR, I'M SURE TO MAKE A BIG HIT. I'LL STORM NEW YORK.
YOU ARE ALL RIGHT JUST BE ON HAND AT THE OPERA HOUSE TONIGHT. YOU'RE BOOKED FOR THE SEASON DON'T DISAPPOINT US.
CONTRACT
MANAGER THEATRICAL SYNDICATE
RULES
MAKE UP
NOW THERE IS NO REASON FOR YOU CARRYING ON LIKE THAT. WAIT TILL YOU SEE. YOU'LL BE SURPRISED.
I KNOW GRAND MA BUT THINK OF YOUR LARGE FAMILY OH STOP AND THINK. OH.
HERE COMES THE POOR OLD FOOL. OH WHAT WILL EVER COME FROM THIS. TO THINK THAT I MUST SIT HERE AND LOOK AT MY POOR OLD GRANDMOTHER
HO HO SHE COMES HO HO HERE COMES THE FAIRY HERE COMES THE FAIRY
HELLO BILL!
TO THE WOODS!
IT'S MINE I SAW IT FIRST!
YOU'RE IT. TAG!
SHOOT IT!
VINTAGE OF '76!
OH I FEEL SO HAPPY I COULD THROW MYSELF AWAY. YIP! YIP!!
GRAND PA WILL TURN OVER IN HIS GRAVE.
I FEEL AS HAPPY AS A BIG SUNFLOWER THATS WAFTED BY THE BREEZES
OH! OH! OH! WHAT SHALL I DO? IF HER CHILDREN ONLY KNEW, I AM GOING MAD. I MUST PROTEST! OH!
OPERA HOUSE
POLICE! RIOT!!!
HELP!!! POLICE
SAVE THE JOIST!! HELP!!
SAVE THE PIECES
POLICE PATROL
AMBULANCE
WAS YOU CALLIN' ME HECKTER? AIRE YE SICK?
NO GRAND MA. I WAS DREAMING I GUESS. I'M ALL RIGHT. I ATE A WELCH RAREBIT LAST NIGHT AND I PRESUME I WAS HAVING NIGHTMARE MUCH OBLIGE GRAND MA GO BACK TO YOUR BED. I'M ALL RIGHT. OH!
SILAS.

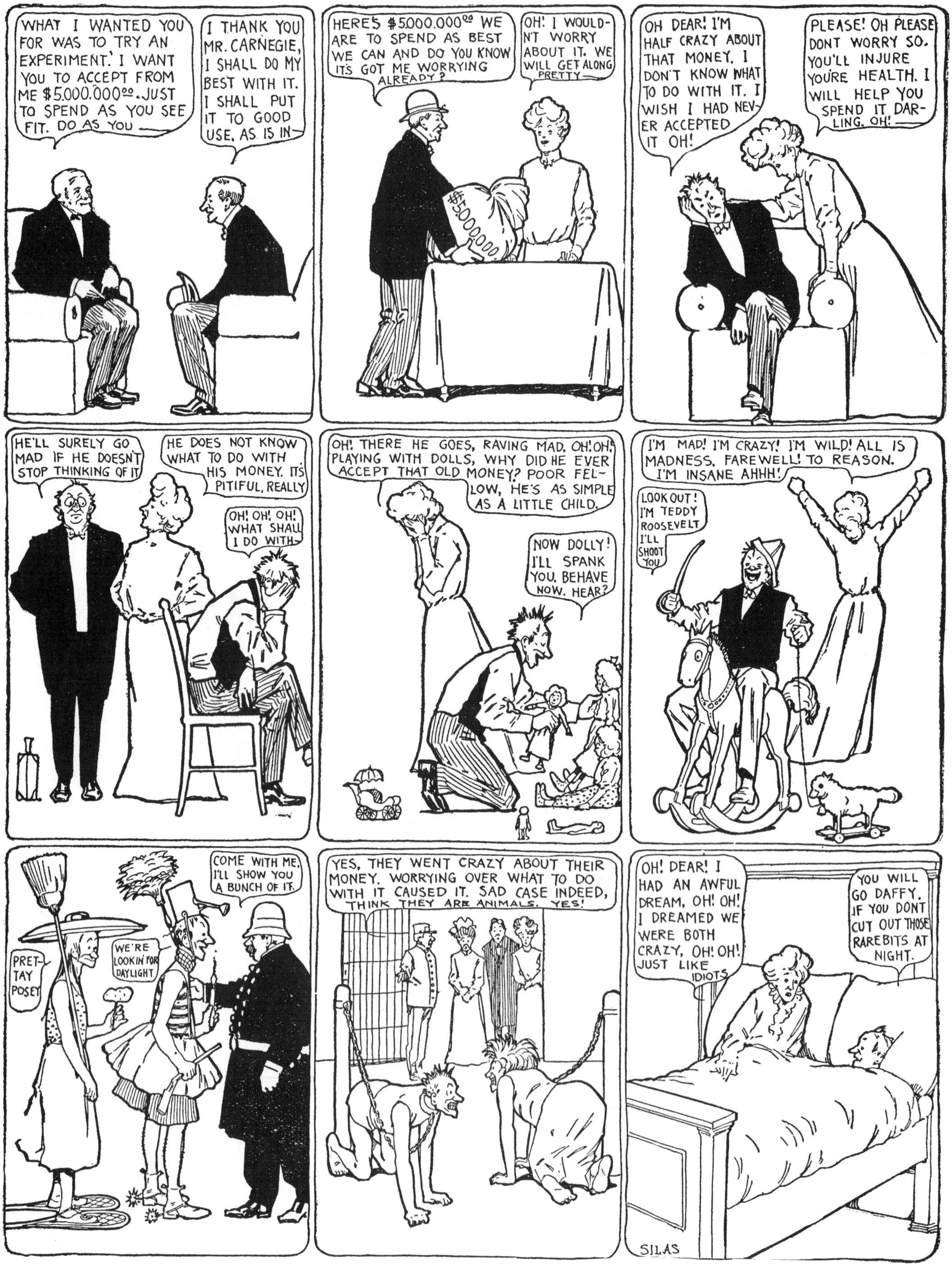

WHAT I WANTED YOU FOR WAS TO TRY AN EXPERIMENT. I WANT YOU TO ACCEPT FROM ME $5.000.000.00 JUST TO SPEND AS YOU SEE FIT. DO AS YOU —
I THANK YOU MR. CARNEGIE, I SHALL DO MY BEST WITH IT. I SHALL PUT IT TO GOOD USE, AS IS IN—
HERE'S $5.000.000.00 WE ARE TO SPEND AS BEST WE CAN AND DO YOU KNOW ITS GOT ME WORRYING ALREADY?
OH! I WOULDN'T WORRY ABOUT IT. WE WILL GET ALONG PRETTY —
$5000000
OH DEAR! I'M HALF CRAZY ABOUT THAT MONEY. I DON'T KNOW WHAT TO DO WITH IT. I WISH I HAD NEVER ACCEPTED IT OH!
PLEASE! OH PLEASE DONT WORRY SO. YOU'LL INJURE YOU'RE HEALTH. I WILL HELP YOU SPEND IT DARLING. OH!
HE'LL SURELY GO MAD IF HE DOESN'T STOP THINKING OF IT
HE DOES NOT KNOW WHAT TO DO WITH HIS MONEY. ITS PITIFUL, REALLY
OH! OH! OH! WHAT SHALL I DO WITH-
OH! THERE HE GOES, RAVING MAD. OH! OH! PLAYING WITH DOLLS, WHY DID HE EVER ACCEPT THAT OLD MONEY? POOR FELLOW, HE'S AS SIMPLE AS A LITTLE CHILD.
NOW DOLLY! I'LL SPANK YOU. BEHAVE NOW. HEAR?
I'M MAD! I'M CRAZY! I'M WILD! ALL IS MADNESS. FAREWELL! TO REASON. I'M INSANE AHHH!
LOOK OUT! I'M TEDDY ROOSEVELT I'LL SHOOT YOU
PRETTAY POSEY
WE'RE LOOKIN' FOR DAYLIGHT
COME WITH ME, I'LL SHOW YOU A BUNCH OF IT.
YES, THEY WENT CRAZY ABOUT THEIR MONEY. WORRYING OVER WHAT TO DO WITH IT CAUSED IT. SAD CASE INDEED, THINK THEY ARE ANIMALS. YES!
OH! DEAR! I HAD AN AWFUL DREAM, OH! OH! I DREAMED WE WERE BOTH CRAZY, OH! OH! JUST LIKE IDIOTS
YOU WILL GO DAFFY, IF YOU DONT CUT OUT THOSE RAREBITS AT NIGHT.
SILAS

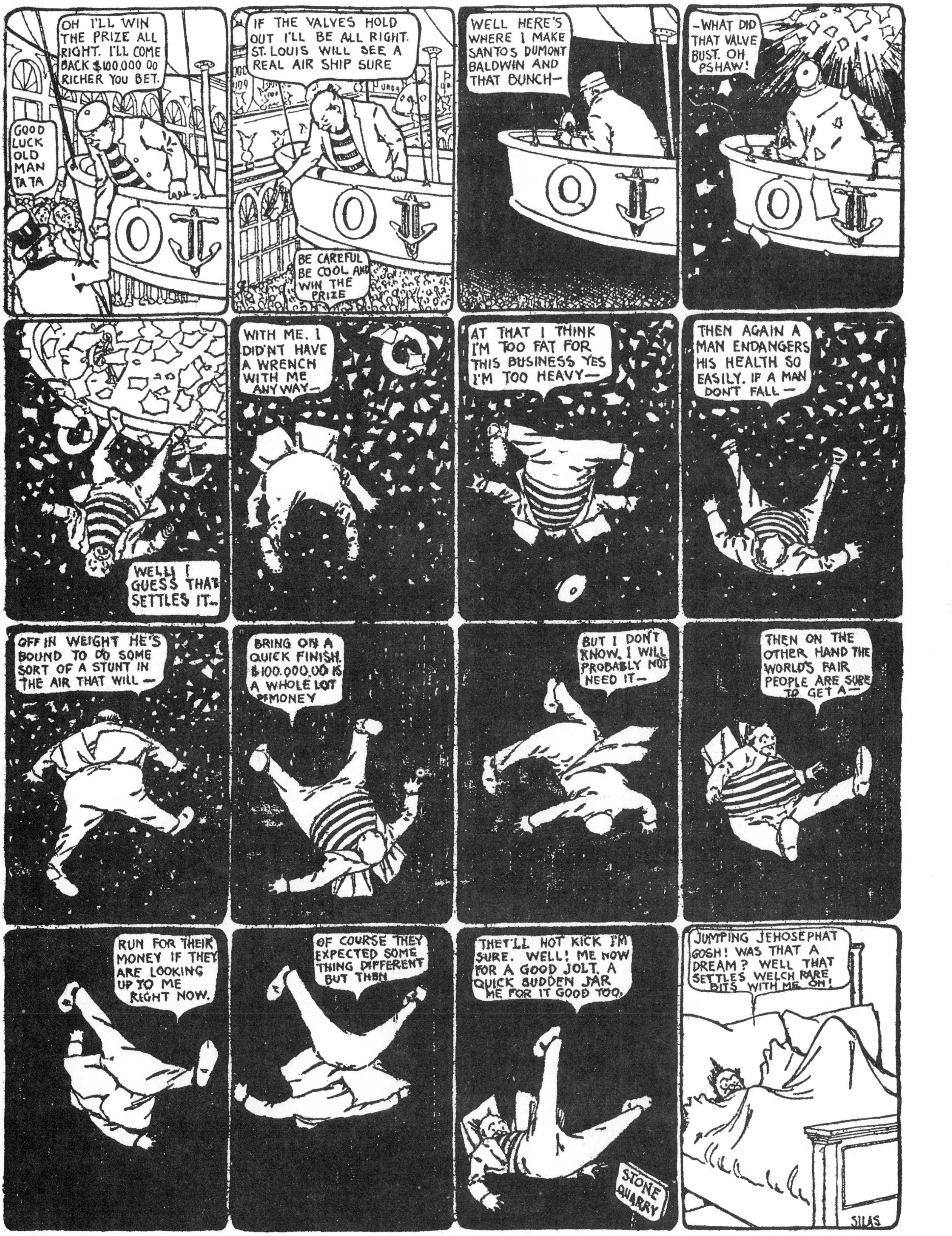
OH I'LL WIN THE PRIZE ALL RIGHT. I'LL COME BACK $100.000 00 RICHER YOU BET.
GOOD LUCK OLD MAN TA TA
IF THE VALVES HOLD OUT I'LL BE ALL RIGHT. ST. LOUIS WILL SEE A REAL AIR SHIP SURE
BE CAREFUL BE COOL AND WIN THE PRIZE
WELL HERE'S WHERE I MAKE SANTOS DUMONT BALDWIN AND THAT BUNCH—
—WHAT DID THAT VALVE BUST. OH PSHAW!
WELL! I GUESS THAT SETTLES IT—
WITH ME. I DIDN'T HAVE A WRENCH WITH ME ANYWAY—
AT THAT I THINK I'M TOO FAT FOR THIS BUSINESS YES I'M TOO HEAVY—
THEN AGAIN A MAN ENDANGERS HIS HEALTH SO EASILY. IF A MAN DON'T FALL—
OFF IN WEIGHT HE'S BOUND TO DO SOME SORT OF A STUNT IN THE AIR THAT WILL—
BRING ON A QUICK FINISH. $100.000.00 IS A WHOLE LOT OF MONEY
BUT I DON'T KNOW. I WILL PROBABLY NOT NEED IT—
THEN ON THE OTHER HAND THE WORLD'S FAIR PEOPLE ARE SURE TO GET A—
RUN FOR THEIR MONEY IF THEY ARE LOOKING UP TO ME RIGHT NOW.
OF COURSE THEY EXPECTED SOME THING DIFFERENT BUT THEN
THEY'LL NOT KICK I'M SURE. WELL! ME NOW FOR A GOOD JOLT. A QUICK SUDDEN JAR ME FOR IT GOOD TOO.
STONE QUARRY
JUMPING JEHOSEPHAT GOSH! WAS THAT A DREAM? WELL THAT SETTLES WELCH RARE BITS WITH ME. OH!
SILAS

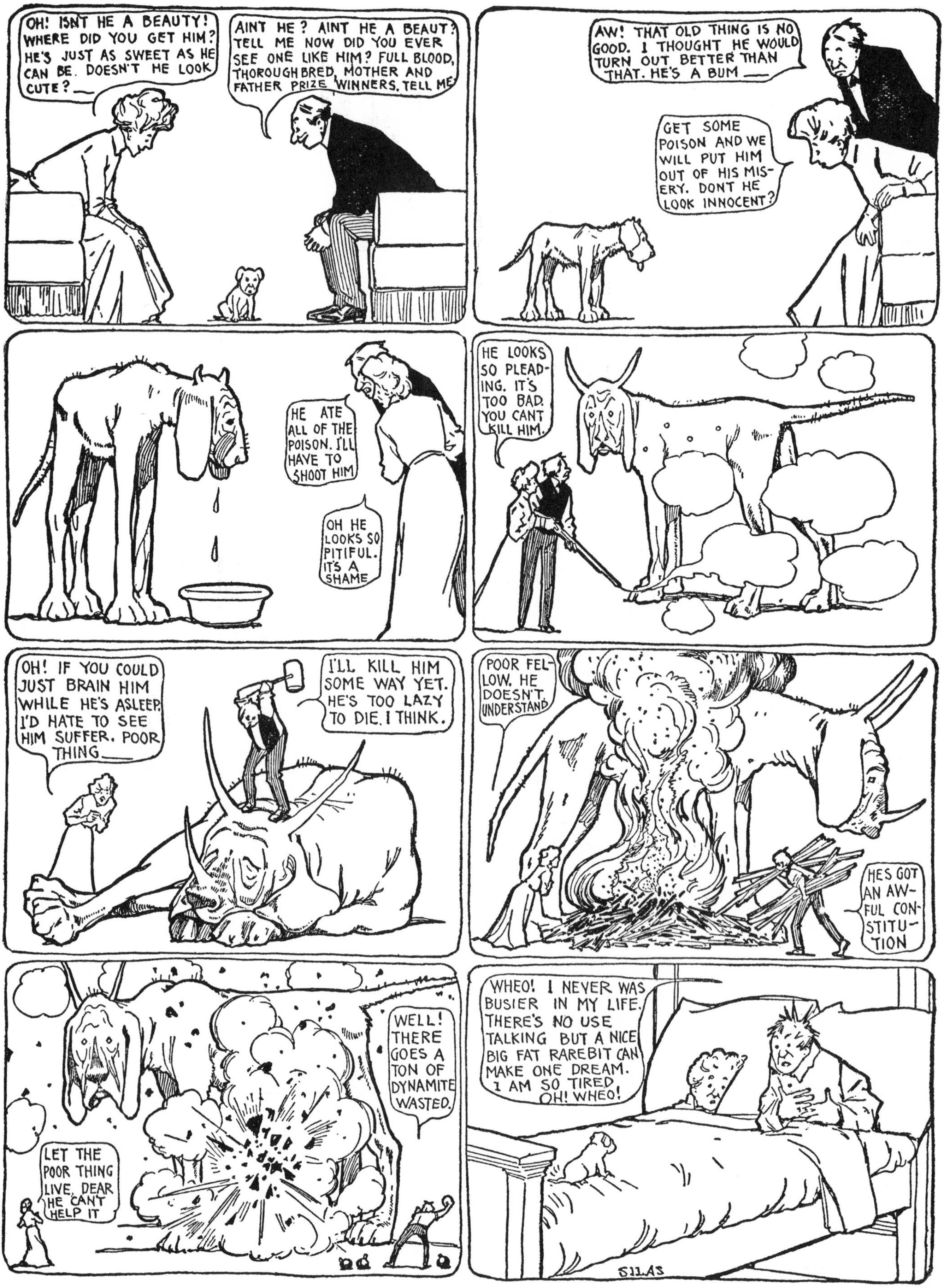
OH! ISN'T HE A BEAUTY! WHERE DID YOU GET HIM? HE'S JUST AS SWEET AS HE CAN BE. DOESN'T HE LOOK CUTE?
AINT HE? AINT HE A BEAUT? TELL ME NOW DID YOU EVER SEE ONE LIKE HIM? FULL BLOOD, THOROUGHBRED, MOTHER AND FATHER PRIZE WINNERS. TELL ME
AW! THAT OLD THING IS NO GOOD. I THOUGHT HE WOULD TURN OUT BETTER THAN THAT. HE'S A BUM
GET SOME POISON AND WE WILL PUT HIM OUT OF HIS MISERY. DONT HE LOOK INNOCENT?
HE ATE ALL OF THE POISON. I'LL HAVE TO SHOOT HIM
OH HE LOOKS SO PITIFUL. IT'S A SHAME
HE LOOKS SO PLEADING. IT'S TOO BAD. YOU CANT KILL HIM.
OH! IF YOU COULD JUST BRAIN HIM WHILE HE'S ASLEEP. I'D HATE TO SEE HIM SUFFER. POOR THING
I'LL KILL HIM SOME WAY YET. HE'S TOO LAZY TO DIE. I THINK.
POOR FELLOW. HE DOESN'T UNDERSTAND
HE'S GOT AN AWFUL CONSTITUTION
WELL! THERE GOES A TON OF DYNAMITE WASTED.
LET THE POOR THING LIVE, DEAR HE CAN'T HELP IT
WHEO! I NEVER WAS BUSIER IN MY LIFE. THERE'S NO USE TALKING BUT A NICE BIG FAT RAREBIT CAN MAKE ONE DREAM. I AM SO TIRED OH! WHEO!
SILAS

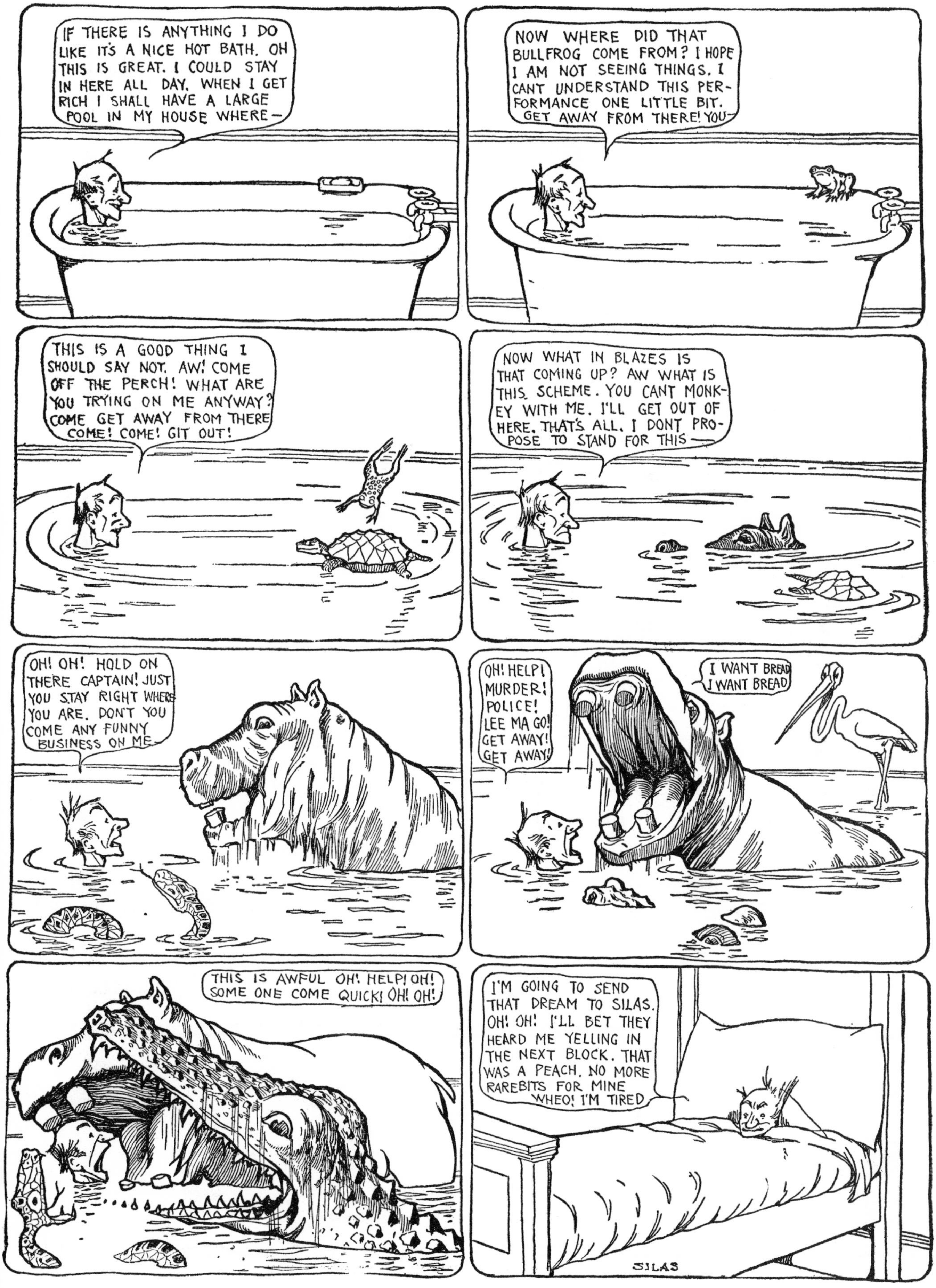
IF THERE IS ANYTHING I DO LIKE IT'S A NICE HOT BATH. OH THIS IS GREAT. I COULD STAY IN HERE ALL DAY. WHEN I GET RICH I SHALL HAVE A LARGE POOL IN MY HOUSE WHERE—
NOW WHERE DID THAT BULLFROG COME FROM? I HOPE I AM NOT SEEING THINGS. I CANT UNDERSTAND THIS PERFORMANCE ONE LITTLE BIT. GET AWAY FROM THERE! YOU—
THIS IS A GOOD THING I SHOULD SAY NOT. AW! COME OFF THE PERCH! WHAT ARE YOU TRYING ON ME ANYWAY? COME GET AWAY FROM THERE COME! COME! GIT OUT!
NOW WHAT IN BLAZES IS THAT COMING UP? AW WHAT IS THIS SCHEME. YOU CANT MONKEY WITH ME. I'LL GET OUT OF HERE. THAT'S ALL. I DONT PROPOSE TO STAND FOR THIS—
OH! OH! HOLD ON THERE CAPTAIN! JUST YOU STAY RIGHT WHERE YOU ARE. DON'T YOU COME ANY FUNNY BUSINESS ON ME—
OH! HELP! MURDER! POLICE! LEE MA GO! GET AWAY! GET AWAY!
I WANT BREAD I WANT BREAD
THIS IS AWFUL OH! HELP! OH! SOME ONE COME QUICK! OH! OH!
I'M GOING TO SEND THAT DREAM TO SILAS. OH! OH! I'LL BET THEY HEARD ME YELLING IN THE NEXT BLOCK. THAT WAS A PEACH. NO MORE RAREBITS FOR MINE WHEO! I'M TIRED
SILAS

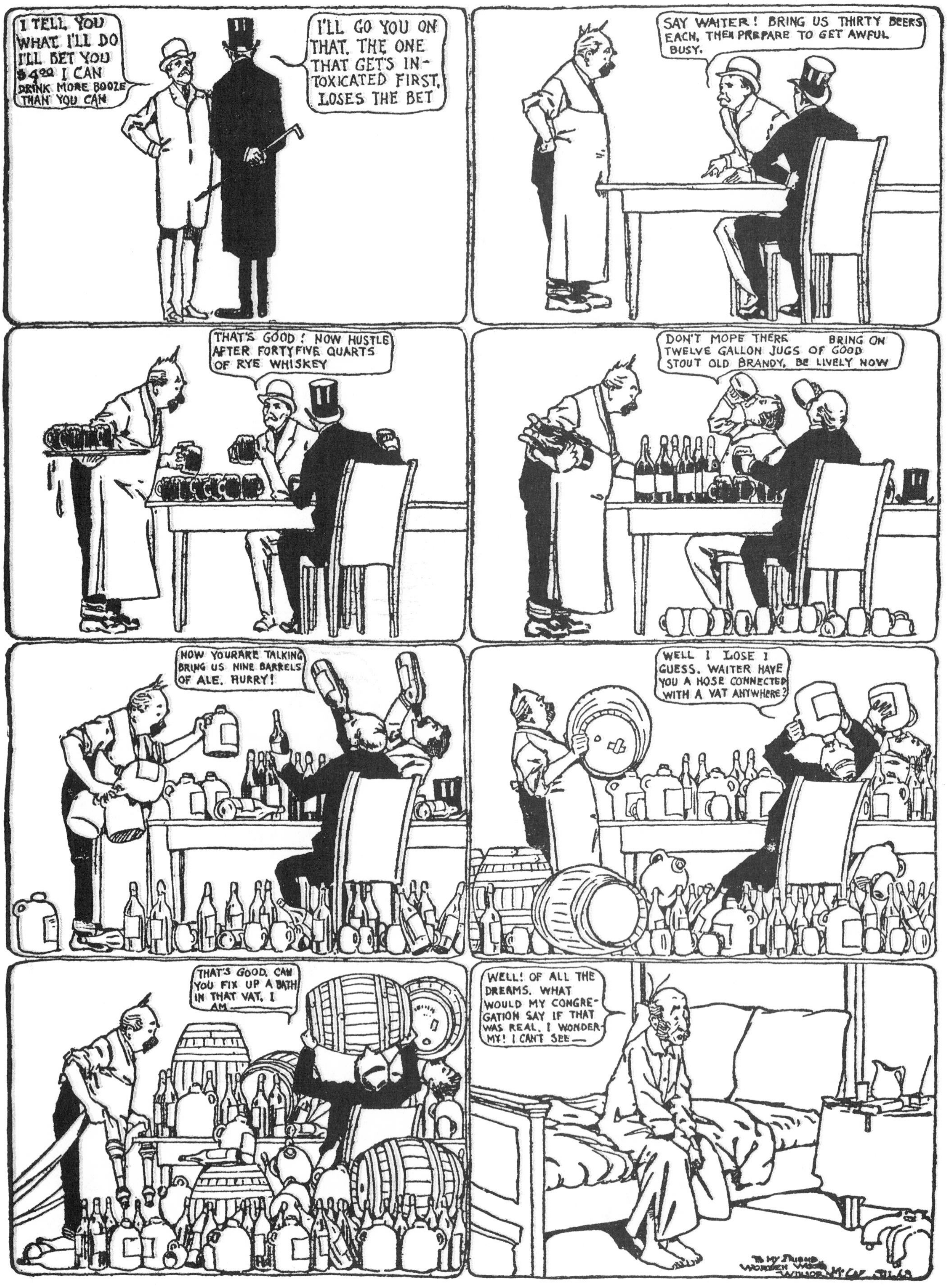
I TELL YOU WHAT I'LL DO I'LL BET YOU $4.00 I CAN DRINK MORE BOOZE THAN YOU CAN
I'LL GO YOU ON THAT. THE ONE THAT GET'S INTOXICATED FIRST, LOSES THE BET
SAY WAITER! BRING US THIRTY BEERS EACH, THEN PREPARE TO GET AWFUL BUSY.
THAT'S GOOD! NOW HUSTLE AFTER FORTYFIVE QUARTS OF RYE WHISKEY
DON'T MOPE THERE BRING ON TWELVE GALLON JUGS OF GOOD STOUT OLD BRANDY, BE LIVELY NOW
NOW YOURARE TALKING BRING US NINE BARRELS OF ALE. HURRY!
WELL I LOSE I GUESS. WAITER HAVE YOU A HOSE CONNECTED WITH A VAT ANYWHERE?
THAT'S GOOD, CAN YOU FIX UP A BATH IN THAT VAT, I AM
WELL! OF ALL THE DREAMS. WHAT WOULD MY CONGREGATION SAY IF THAT WAS REAL. I WONDER. MY! I CAN'T SEE —

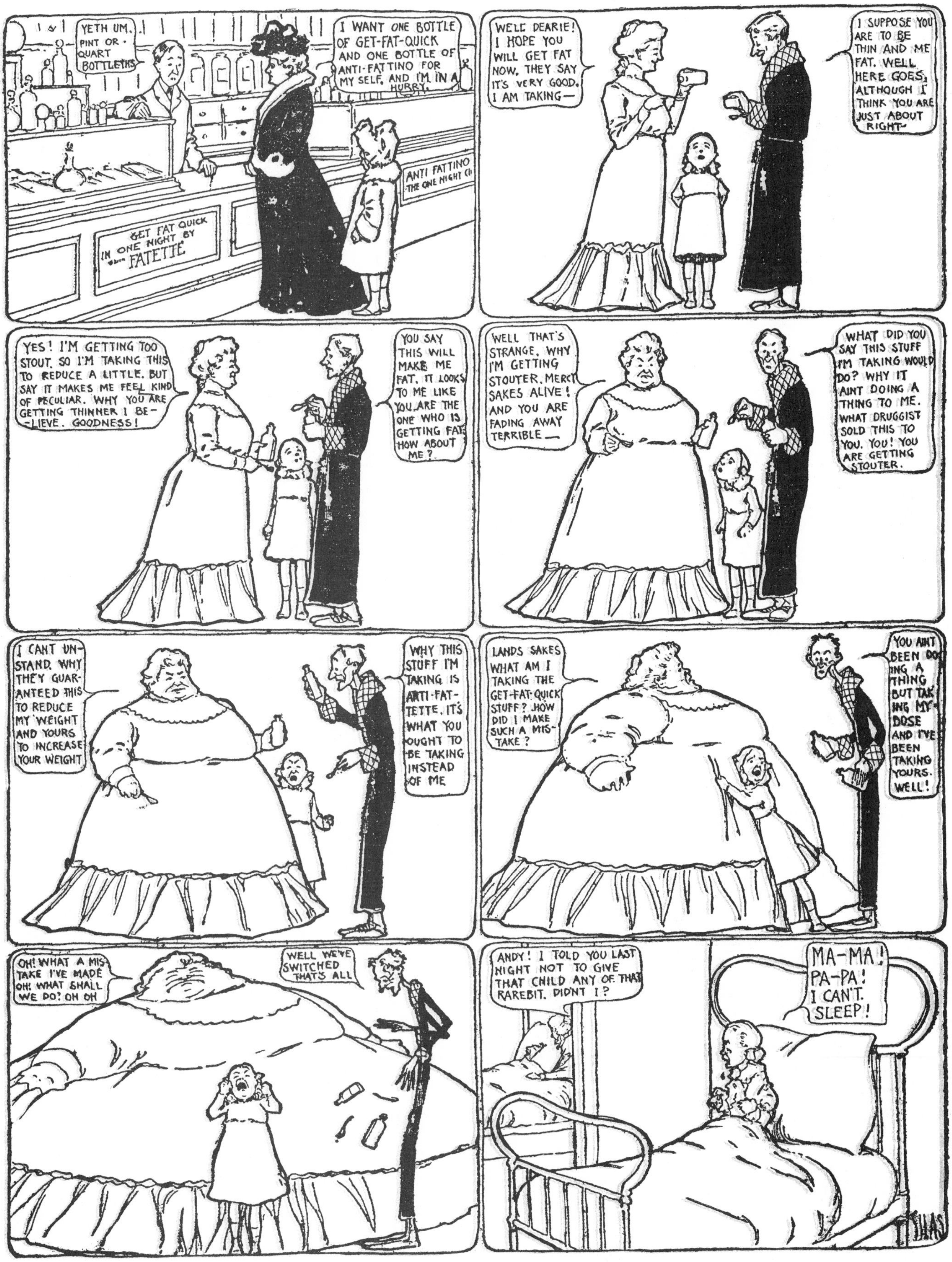
YETH UM. PINT OR QUART BOTTLEYTH?
I WANT ONE BOTTLE OF GET-FAT-QUICK AND ONE BOTTLE OF ANTI-FATTINO FOR MY SELF. AND I'M IN A HURRY.
ANTI FATTINO THE ONE NIGHT
GET FAT QUICK IN ONE NIGHT BY FATETTE
WELL DEARIE! I HOPE YOU WILL GET FAT NOW. THEY SAY IT'S VERY GOOD. I AM TAKING—
I SUPPOSE YOU ARE TO BE THIN AND ME FAT. WELL HERE GOES, ALTHOUGH I THINK YOU ARE JUST ABOUT RIGHT—
YES! I'M GETTING TOO STOUT. SO I'M TAKING THIS TO REDUCE A LITTLE. BUT SAY IT MAKES ME FEEL KIND OF PECULIAR. WHY YOU ARE GETTING THINNER I BE--LIEVE. GOODNESS!
YOU SAY THIS WILL MAKE ME FAT. IT LOOKS TO ME LIKE YOU ARE THE ONE WHO IS GETTING FAT. HOW ABOUT ME?
WELL THAT'S STRANGE. WHY I'M GETTING STOUTER. MERCY SAKES ALIVE! AND YOU ARE FADING AWAY TERRIBLE—
WHAT DID YOU SAY THIS STUFF I'M TAKING WOULD DO? WHY IT AINT DOING A THING TO ME. WHAT DRUGGIST SOLD THIS TO YOU. YOU! YOU ARE GETTING STOUTER.
I CANT UNSTAND. WHY THEY GUARANTEED THIS TO REDUCE MY WEIGHT AND YOURS TO INCREASE YOUR WEIGHT
WHY THIS STUFF I'M TAKING IS ANTI-FAT-TETTE. IT'S WHAT YOU OUGHT TO BE TAKING INSTEAD OF ME
LANDS SAKES WHAT AM I TAKING THE GET-FAT-QUICK STUFF? HOW DID I MAKE SUCH A MISTAKE?
YOU AINT BEEN DOING A THING BUT TAKING MY DOSE AND I'VE BEEN TAKING YOURS. WELL!
OH! WHAT A MISTAKE I'VE MADE OH! WHAT SHALL WE DO? OH OH
WELL WE'VE SWITCHED THAT'S ALL
ANDY! I TOLD YOU LAST NIGHT NOT TO GIVE THAT CHILD ANY OF THAT RAREBIT. DIDN'T I?
MA-MA! PA-PA! I CAN'T SLEEP!
SILAS

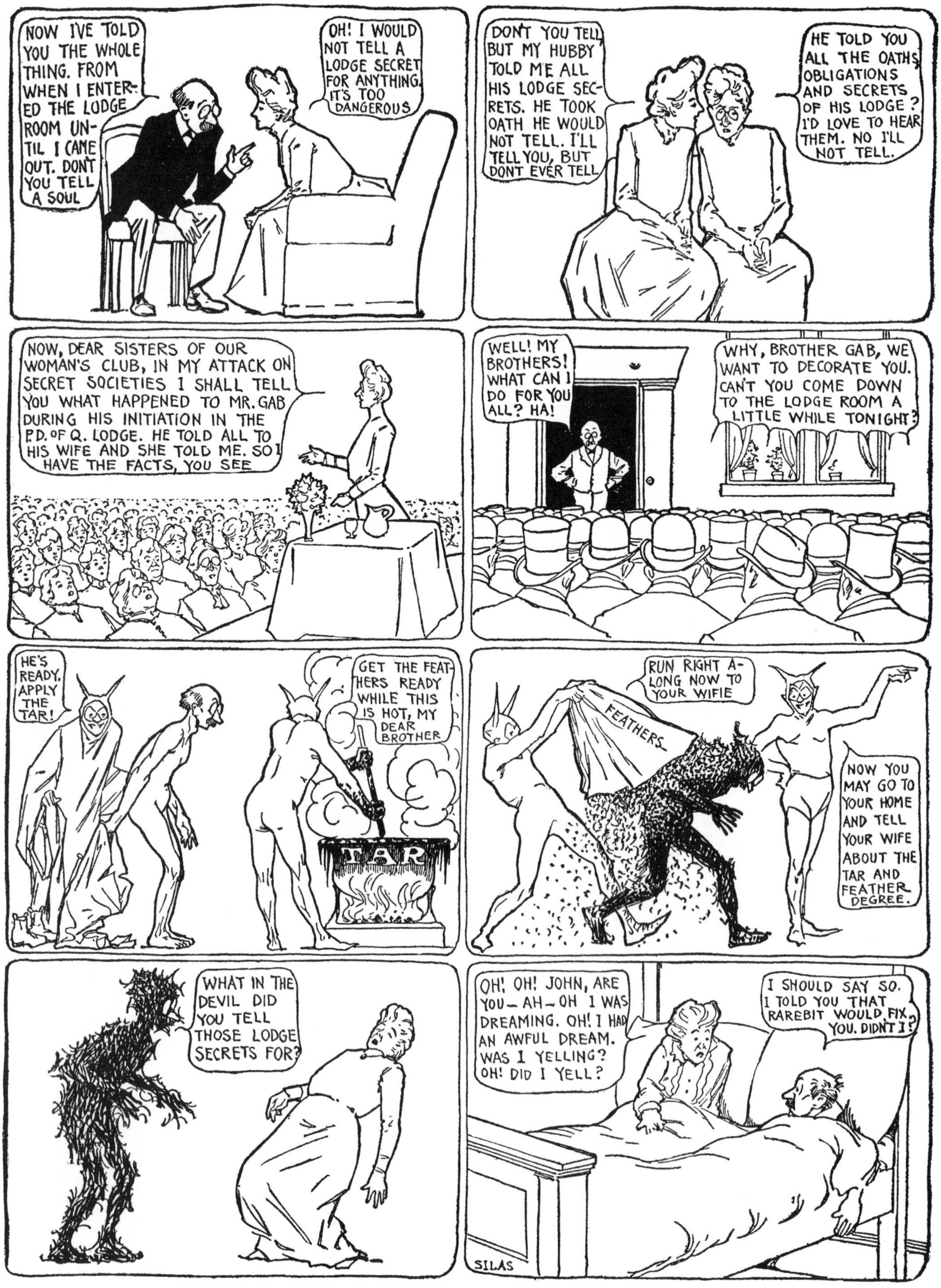
NOW I'VE TOLD YOU THE WHOLE THING. FROM WHEN I ENTERED THE LODGE ROOM UNTIL I CAME OUT. DON'T YOU TELL A SOUL
OH! I WOULD NOT TELL A LODGE SECRET FOR ANYTHING. IT'S TOO DANGEROUS
DON'T YOU TELL BUT MY HUBBY TOLD ME ALL HIS LODGE SECRETS. HE TOOK OATH HE WOULD NOT TELL. I'LL TELL YOU, BUT DONT EVER TELL
HE TOLD YOU ALL THE OATHS, OBLIGATIONS AND SECRETS OF HIS LODGE? I'D LOVE TO HEAR THEM. NO I'LL NOT TELL.
NOW, DEAR SISTERS OF OUR WOMAN'S CLUB, IN MY ATTACK ON SECRET SOCIETIES I SHALL TELL YOU WHAT HAPPENED TO MR. GAB DURING HIS INITIATION IN THE P.D. OF Q. LODGE. HE TOLD ALL TO HIS WIFE AND SHE TOLD ME. SO I HAVE THE FACTS, YOU SEE
WELL! MY BROTHERS! WHAT CAN I DO FOR YOU ALL? HA!
WHY, BROTHER GAB, WE WANT TO DECORATE YOU. CAN'T YOU COME DOWN TO THE LODGE ROOM A LITTLE WHILE TONIGHT?
HE'S READY. APPLY THE TAR!
GET THE FEATHERS READY WHILE THIS IS HOT, MY DEAR BROTHER
TAR
RUN RIGHT ALONG NOW TO YOUR WIFIE
FEATHERS
NOW YOU MAY GO TO YOUR HOME AND TELL YOUR WIFE ABOUT THE TAR AND FEATHER DEGREE.
WHAT IN THE DEVIL DID YOU TELL THOSE LODGE SECRETS FOR?
OH! OH! JOHN, ARE YOU—AH—OH I WAS DREAMING. OH! I HAD AN AWFUL DREAM. WAS I YELLING? OH! DID I YELL?
I SHOULD SAY SO. I TOLD YOU THAT RAREBIT WOULD FIX YOU. DIDN'T I?
SILAS

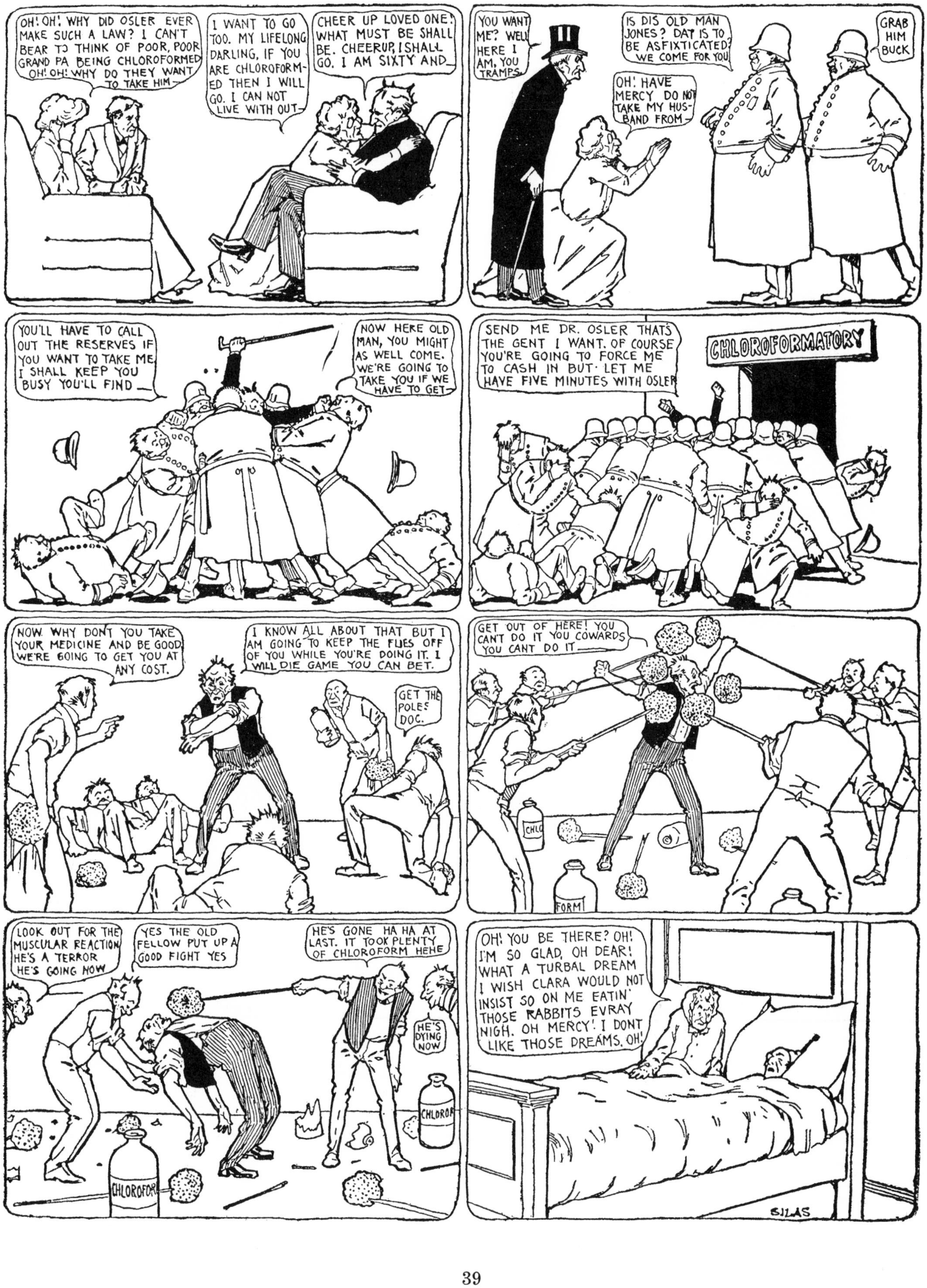

OH! OH! WHY DID OSLER EVER MAKE SUCH A LAW? I CAN'T BEAR TO THINK OF POOR, POOR GRAND PA BEING CHLOROFORMED OH! OH! WHY DO THEY WANT TO TAKE HIM
I WANT TO GO TOO. MY LIFELONG DARLING, IF YOU ARE CHLOROFORMED THEN I WILL GO. I CAN NOT LIVE WITH OUT
CHEER UP LOVED ONE! WHAT MUST BE SHALL BE. CHEERUP, I SHALL GO. I AM SIXTY AND
YOU WANT ME? WELL HERE I AM, YOU TRAMPS
IS DIS OLD MAN JONES? DAT IS TO BE ASFIXTICATED? WE COME FOR YOU
GRAB HIM BUCK
OH! HAVE MERCY DO NOT TAKE MY HUSBAND FROM
YOU'LL HAVE TO CALL OUT THE RESERVES IF YOU WANT TO TAKE ME I SHALL KEEP YOU BUSY YOU'LL FIND
NOW HERE OLD MAN, YOU MIGHT AS WELL COME. WE'RE GOING TO TAKE YOU IF WE HAVE TO GET
SEND ME DR. OSLER THATS THE GENT I WANT. OF COURSE YOU'RE GOING TO FORCE ME TO CASH IN BUT· LET ME HAVE FIVE MINUTES WITH OSLER
CHLOROFORMATORY
NOW. WHY DONT YOU TAKE YOUR MEDICINE AND BE GOOD WE'RE GOING TO GET YOU AT ANY COST.
I KNOW ALL ABOUT THAT BUT I AM GOING TO KEEP THE FLIES OFF OF YOU WHILE YOU'RE DOING IT. I WILL DIE GAME YOU CAN BET.
GET THE POLES DOC.
GET OUT OF HERE! YOU CAN'T DO IT YOU COWARDS YOU CANT DO IT
CHLO
FORM
LOOK OUT FOR THE MUSCULAR REACTION HE'S A TERROR HE'S GOING NOW
YES THE OLD FELLOW PUT UP A GOOD FIGHT YES
HE'S GONE HA HA AT LAST. IT TOOK PLENTY OF CHLOROFORM HEHE
HE'S DYING NOW
CHLOROF
CHLOROFOR
OH! YOU BE THERE? OH! I'M SO GLAD, OH DEAR! WHAT A TURBAL DREAM I WISH CLARA WOULD NOT INSIST SO ON ME EATIN' THOSE RABBITS EVRAY NIGH. OH MERCY! I DONT LIKE THOSE DREAMS. OH!
SILAS

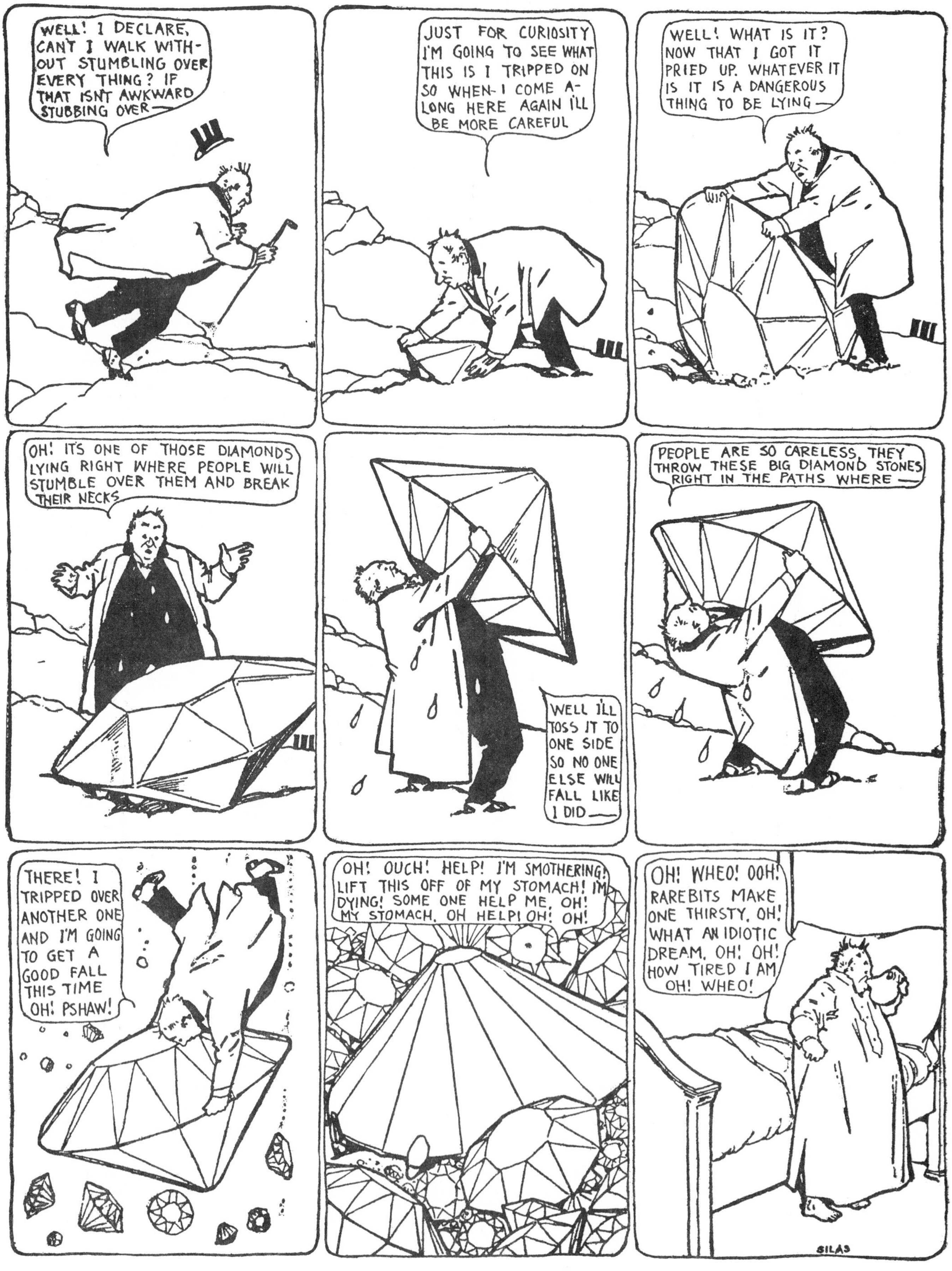
WELL! I DECLARE, CAN'T I WALK WITH-OUT STUMBLING OVER EVERY THING? IF THAT ISN'T AWKWARD STUBBING OVER—
JUST FOR CURIOSITY I'M GOING TO SEE WHAT THIS IS I TRIPPED ON SO WHEN I COME A-LONG HERE AGAIN I'LL BE MORE CAREFUL
WELL! WHAT IS IT? NOW THAT I GOT IT PRIED UP. WHATEVER IT IS IT IS A DANGEROUS THING TO BE LYING—
OH! IT'S ONE OF THOSE DIAMONDS LYING RIGHT WHERE PEOPLE WILL STUMBLE OVER THEM AND BREAK THEIR NECKS
WELL I'LL TOSS IT TO ONE SIDE SO NO ONE ELSE WILL FALL LIKE I DID—
PEOPLE ARE SO CARELESS, THEY THROW THESE BIG DIAMOND STONES RIGHT IN THE PATHS WHERE—
THERE! I TRIPPED OVER ANOTHER ONE AND I'M GOING TO GET A GOOD FALL THIS TIME OH! PSHAW!
OH! OUCH! HELP! I'M SMOTHERING! LIFT THIS OFF OF MY STOMACH! I'M DYING! SOME ONE HELP ME. OH! MY STOMACH. OH HELP! OH! OH!
OH! WHEO! OOH! RAREBITS MAKE ONE THIRSTY. OH! WHAT AN IDIOTIC DREAM. OH! OH! HOW TIRED I AM OH! WHEO!
SILAS

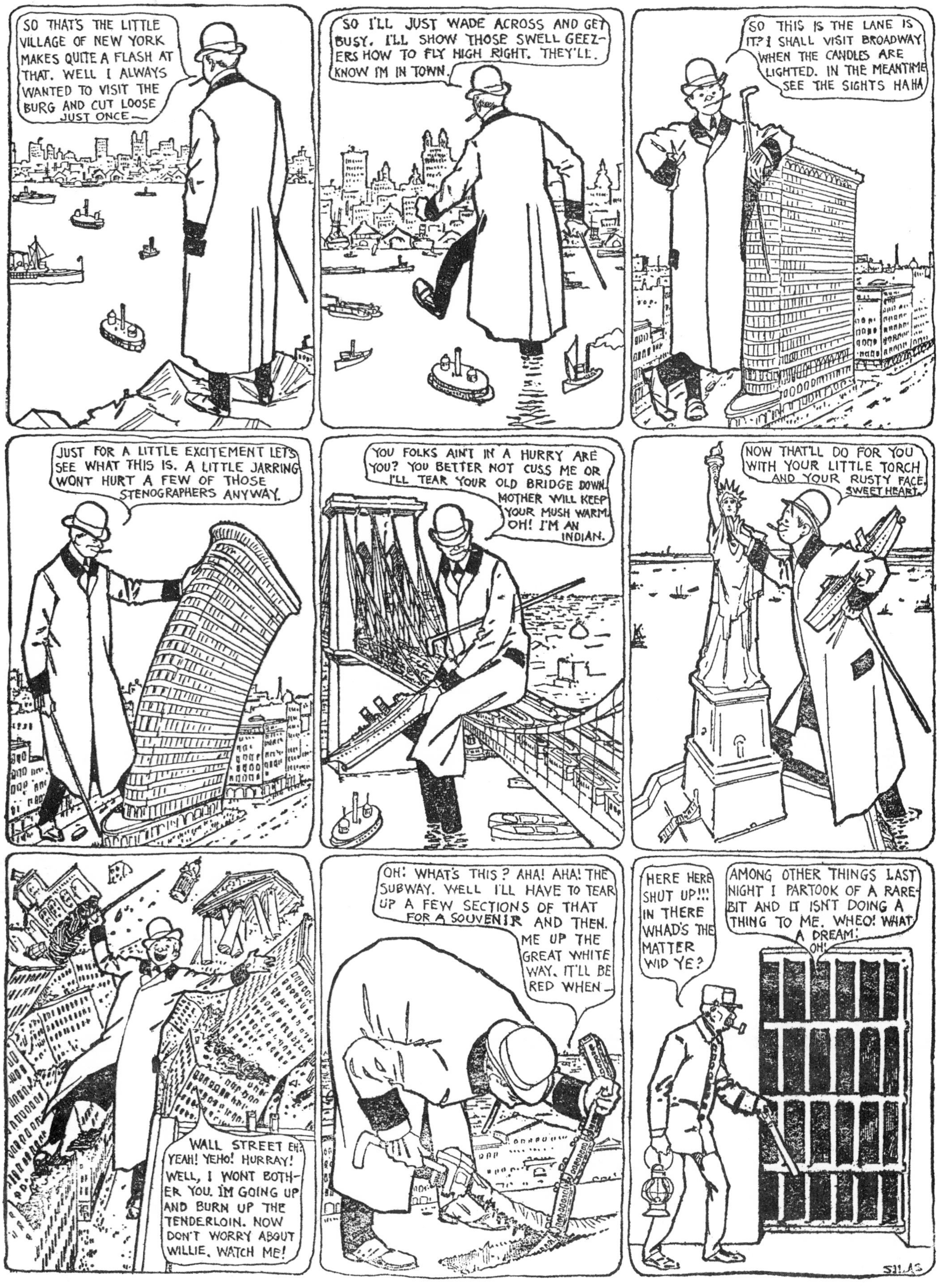
SO THAT'S THE LITTLE VILLAGE OF NEW YORK MAKES QUITE A FLASH AT THAT. WELL I ALWAYS WANTED TO VISIT THE BURG AND CUT LOOSE JUST ONCE—
SO I'LL JUST WADE ACROSS AND GET BUSY. I'LL SHOW THOSE SWELL GEEZERS HOW TO FLY HIGH RIGHT. THEY'LL KNOW I'M IN TOWN.
SO THIS IS THE LANE IS IT? I SHALL VISIT BROADWAY WHEN THE CANDLES ARE LIGHTED. IN THE MEANTIME SEE THE SIGHTS HA HA
JUST FOR A LITTLE EXCITEMENT LET'S SEE WHAT THIS IS. A LITTLE JARRING WONT HURT A FEW OF THOSE STENOGRAPHERS ANYWAY.
YOU FOLKS AIN'T IN A HURRY ARE YOU? YOU BETTER NOT CUSS ME OR I'LL TEAR YOUR OLD BRIDGE DOWN. MOTHER WILL KEEP YOUR MUSH WARM. OH! I'M AN INDIAN.
NOW THAT'LL DO FOR YOU WITH YOUR LITTLE TORCH AND YOUR RUSTY FACE, SWEETHEART.
WALL STREET EH? YEAH! YEHO! HURRAY! WELL, I WONT BOTHER YOU. I'M GOING UP AND BURN UP THE TENDERLOIN. NOW DON'T WORRY ABOUT WILLIE. WATCH ME!
OH! WHAT'S THIS? AHA! AHA! THE SUBWAY. WELL I'LL HAVE TO TEAR UP A FEW SECTIONS OF THAT FOR A SOUVENIR AND THEN. ME UP THE GREAT WHITE WAY. IT'LL BE RED WHEN—
HERE HERE SHUT UP!!! IN THERE WHAD'S THE MATTER WID YE?
AMONG OTHER THINGS LAST NIGHT I PARTOOK OF A RAREBIT AND IT ISN'T DOING A THING TO ME. WHEO! WHAT A DREAM! OH!
SILAS

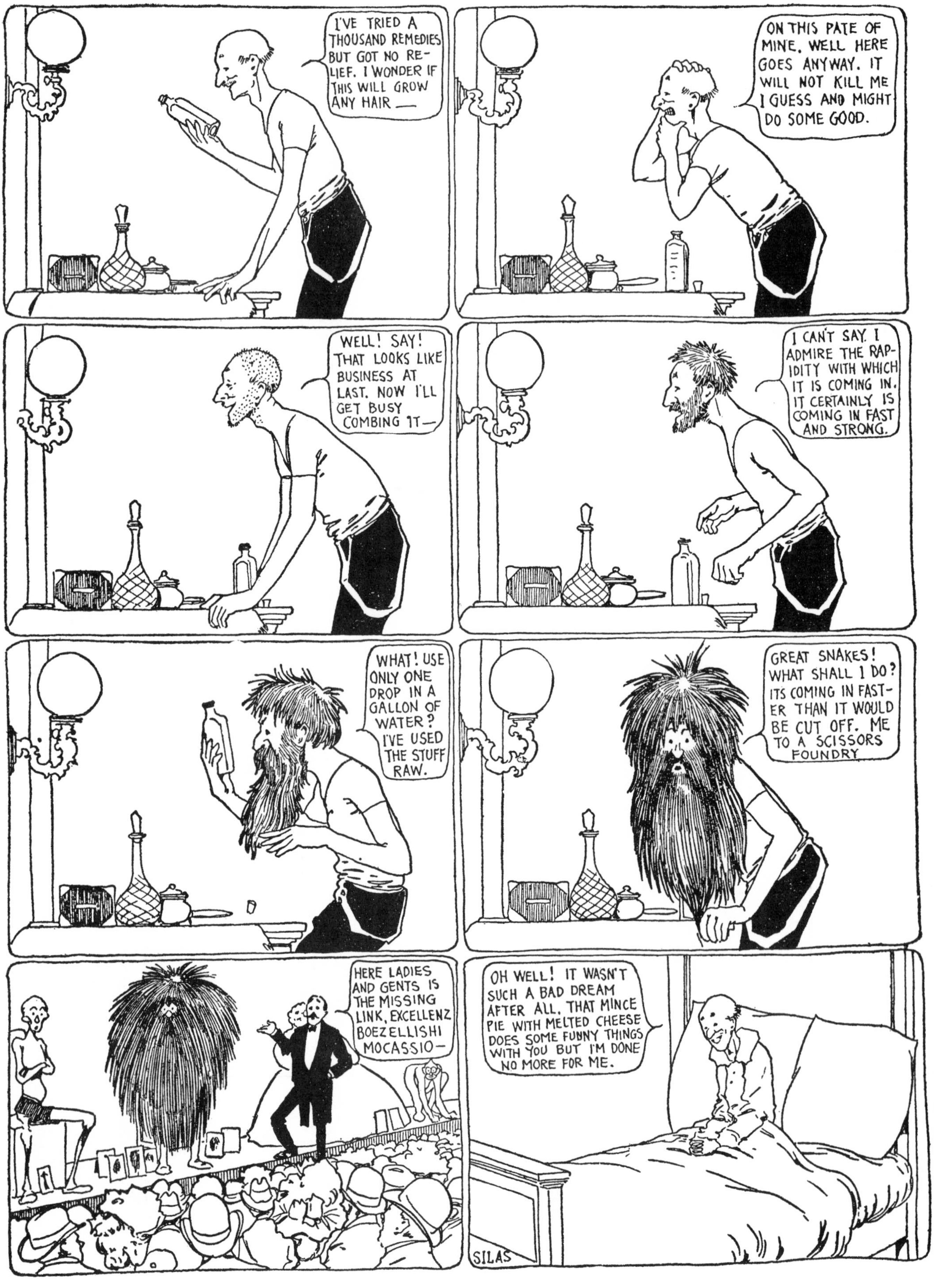
I'VE TRIED A THOUSAND REMEDIES BUT GOT NO RELIEF. I WONDER IF THIS WILL GROW ANY HAIR —
ON THIS PATE OF MINE. WELL HERE GOES ANYWAY. IT WILL NOT KILL ME I GUESS AND MIGHT DO SOME GOOD.
WELL! SAY! THAT LOOKS LIKE BUSINESS AT LAST. NOW I'LL GET BUSY COMBING IT—
I CAN'T SAY. I ADMIRE THE RAPIDITY WITH WHICH IT IS COMING IN. IT CERTAINLY IS COMING IN FAST AND STRONG.
WHAT! USE ONLY ONE DROP IN A GALLON OF WATER? I'VE USED THE STUFF RAW.
GREAT SNAKES! WHAT SHALL I DO? ITS COMING IN FASTER THAN IT WOULD BE CUT OFF. ME TO A SCISSORS FOUNDRY
HERE LADIES AND GENTS IS THE MISSING LINK, EXCELLENZ BOEZELLISHI MOCASSIO—
OH WELL! IT WASN'T SUCH A BAD DREAM AFTER ALL. THAT MINCE PIE WITH MELTED CHEESE DOES SOME FUNNY THINGS WITH YOU BUT I'M DONE NO MORE FOR ME.
SILAS

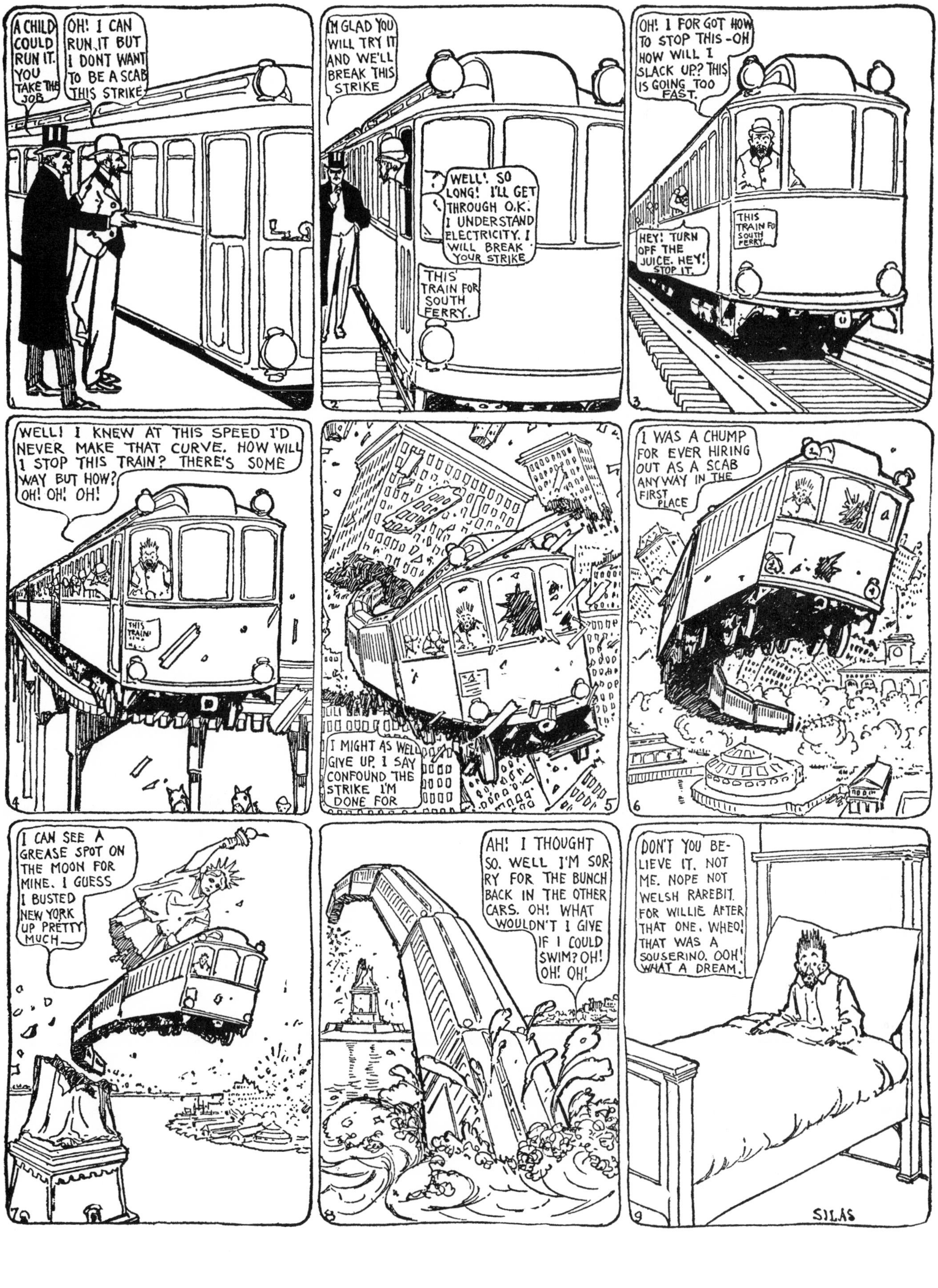
A CHILD COULD RUN IT. YOU TAKE THE JOB
OH! I CAN RUN IT BUT I DONT WANT TO BE A SCAB THIS STRIKE
I'M GLAD YOU WILL TRY IT AND WE'LL BREAK THIS STRIKE
WELL! SO LONG! I'LL GET THROUGH O.K. I UNDERSTAND ELECTRICITY. I WILL BREAK YOUR STRIKE
THIS TRAIN FOR SOUTH FERRY.
OH! I FOR GOT HOW TO STOP THIS - OH HOW WILL I SLACK UP? THIS IS GOING TOO FAST.
HEY! TURN OFF THE JUICE. HEY! STOP IT.
THIS TRAIN FO SOUTH FERRY.
WELL! I KNEW AT THIS SPEED I'D NEVER MAKE THAT CURVE. HOW WILL I STOP THIS TRAIN? THERE'S SOME WAY BUT HOW? OH! OH! OH!
I MIGHT AS WELL GIVE UP. I SAY CONFOUND THE STRIKE I'M DONE FOR
I WAS A CHUMP FOR EVER HIRING OUT AS A SCAB ANYWAY IN THE FIRST PLACE
I CAN SEE A GREASE SPOT ON THE MOON FOR MINE. I GUESS I BUSTED NEW YORK UP PRETTY MUCH—
AH! I THOUGHT SO. WELL I'M SORRY FOR THE BUNCH BACK IN THE OTHER CARS. OH! WHAT WOULDN'T I GIVE IF I COULD SWIM? OH! OH! OH!
DON'T YOU BELIEVE IT. NOT ME. NOPE NOT WELSH RAREBIT FOR WILLIE AFTER THAT ONE. WHEO! THAT WAS A SOUSERINO. OOH! WHAT A DREAM.
SILAS

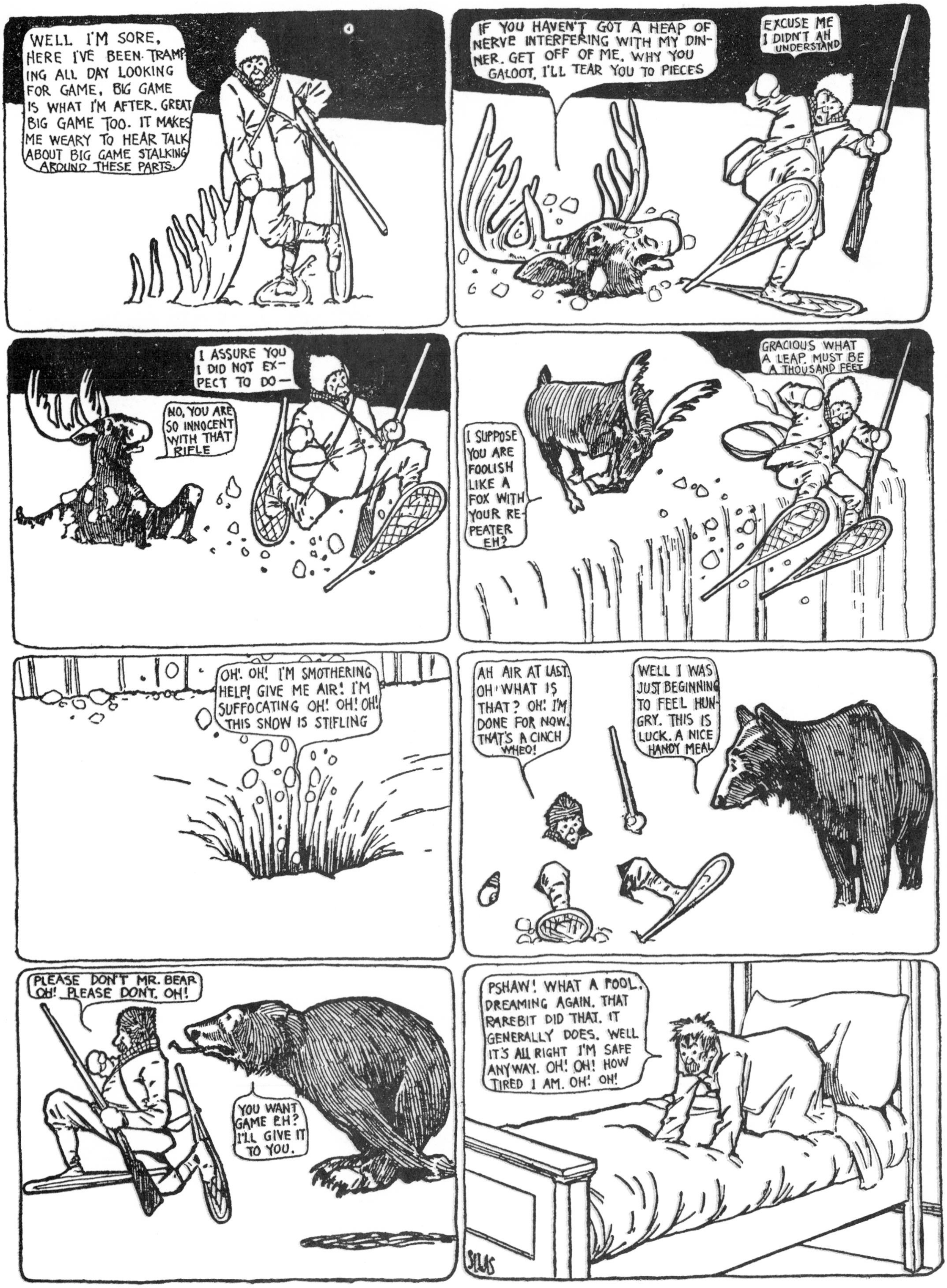
WELL I'M SORE, HERE I'VE BEEN TRAMPING ALL DAY LOOKING FOR GAME. BIG GAME IS WHAT I'M AFTER. GREAT BIG GAME TOO. IT MAKES ME WEARY TO HEAR TALK ABOUT BIG GAME STALKING AROUND THESE PARTS.
IF YOU HAVEN'T GOT A HEAP OF NERVE INTERFERING WITH MY DINNER. GET OFF OF ME. WHY YOU GALOOT, I'LL TEAR YOU TO PIECES
EXCUSE ME I DIDN'T AH UNDERSTAND
I ASSURE YOU I DID NOT EXPECT TO DO—
NO, YOU ARE SO INNOCENT WITH THAT RIFLE
GRACIOUS WHAT A LEAP. MUST BE A THOUSAND FEET
I SUPPOSE YOU ARE FOOLISH LIKE A FOX WITH YOUR REPEATER EH?
OH! OH! I'M SMOTHERING HELP! GIVE ME AIR! I'M SUFFOCATING OH! OH! OH! THIS SNOW IS STIFLING
AH AIR AT LAST. OH WHAT IS THAT? OH! I'M DONE FOR NOW. THAT'S A CINCH WHEO!
WELL I WAS JUST BEGINNING TO FEEL HUNGRY. THIS IS LUCK. A NICE HANDY MEAL
PLEASE DON'T MR. BEAR OH! PLEASE DON'T. OH!
YOU WANT GAME EH? I'LL GIVE IT TO YOU.
PSHAW! WHAT A FOOL. DREAMING AGAIN. THAT RAREBIT DID THAT. IT GENERALLY DOES. WELL IT'S ALL RIGHT I'M SAFE ANYWAY. OH! OH! HOW TIRED I AM. OH! OH!
SILAS

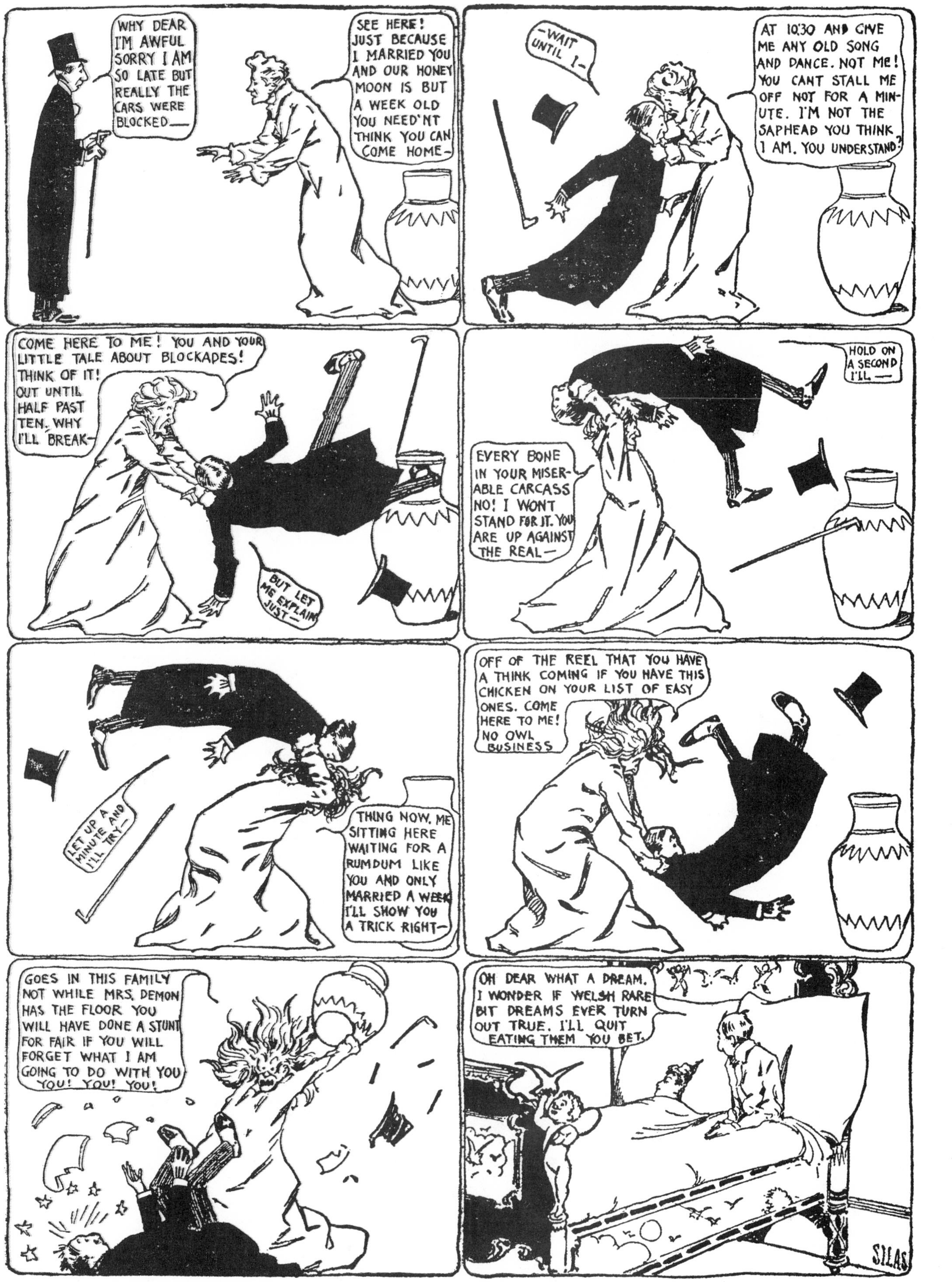
WHY DEAR I'M AWFUL SORRY I AM SO LATE BUT REALLY THE CARS WERE BLOCKED—
SEE HERE! JUST BECAUSE I MARRIED YOU AND OUR HONEY MOON IS BUT A WEEK OLD YOU NEED'NT THINK YOU CAN COME HOME—
—WAIT UNTIL I—
AT 10.30 AND GIVE ME ANY OLD SONG AND DANCE. NOT ME! YOU CANT STALL ME OFF NOT FOR A MINUTE. I'M NOT THE SAPHEAD YOU THINK I AM. YOU UNDERSTAND?
COME HERE TO ME! YOU AND YOUR LITTLE TALE ABOUT BLOCKADES! THINK OF IT! OUT UNTIL HALF PAST TEN. WHY I'LL BREAK—
BUT LET ME EXPLAIN JUST—
HOLD ON A SECOND I'LL—
EVERY BONE IN YOUR MISERABLE CARCASS NO! I WONT STAND FOR IT. YOU ARE UP AGAINST THE REAL—
LET UP A MINUTE AND I'LL TRY—
THING NOW. ME SITTING HERE WAITING FOR A RUMDUM LIKE YOU AND ONLY MARRIED A WEEK I'LL SHOW YOU A TRICK RIGHT—
OFF OF THE REEL THAT YOU HAVE A THINK COMING IF YOU HAVE THIS CHICKEN ON YOUR LIST OF EASY ONES. COME HERE TO ME! NO OWL BUSINESS
GOES IN THIS FAMILY NOT WHILE MRS. DEMON HAS THE FLOOR YOU WILL HAVE DONE A STUNT FOR FAIR IF YOU WILL FORGET WHAT I AM GOING TO DO WITH YOU YOU! YOU! YOU!
OH DEAR WHAT A DREAM. I WONDER IF WELSH RARE BIT DREAMS EVER TURN OUT TRUE. I'LL QUIT EATING THEM YOU BET.
SILAS

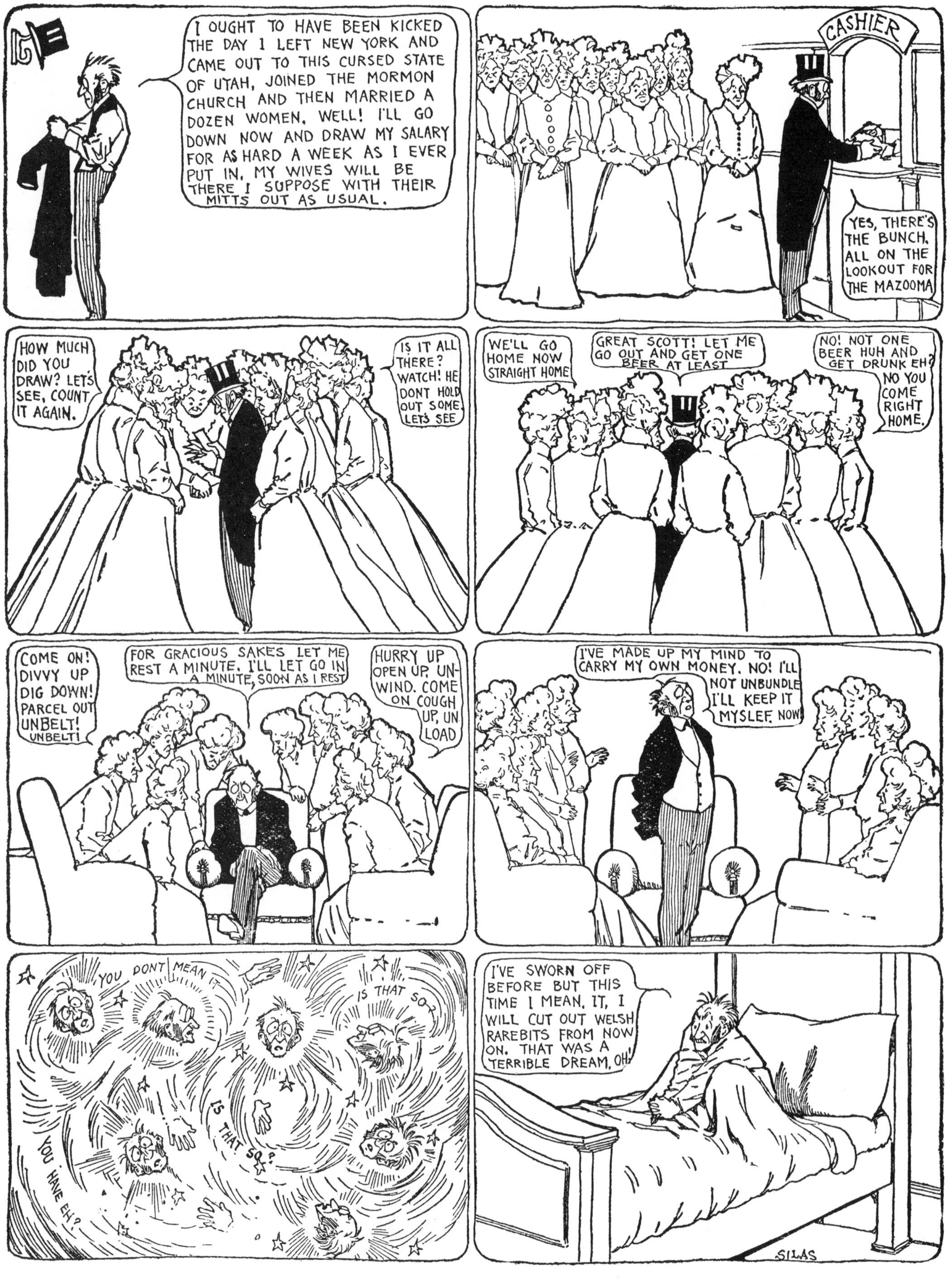
I OUGHT TO HAVE BEEN KICKED THE DAY I LEFT NEW YORK AND CAME OUT TO THIS CURSED STATE OF UTAH, JOINED THE MORMON CHURCH AND THEN MARRIED A DOZEN WOMEN. WELL! I'LL GO DOWN NOW AND DRAW MY SALARY FOR AS HARD A WEEK AS I EVER PUT IN. MY WIVES WILL BE THERE I SUPPOSE WITH THEIR MITTS OUT AS USUAL.
CASHIER
YES, THERE'S THE BUNCH, ALL ON THE LOOKOUT FOR THE MAZOOMA
HOW MUCH DID YOU DRAW? LET'S SEE, COUNT IT AGAIN.
IS IT ALL THERE? WATCH! HE DONT HOLD OUT SOME. LET'S SEE
WE'LL GO HOME NOW STRAIGHT HOME
GREAT SCOTT! LET ME GO OUT AND GET ONE BEER AT LEAST
NO! NOT ONE BEER HUH AND GET DRUNK EH? NO YOU COME RIGHT HOME.
COME ON! DIVVY UP DIG DOWN! PARCEL OUT UNBELT! UNBELT!
FOR GRACIOUS SAKES LET ME REST A MINUTE. I'LL LET GO IN A MINUTE, SOON AS I REST
HURRY UP OPEN UP. UNWIND. COME ON COUGH UP, UNLOAD
I'VE MADE UP MY MIND TO CARRY MY OWN MONEY. NO! I'LL NOT UNBUNDLE I'LL KEEP IT MYSLEF NOW
YOU DONT MEAN IT
IS THAT SO?
IS THAT SO?
YOU HAVE EH?
I'VE SWORN OFF BEFORE BUT THIS TIME I MEAN IT, I WILL CUT OUT WELSH RAREBITS FROM NOW ON. THAT WAS A TERRIBLE DREAM. OH!
SILAS

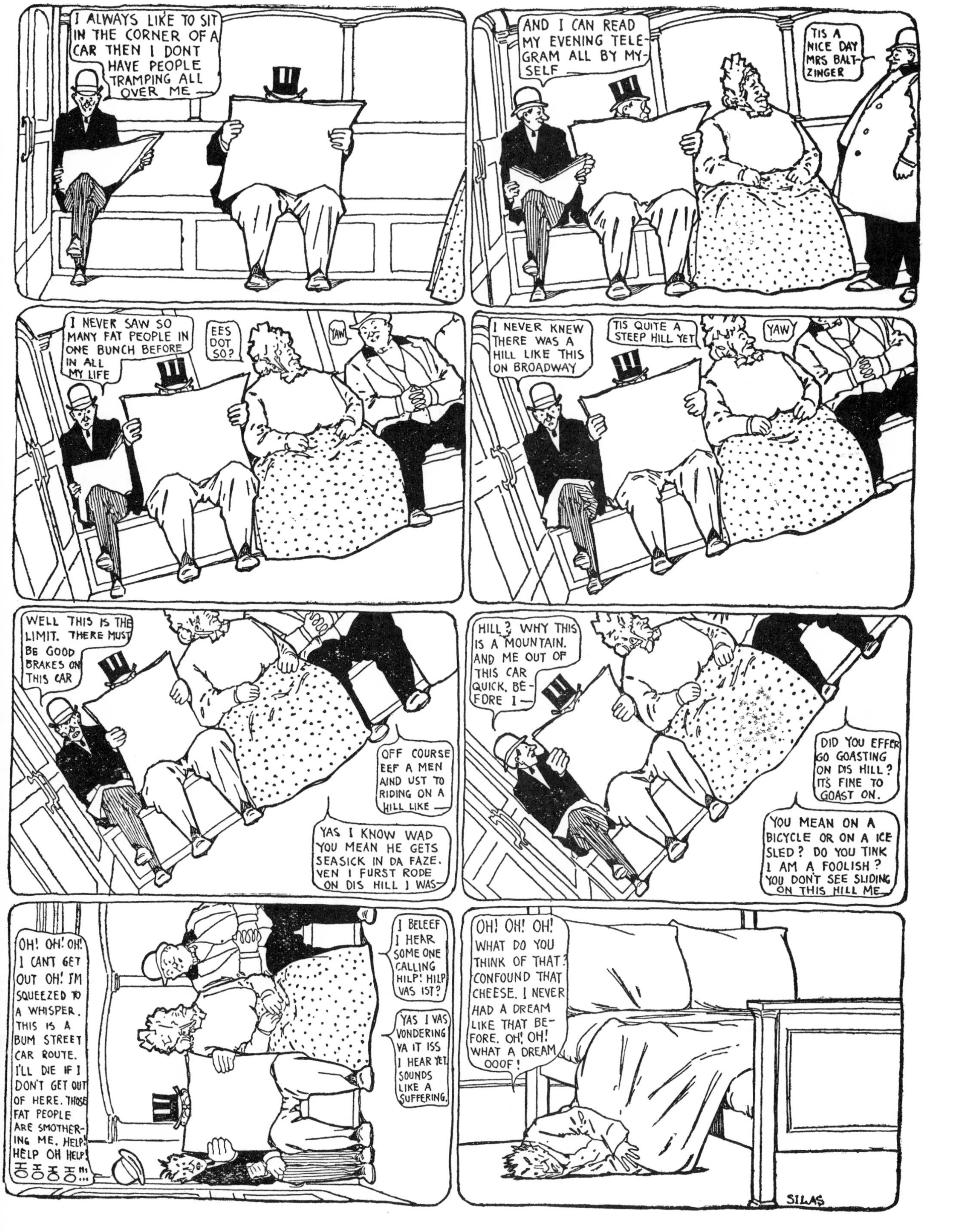

I ALWAYS LIKE TO SIT IN THE CORNER OF A CAR THEN I DONT HAVE PEOPLE TRAMPING ALL OVER ME —
AND I CAN READ MY EVENING TELEGRAM ALL BY MYSELF —
TIS A NICE DAY MRS BALTZINGER
I NEVER SAW SO MANY FAT PEOPLE IN ONE BUNCH BEFORE IN ALL MY LIFE
EES DOT SO?
YAW
I NEVER KNEW THERE WAS A HILL LIKE THIS ON BROADWAY
TIS QUITE A STEEP HILL YET
YAW
WELL THIS IS THE LIMIT. THERE MUST BE GOOD BRAKES ON THIS CAR
OFF COURSE EEF A MEN AIND UST TO RIDING ON A HILL LIKE —
YAS I KNOW WAD YOU MEAN HE GETS SEASICK IN DA FAZE. VEN I FURST RODE ON DIS HILL I WAS—
HILL? WHY THIS IS A MOUNTAIN. AND ME OUT OF THIS CAR QUICK, BEFORE I —
DID YOU EFFER GO GOASTING ON DIS HILL? IT'S FINE TO GOAST ON.
YOU MEAN ON A BICYCLE OR ON A ICE SLED? DO YOU TINK I AM A FOOLISH? YOU DON'T SEE SLIDING ON THIS HILL ME —
OH! OH! OH! I CANT GET OUT OH! I'M SQUEEZED TO A WHISPER. THIS IS A BUM STREET CAR ROUTE. I'LL DIE IF I DON'T GET OUT OF HERE. THOSE FAT PEOPLE ARE SMOTHERING ME. HELP! HELP OH HELP!
I BELEEF I HEAR SOME ONE CALLING HILP! HILP VAS IST?
YAS I VAS VONDERING VA IT ISS I HEAR YET. SOUNDS LIKE A SUFFERING.
OH! OH! OH! WHAT DO YOU THINK OF THAT? CONFOUND THAT CHEESE. I NEVER HAD A DREAM LIKE THAT BEFORE. OH! OH! WHAT A DREAM OOOF!
SILAS

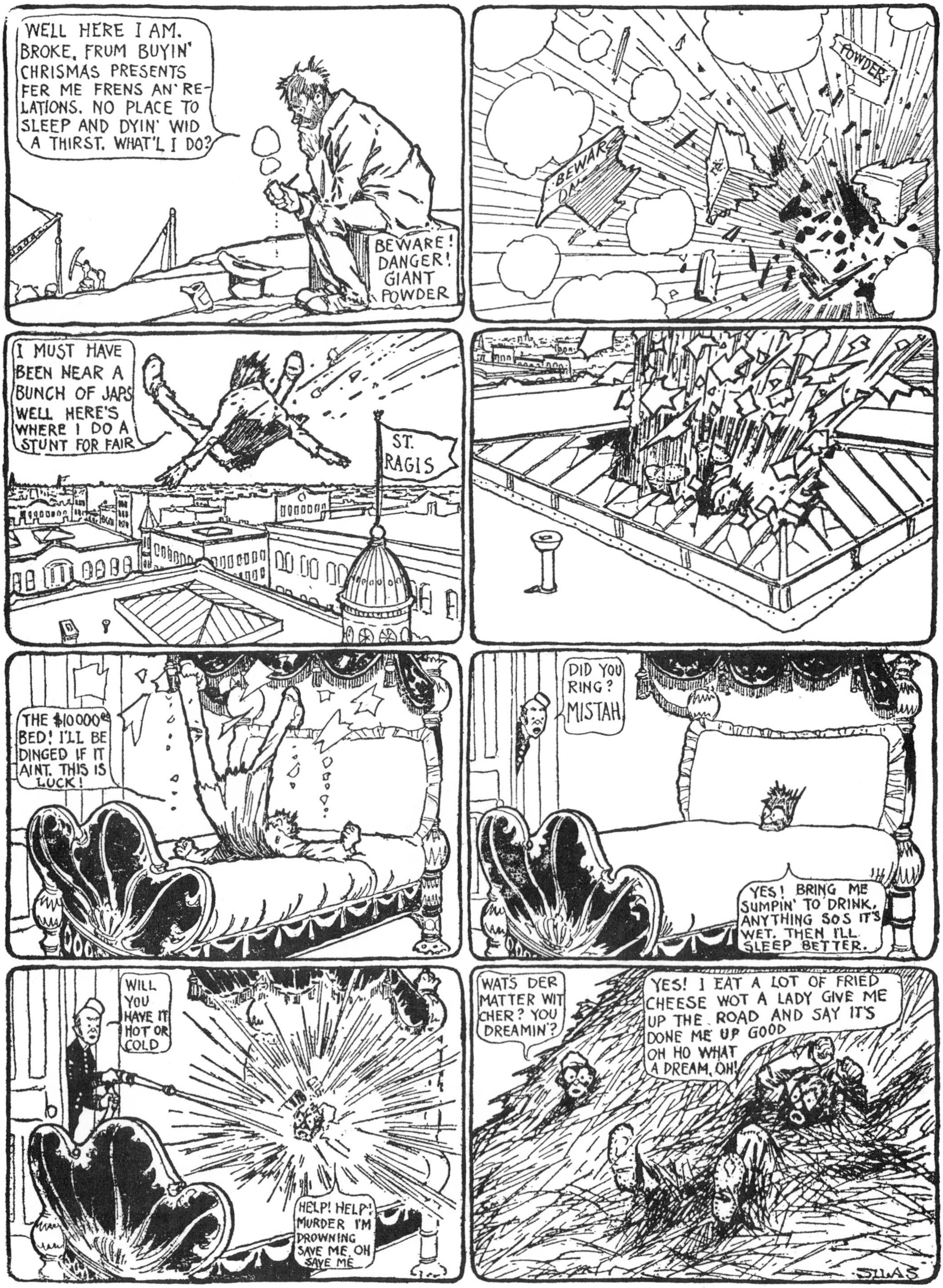
WELL HERE I AM. BROKE, FRUM BUYIN' CHRISMAS PRESENTS FER ME FRENS AN' RE-LATIONS. NO PLACE TO SLEEP AND DYIN' WID A THIRST. WHAT'L I DO?
BEWARE! DANGER! GIANT POWDER
POWDER
I MUST HAVE BEEN NEAR A BUNCH OF JAPS WELL HERE'S WHERE I DO A STUNT FOR FAIR
ST. RAGIS
THE $10000.00 BED! I'LL BE DINGED IF IT AINT. THIS IS LUCK!
DID YOU RING? MISTAH
YES! BRING ME SUMPIN' TO DRINK, ANYTHING SO'S IT'S WET. THEN I'LL SLEEP BETTER.
WILL YOU HAVE IT HOT OR COLD
HELP! HELP! MURDER I'M DROWNING SAVE ME OH SAVE ME
WATS DER MATTER WIT CHER? YOU DREAMIN'?
YES! I EAT A LOT OF FRIED CHEESE WOT A LADY GIVE ME UP THE ROAD AND SAY IT'S DONE ME UP GOOD OH HO WHAT A DREAM, OH!
SILAS

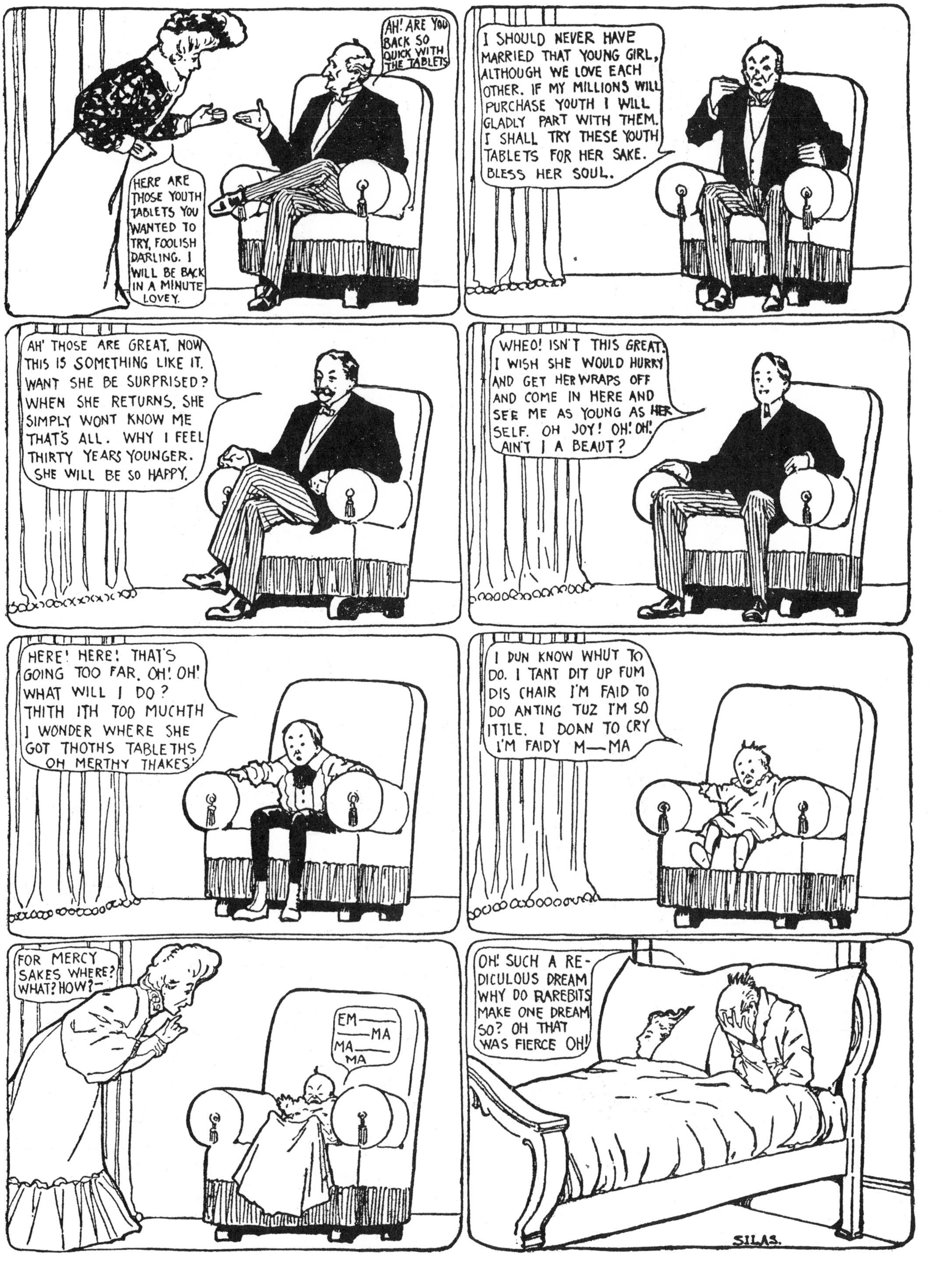
AH! ARE YOU BACK SO QUICK WITH THE TABLETS
HERE ARE THOSE YOUTH TABLETS YOU WANTED TO TRY, FOOLISH DARLING. I WILL BE BACK IN A MINUTE LOVEY.
I SHOULD NEVER HAVE MARRIED THAT YOUNG GIRL, ALTHOUGH WE LOVE EACH OTHER. IF MY MILLIONS WILL PURCHASE YOUTH I WILL GLADLY PART WITH THEM. I SHALL TRY THESE YOUTH TABLETS FOR HER SAKE. BLESS HER SOUL.
AH' THOSE ARE GREAT. NOW THIS IS SOMETHING LIKE IT. WANT SHE BE SURPRISED? WHEN SHE RETURNS, SHE SIMPLY WONT KNOW ME THAT'S ALL. WHY I FEEL THIRTY YEARS YOUNGER. SHE WILL BE SO HAPPY.
WHEO! ISN'T THIS GREAT. I WISH SHE WOULD HURRY AND GET HER WRAPS OFF AND COME IN HERE AND SEE ME AS YOUNG AS HER SELF. OH JOY! OH! OH! AIN'T I A BEAUT?
HERE! HERE! THAT'S GOING TOO FAR. OH! OH! WHAT WILL I DO? THITH ITH TOO MUCHTH I WONDER WHERE SHE GOT THOTHS TABLETHS OH MERTHY THAKES!
I DUN KNOW WHUT TO DO. I TANT DIT UP FUM DIS CHAIR I'M FAID TO DO ANTING TUZ I'M SO ITTLE. I DOAN TO CRY I'M FAIDY M—MA
FOR MERCY SAKES WHERE? WHAT? HOW?—
EM—— ——MA MA—— MA
OH! SUCH A REDICULOUS DREAM WHY DO RAREBITS MAKE ONE DREAM SO? OH THAT WAS FIERCE OH!
SILAS.

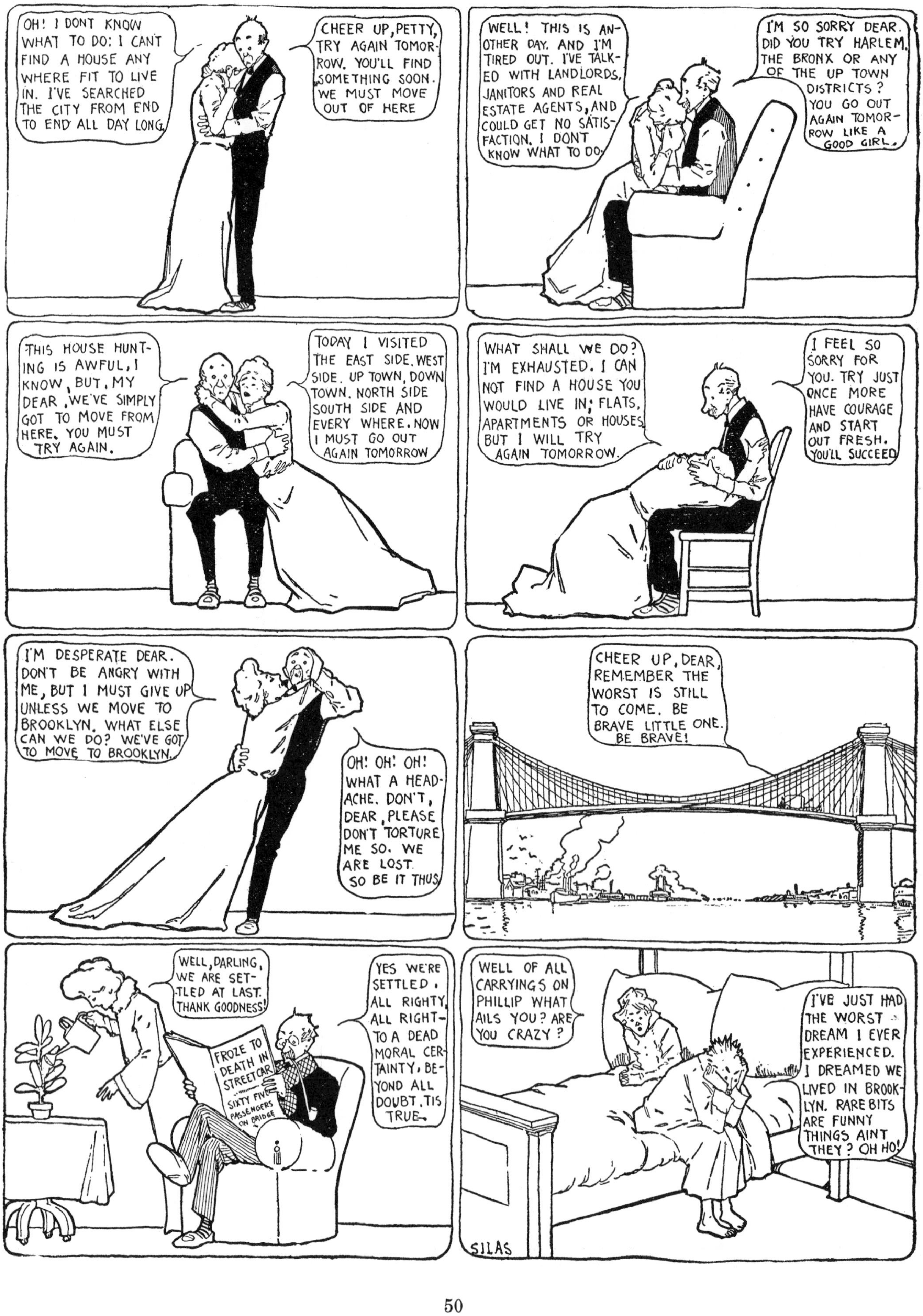
OH! I DONT KNOW WHAT TO DO: I CAN'T FIND A HOUSE ANY WHERE FIT TO LIVE IN. I'VE SEARCHED THE CITY FROM END TO END ALL DAY LONG.
CHEER UP, PETTY, TRY AGAIN TOMORROW. YOU'LL FIND SOMETHING SOON. WE MUST MOVE OUT OF HERE
WELL! THIS IS ANOTHER DAY. AND I'M TIRED OUT. I'VE TALKED WITH LANDLORDS, JANITORS AND REAL ESTATE AGENTS, AND COULD GET NO SATISFACTION. I DONT KNOW WHAT TO DO.
I'M SO SORRY DEAR. DID YOU TRY HARLEM, THE BRONX OR ANY OF THE UP TOWN DISTRICTS? YOU GO OUT AGAIN TOMORROW LIKE A GOOD GIRL.
THIS HOUSE HUNTING IS AWFUL, I KNOW, BUT, MY DEAR, WE'VE SIMPLY GOT TO MOVE FROM HERE. YOU MUST TRY AGAIN.
TODAY I VISITED THE EAST SIDE. WEST SIDE. UP TOWN, DOWN TOWN. NORTH SIDE SOUTH SIDE AND EVERY WHERE. NOW I MUST GO OUT AGAIN TOMORROW
WHAT SHALL WE DO? I'M EXHAUSTED. I CAN NOT FIND A HOUSE YOU WOULD LIVE IN; FLATS, APARTMENTS OR HOUSES BUT I WILL TRY AGAIN TOMORROW.
I FEEL SO SORRY FOR YOU. TRY JUST ONCE MORE HAVE COURAGE AND START OUT FRESH. YOU'LL SUCCEED
I'M DESPERATE DEAR. DON'T BE ANGRY WITH ME, BUT I MUST GIVE UP UNLESS WE MOVE TO BROOKLYN. WHAT ELSE CAN WE DO? WE'VE GOT TO MOVE TO BROOKLYN.
OH! OH! OH! WHAT A HEADACHE. DON'T, DEAR, PLEASE DON'T TORTURE ME SO. WE ARE LOST. SO BE IT THUS
CHEER UP, DEAR, REMEMBER THE WORST IS STILL TO COME. BE BRAVE LITTLE ONE. BE BRAVE!
WELL, DARLING, WE ARE SETTLED AT LAST. THANK GOODNESS!
FROZE TO DEATH IN STREETCAR
SIXTY FIVE PASSENGERS ON BRIDGE
YES WE'RE SETTLED, ALL RIGHTY, ALL RIGHT-TO A DEAD MORAL CERTAINTY, BEYOND ALL DOUBT, TIS TRUE.
WELL OF ALL CARRYINGS ON PHILLIP WHAT AILS YOU? ARE YOU CRAZY?
I'VE JUST HAD THE WORST DREAM I EVER EXPERIENCED. I DREAMED WE LIVED IN BROOKLYN. RARE BITS ARE FUNNY THINGS AINT THEY? OH HO!
SILAS

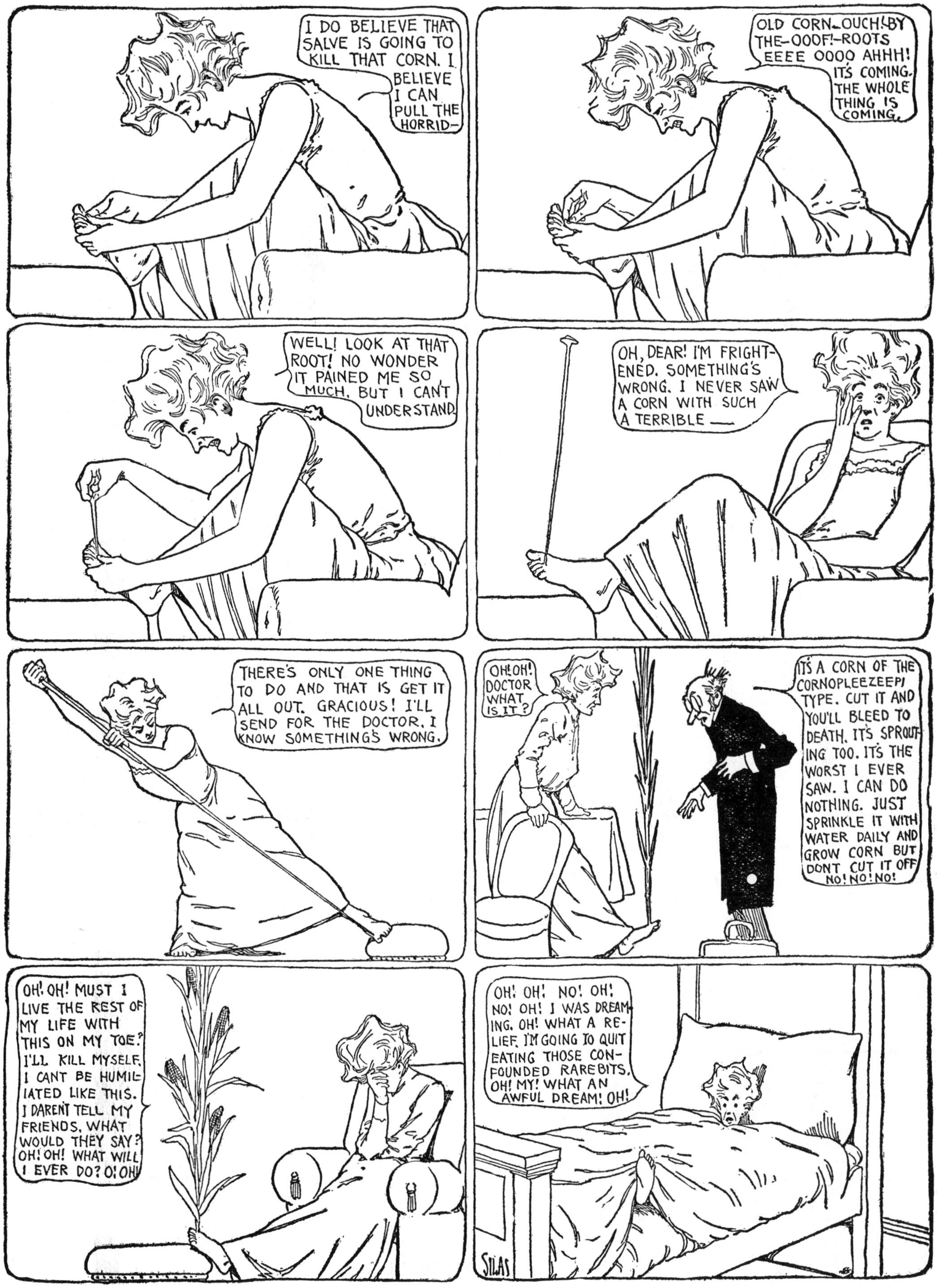
I DO BELIEVE THAT SALVE IS GOING TO KILL THAT CORN. I BELIEVE I CAN PULL THE HORRID—
OLD CORN—OUCH! BY THE—OOOF!—ROOTS EEEE OOOO AHHH! IT'S COMING. THE WHOLE THING IS COMING.
WELL! LOOK AT THAT ROOT! NO WONDER IT PAINED ME SO MUCH. BUT I CAN'T UNDERSTAND
OH, DEAR! I'M FRIGHTENED. SOMETHING'S WRONG. I NEVER SAW A CORN WITH SUCH A TERRIBLE —
THERE'S ONLY ONE THING TO DO AND THAT IS GET IT ALL OUT. GRACIOUS! I'LL SEND FOR THE DOCTOR. I KNOW SOMETHING'S WRONG.
OH! OH! DOCTOR WHAT IS IT?
IT'S A CORN OF THE CORNOPLEEZEEPI TYPE. CUT IT AND YOU'LL BLEED TO DEATH. IT'S SPROUTING TOO. IT'S THE WORST I EVER SAW. I CAN DO NOTHING. JUST SPRINKLE IT WITH WATER DAILY AND GROW CORN BUT DONT CUT IT OFF NO! NO! NO!
OH! OH! MUST I LIVE THE REST OF MY LIFE WITH THIS ON MY TOE? I'LL KILL MYSELF. I CANT BE HUMILIATED LIKE THIS. I DAREN'T TELL MY FRIENDS. WHAT WOULD THEY SAY? OH! OH! WHAT WILL I EVER DO? O! OH!
OH! OH! NO! OH! NO! OH! I WAS DREAMING. OH! WHAT A RELIEF. I'M GOING TO QUIT EATING THOSE CONFOUNDED RAREBITS. OH! MY! WHAT AN AWFUL DREAM! OH!
SILAS

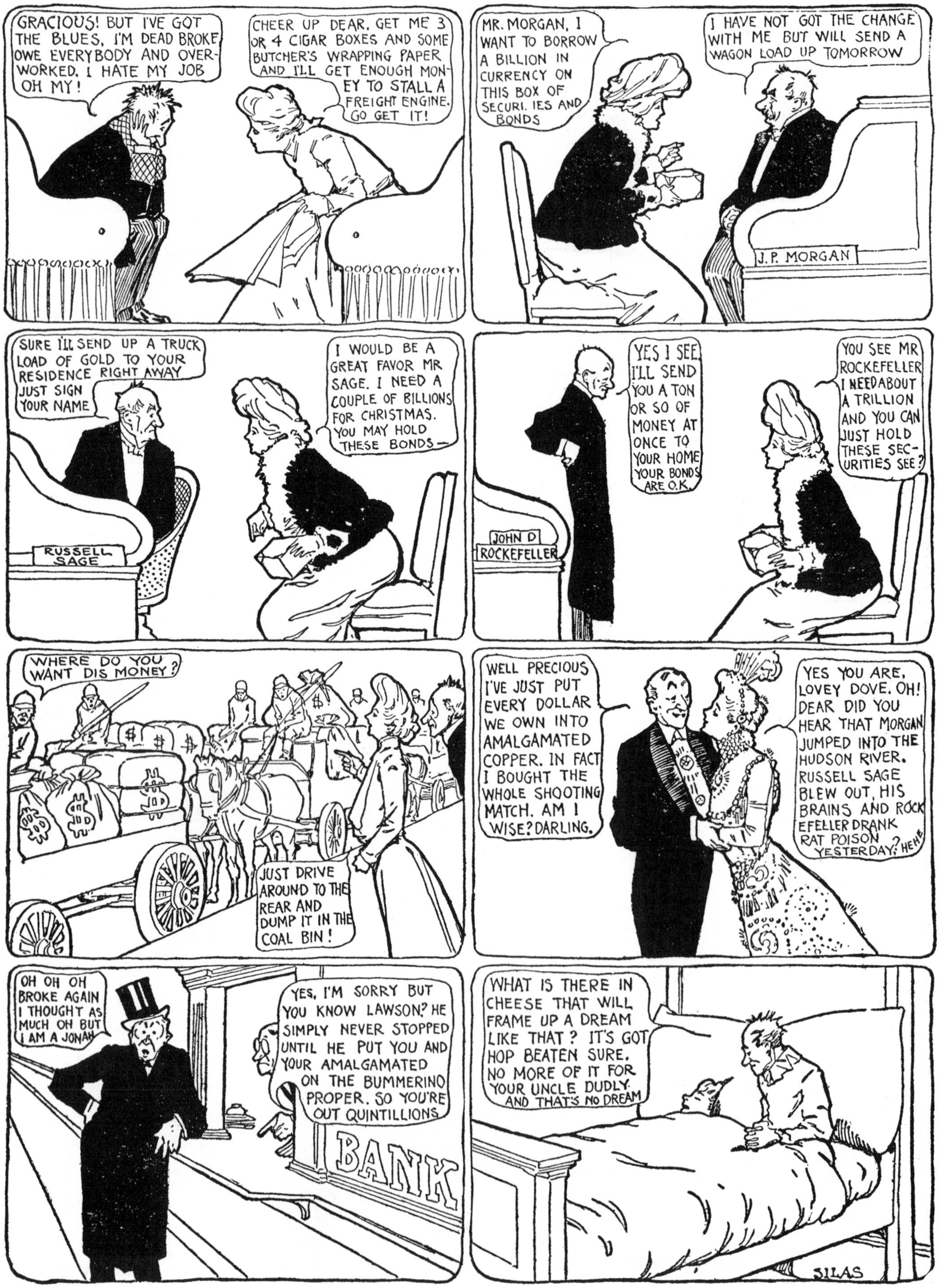
GRACIOUS! BUT I'VE GOT THE BLUES, I'M DEAD BROKE OWE EVERYBODY AND OVER-WORKED, I HATE MY JOB OH MY!
CHEER UP DEAR, GET ME 3 OR 4 CIGAR BOXES AND SOME BUTCHER'S WRAPPING PAPER AND I'LL GET ENOUGH MONEY TO STALL A FREIGHT ENGINE. GO GET IT!
MR. MORGAN, I WANT TO BORROW A BILLION IN CURRENCY ON THIS BOX OF SECURI. IES AND BONDS
I HAVE NOT GOT THE CHANGE WITH ME BUT WILL SEND A WAGON LOAD UP TOMORROW
J. P. MORGAN
SURE I'LL SEND UP A TRUCK LOAD OF GOLD TO YOUR RESIDENCE RIGHT AWAY JUST SIGN YOUR NAME
I WOULD BE A GREAT FAVOR MR SAGE. I NEED A COUPLE OF BILLIONS FOR CHRISTMAS. YOU MAY HOLD THESE BONDS—
RUSSELL SAGE
YES I SEE. I'LL SEND YOU A TON OR SO OF MONEY AT ONCE TO YOUR HOME YOUR BONDS ARE O.K.
YOU SEE MR ROCKEFELLER I NEED ABOUT A TRILLION AND YOU CAN JUST HOLD THESE SECURITIES SEE?
JOHN D ROCKEFELLER
WHERE DO YOU WANT DIS MONEY?
JUST DRIVE AROUND TO THE REAR AND DUMP IT IN THE COAL BIN!
WELL PRECIOUS I'VE JUST PUT EVERY DOLLAR WE OWN INTO AMALGAMATED COPPER. IN FACT I BOUGHT THE WHOLE SHOOTING MATCH. AM I WISE? DARLING.
YES YOU ARE, LOVEY DOVE. OH! DEAR DID YOU HEAR THAT MORGAN JUMPED INTO THE HUDSON RIVER. RUSSELL SAGE BLEW OUT, HIS BRAINS AND ROCKEFELLER DRANK RAT POISON YESTERDAY? HEHE
OH OH OH BROKE AGAIN I THOUGHT AS MUCH OH BUT I AM A JONAH
YES, I'M SORRY BUT YOU KNOW LAWSON? HE SIMPLY NEVER STOPPED UNTIL HE PUT YOU AND YOUR AMALGAMATED ON THE BUMMERINO PROPER. SO YOU'RE OUT QUINTILLIONS
BANK
WHAT IS THERE IN CHEESE THAT WILL FRAME UP A DREAM LIKE THAT? IT'S GOT HOP BEATEN SURE. NO MORE OF IT FOR YOUR UNCLE DUDLY. AND THAT'S NO DREAM
SILAS

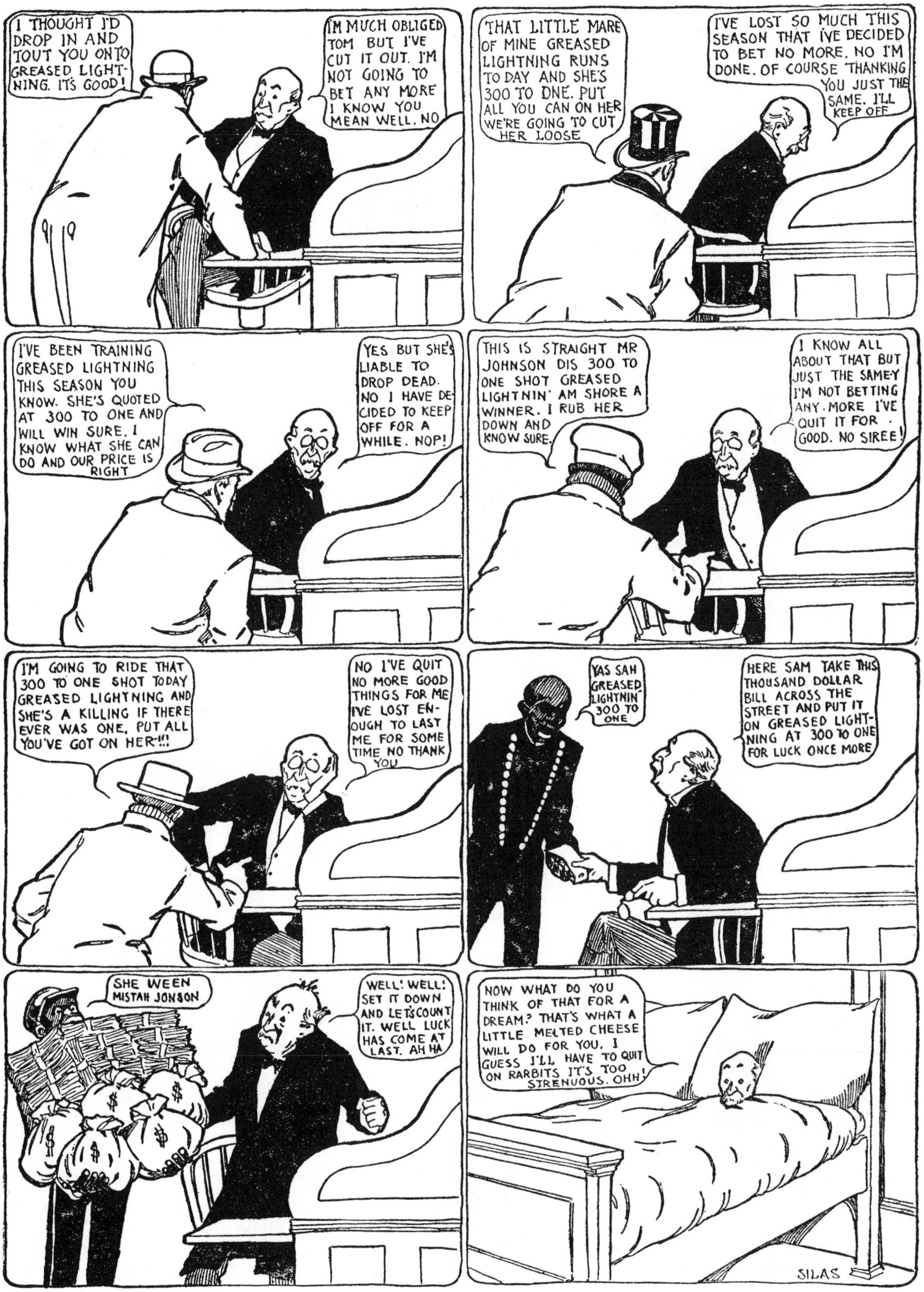
I THOUGHT I'D DROP IN AND TOUT YOU ONTO GREASED LIGHTNING. IT'S GOOD!
I'M MUCH OBLIGED TOM BUT I'VE CUT IT OUT. I'M NOT GOING TO BET ANY MORE I KNOW YOU MEAN WELL. NO
THAT LITTLE MARE OF MINE GREASED LIGHTNING RUNS TO DAY AND SHE'S 300 TO ONE. PUT ALL YOU CAN ON HER WE'RE GOING TO CUT HER LOOSE
I'VE LOST SO MUCH THIS SEASON THAT I'VE DECIDED TO BET NO MORE. NO I'M DONE. OF COURSE THANKING YOU JUST THE SAME. I'LL KEEP OFF
I'VE BEEN TRAINING GREASED LIGHTNING THIS SEASON YOU KNOW. SHE'S QUOTED AT 300 TO ONE AND WILL WIN SURE. I KNOW WHAT SHE CAN DO AND OUR PRICE IS RIGHT
YES BUT SHE'S LIABLE TO DROP DEAD. NO I HAVE DECIDED TO KEEP OFF FOR A WHILE. NOP!
THIS IS STRAIGHT MR JOHNSON DIS 300 TO ONE SHOT GREASED LIGHTNIN' AM SHORE A WINNER. I RUB HER DOWN AND KNOW SURE.
I KNOW ALL ABOUT THAT BUT JUST THE SAME I'M NOT BETTING ANY MORE I'VE QUIT IT FOR GOOD. NO SIREE!
I'M GOING TO RIDE THAT 300 TO ONE SHOT TODAY GREASED LIGHTNING AND SHE'S A KILLING IF THERE EVER WAS ONE. PUT ALL YOU'VE GOT ON HER!!!
NO I'VE QUIT NO MORE GOOD THINGS FOR ME I'VE LOST ENOUGH TO LAST ME FOR SOME TIME NO THANK YOU
YAS SAH GREASED LIGHTNIN' 300 TO ONE
HERE SAM TAKE THIS THOUSAND DOLLAR BILL ACROSS THE STREET AND PUT IT ON GREASED LIGHTNING AT 300 TO ONE FOR LUCK ONCE MORE
SHE WEEN MISTAH JONSON
WELL! WELL! SET IT DOWN AND LET'S COUNT IT. WELL LUCK HAS COME AT LAST. AH HA
NOW WHAT DO YOU THINK OF THAT FOR A DREAM? THAT'S WHAT A LITTLE MELTED CHEESE WILL DO FOR YOU. I GUESS I'LL HAVE TO QUIT ON RARBITS IT'S TOO STRENUOUS. OHH!
SILAS

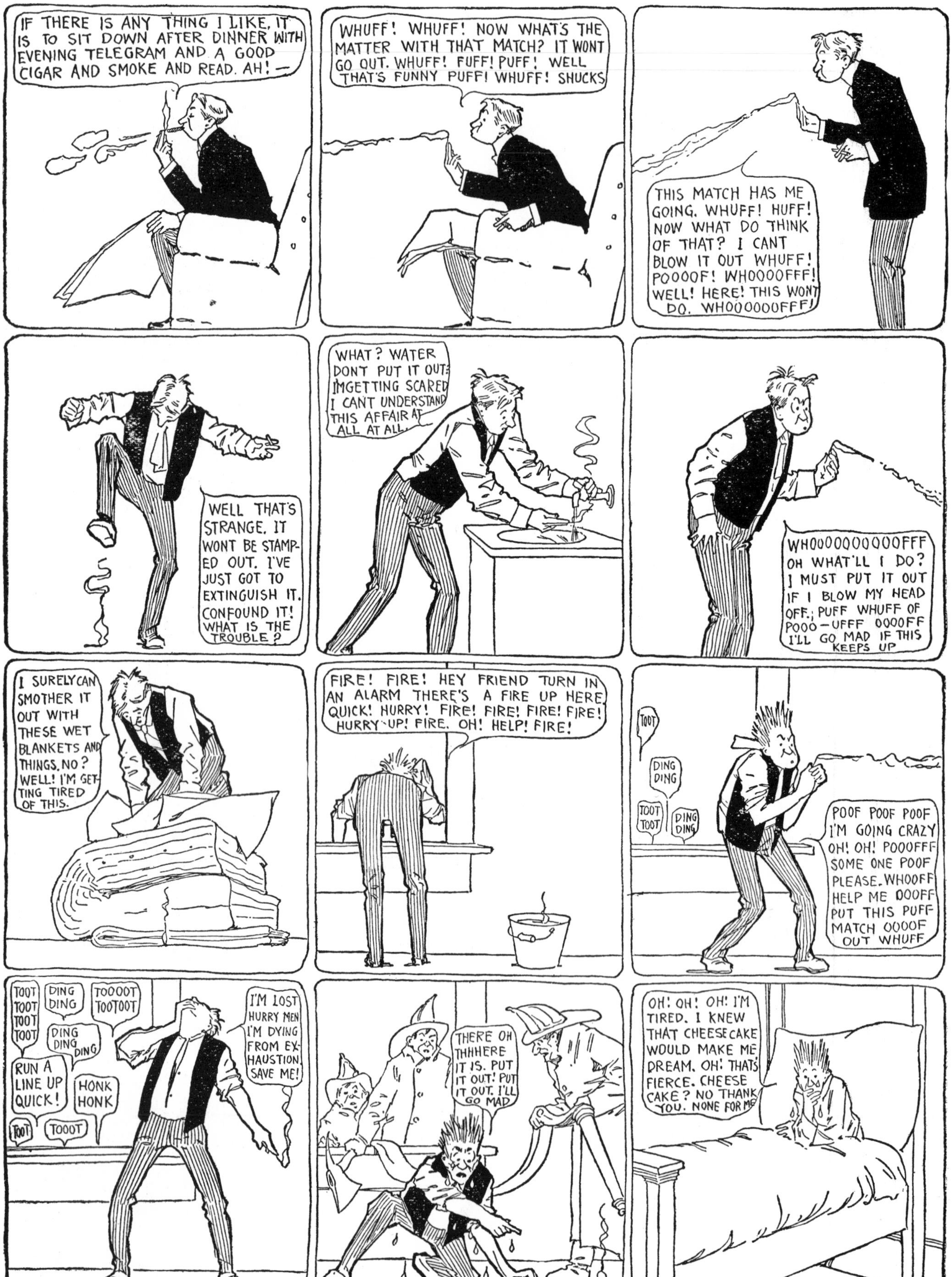
IF THERE IS ANY THING I LIKE, IT IS TO SIT DOWN AFTER DINNER WITH EVENING TELEGRAM AND A GOOD CIGAR AND SMOKE AND READ. AH! —
WHUFF! WHUFF! NOW WHAT'S THE MATTER WITH THAT MATCH? IT WONT GO OUT. WHUFF! FUFF! PUFF! WELL THAT'S FUNNY PUFF! WHUFF! SHUCKS
THIS MATCH HAS ME GOING. WHUFF! HUFF! NOW WHAT DO THINK OF THAT? I CANT BLOW IT OUT WHUFF! POOOOF! WHOOOOFFF! WELL! HERE! THIS WONT DO. WHOOOOOOFFF!
WELL THAT'S STRANGE. IT WONT BE STAMPED OUT. I'VE JUST GOT TO EXTINGUISH IT. CONFOUND IT! WHAT IS THE TROUBLE?
WHAT? WATER DONT PUT IT OUT: IMGETTING SCARED I CANT UNDERSTAND THIS AFFAIR AT ALL AT ALL.
WHOOOOOOOOOOFFF OH WHAT'LL I DO? I MUST PUT IT OUT IF I BLOW MY HEAD OFF. PUFF WHUFF OF POOO—UFFF OOOOFF I'LL GO MAD IF THIS KEEPS UP
I SURELY CAN SMOTHER IT OUT WITH THESE WET BLANKETS AND THINGS. NO? WELL! I'M GETTING TIRED OF THIS.
FIRE! FIRE! HEY FRIEND TURN IN AN ALARM THERE'S A FIRE UP HERE QUICK! HURRY! FIRE! FIRE! FIRE! FIRE! HURRY UP! FIRE. OH! HELP! FIRE!
TOOT
DING DING
TOOT TOOT
DING DING
POOF POOF POOF I'M GOING CRAZY OH! OH! POOOFFF SOME ONE POOF PLEASE. WHOOFF HELP ME OOOFF PUT THIS PUFF MATCH OOOOF OUT WHUFF
TOOT TOOT TOOT TOOT
DING DING
TOOOOT TOOTOOT
DING DING DING
RUN A LINE UP QUICK!
HONK HONK
TOOT
TOOOT
I'M LOST HURRY MEN I'M DYING FROM EXHAUSTION SAVE ME!
THERE OH THHHERE IT IS. PUT IT OUT! PUT IT OUT. I'LL GO MAD
OH! OH! OH! I'M TIRED. I KNEW THAT CHEESE CAKE WOULD MAKE ME DREAM. OH! THATS FIERCE. CHEESE CAKE? NO THANK YOU. NONE FOR ME
SILAS

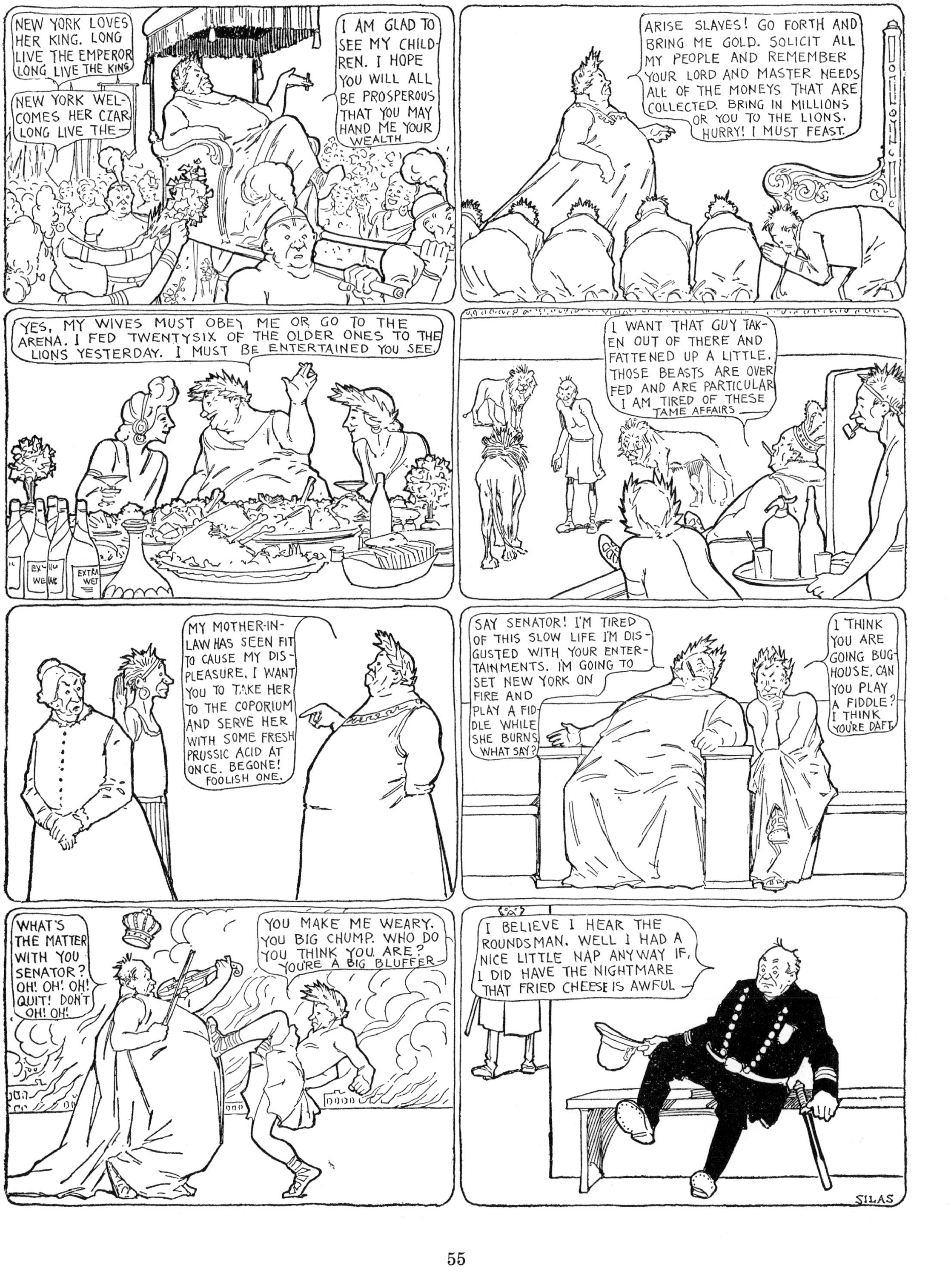
NEW YORK LOVES HER KING. LONG LIVE THE EMPEROR LONG LIVE THE KING
NEW YORK WELCOMES HER CZAR LONG LIVE THE—
I AM GLAD TO SEE MY CHILDREN. I HOPE YOU WILL ALL BE PROSPEROUS THAT YOU MAY HAND ME YOUR WEALTH
ARISE SLAVES! GO FORTH AND BRING ME GOLD. SOLICIT ALL MY PEOPLE AND REMEMBER YOUR LORD AND MASTER NEEDS ALL OF THE MONEYS THAT ARE COLLECTED. BRING IN MILLIONS OR YOU TO THE LIONS. HURRY! I MUST FEAST.
YES, MY WIVES MUST OBEY ME OR GO TO THE ARENA. I FED TWENTYSIX OF THE OLDER ONES TO THE LIONS YESTERDAY. I MUST BE ENTERTAINED YOU SEE.
EXTRA WET
I WANT THAT GUY TAKEN OUT OF THERE AND FATTENED UP A LITTLE. THOSE BEASTS ARE OVER FED AND ARE PARTICULAR I AM TIRED OF THESE TAME AFFAIRS
MY MOTHER-IN-LAW HAS SEEN FIT TO CAUSE MY DISPLEASURE, I WANT YOU TO TAKE HER TO THE COPORIUM AND SERVE HER WITH SOME FRESH PRUSSIC ACID AT ONCE. BEGONE! FOOLISH ONE.
SAY SENATOR! I'M TIRED OF THIS SLOW LIFE I'M DISGUSTED WITH YOUR ENTERTAINMENTS. I'M GOING TO SET NEW YORK ON FIRE AND PLAY A FIDDLE WHILE SHE BURNS. WHAT SAY?
I THINK YOU ARE GOING BUGHOUSE. CAN YOU PLAY A FIDDLE? I THINK YOU'RE DAFT.
WHAT'S THE MATTER WITH YOU SENATOR? OH! OH! OH! QUIT! DON'T OH! OH!
YOU MAKE ME WEARY. YOU BIG CHUMP. WHO DO YOU THINK YOU ARE? YOU'RE A BIG BLUFFER
I BELIEVE I HEAR THE ROUNDSMAN. WELL I HAD A NICE LITTLE NAP ANYWAY IF, I DID HAVE THE NIGHTMARE THAT FRIED CHEESE IS AWFUL
SILAS

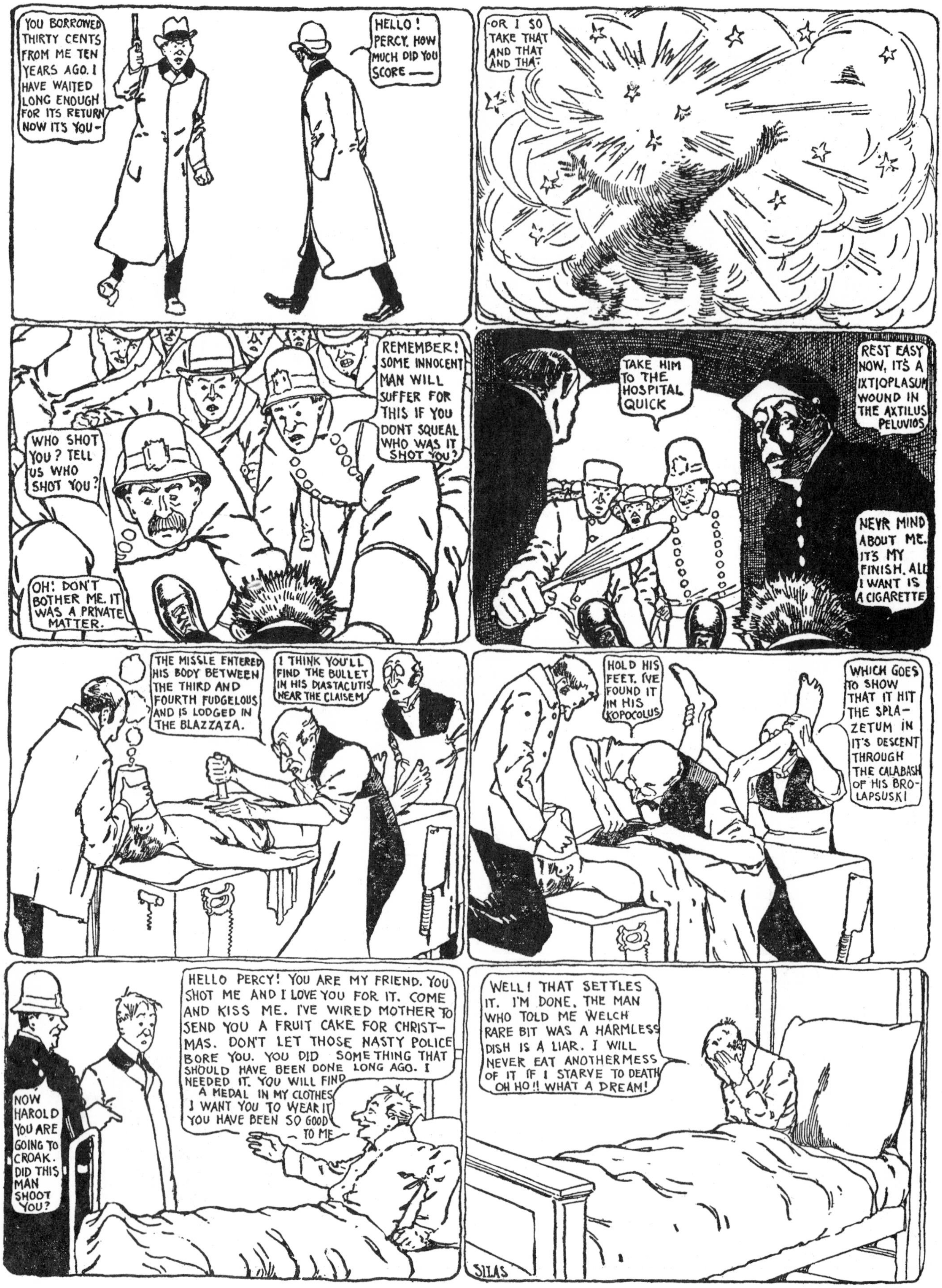
YOU BORROWED THIRTY CENTS FROM ME TEN YEARS AGO. I HAVE WAITED LONG ENOUGH FOR ITS RETURN NOW IT'S YOU-
HELLO! PERCY. HOW MUCH DID YOU SCORE ——
-OR I SO TAKE THAT AND THAT AND THAT.
REMEMBER! SOME INNOCENT MAN WILL SUFFER FOR THIS IF YOU DONT SQUEAL WHO WAS IT SHOT YOU?
WHO SHOT YOU? TELL US WHO SHOT YOU?
OH! DON'T BOTHER ME. IT WAS A PRIVATE MATTER.
TAKE HIM TO THE HOSPITAL QUICK
REST EASY NOW, IT'S A IXTIOPLASUM WOUND IN THE AXTILUS PELUVIOS
NEVR MIND ABOUT ME. IT'S MY FINISH. ALL I WANT IS A CIGARETTE
THE MISSLE ENTERED HIS BODY BETWEEN THE THIRD AND FOURTH FUDGELOUS AND IS LODGED IN THE BLAZZAZA.
I THINK YOU'LL FIND THE BULLET IN HIS DIASTACUTIS NEAR THE CLAISEM
HOLD HIS FEET. I'VE FOUND IT IN HIS KOPOCOLUS
WHICH GOES TO SHOW THAT IT HIT THE SPLAZETUM IN IT'S DESCENT THROUGH THE CALABASH OF HIS BROLAPSUSKI
HELLO PERCY! YOU ARE MY FRIEND. YOU SHOT ME AND I LOVE YOU FOR IT. COME AND KISS ME. I'VE WIRED MOTHER TO SEND YOU A FRUIT CAKE FOR CHRISTMAS. DON'T LET THOSE NASTY POLICE BORE YOU. YOU DID SOMETHING THAT SHOULD HAVE BEEN DONE LONG AGO. I NEEDED IT. YOU WILL FIND A MEDAL IN MY CLOTHES I WANT YOU TO WEAR IT YOU HAVE BEEN SO GOOD TO ME
NOW HAROLD YOU ARE GOING TO CROAK. DID THIS MAN SHOOT YOU?
WELL! THAT SETTLES IT. I'M DONE. THE MAN WHO TOLD ME WELCH RARE BIT WAS A HARMLESS DISH IS A LIAR. I WILL NEVER EAT ANOTHER MESS OF IT IF I STARVE TO DEATH OH HO!! WHAT A DREAM!
SILAS

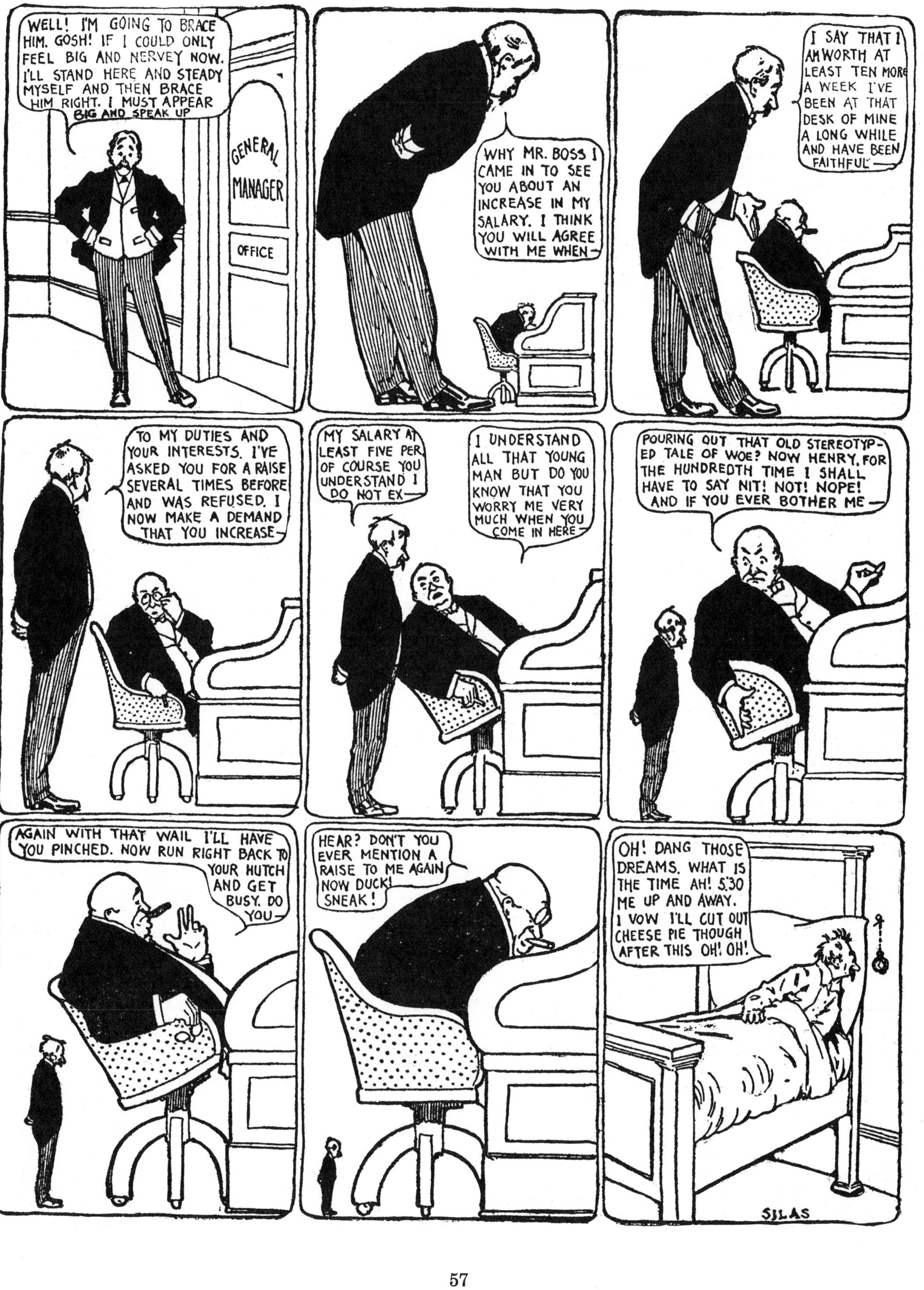
WELL! I'M GOING TO BRACE HIM. GOSH! IF I COULD ONLY FEEL BIG AND NERVEY NOW. I'LL STAND HERE AND STEADY MYSELF AND THEN BRACE HIM RIGHT. I MUST APPEAR BIG AND SPEAK UP
GENERAL MANAGER
OFFICE
WHY MR. BOSS I CAME IN TO SEE YOU ABOUT AN INCREASE IN MY SALARY. I THINK YOU WILL AGREE WITH ME WHEN—
I SAY THAT I AM WORTH AT LEAST TEN MORE A WEEK I'VE BEEN AT THAT DESK OF MINE A LONG WHILE AND HAVE BEEN FAITHFUL—
TO MY DUTIES AND YOUR INTERESTS. I'VE ASKED YOU FOR A RAISE SEVERAL TIMES BEFORE AND WAS REFUSED. I NOW MAKE A DEMAND THAT YOU INCREASE—
MY SALARY AT LEAST FIVE PER OF COURSE YOU UNDERSTAND I DO NOT EX—
I UNDERSTAND ALL THAT YOUNG MAN BUT DO YOU KNOW THAT YOU WORRY ME VERY MUCH WHEN YOU COME IN HERE—
POURING OUT THAT OLD STEREOTYPED TALE OF WOE? NOW HENRY, FOR THE HUNDREDTH TIME I SHALL HAVE TO SAY NIT! NOT! NOPE! AND IF YOU EVER BOTHER ME—
AGAIN WITH THAT WAIL I'LL HAVE YOU PINCHED. NOW RUN RIGHT BACK TO YOUR HUTCH AND GET BUSY. DO YOU—
HEAR? DON'T YOU EVER MENTION A RAISE TO ME AGAIN NOW DUCK! SNEAK!
OH! DANG THOSE DREAMS. WHAT IS THE TIME AH! 5.30 ME UP AND AWAY. I VOW I'LL CUT OUT CHEESE PIE THOUGH AFTER THIS OH! OH!
SILAS

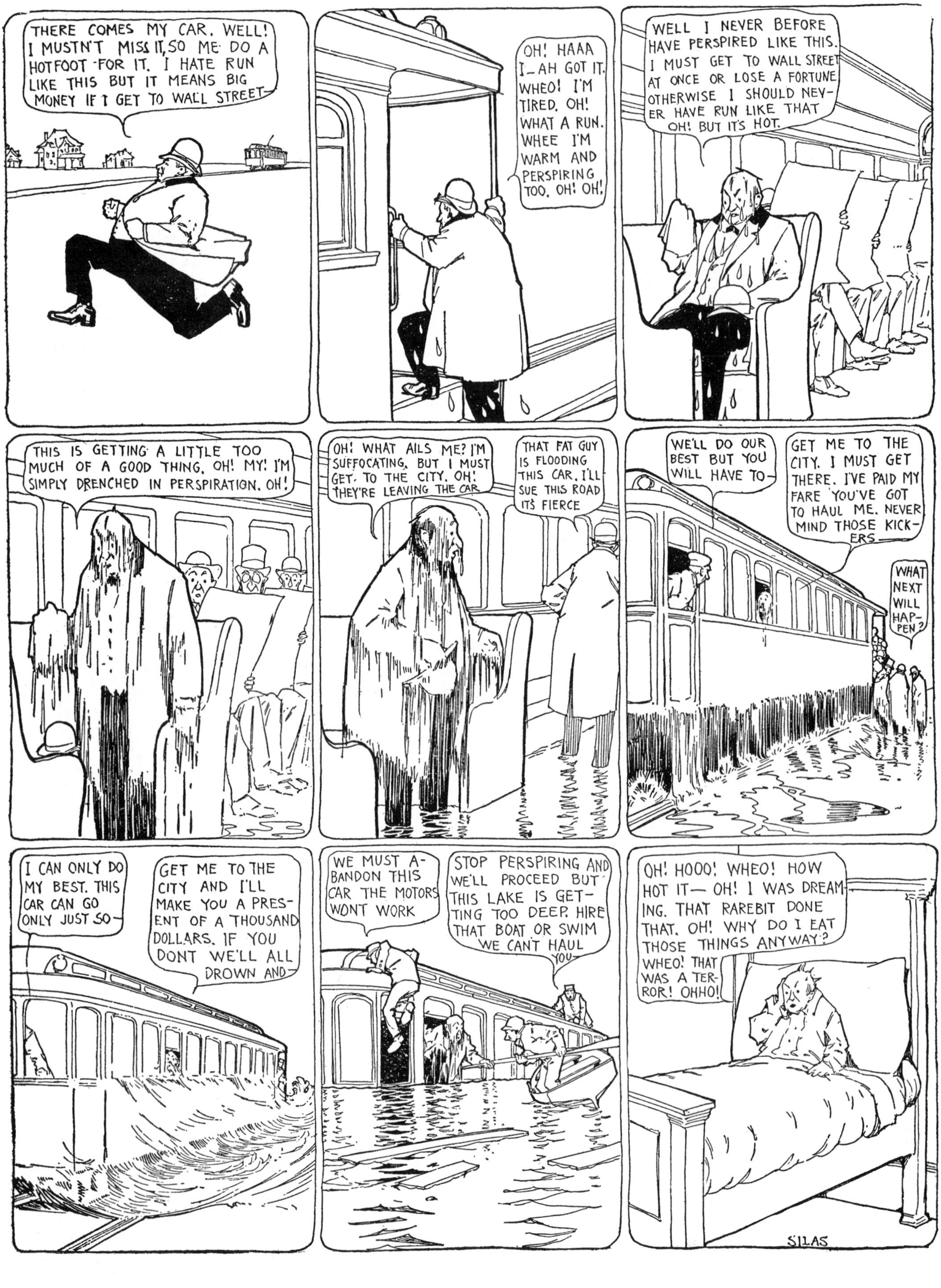
THERE COMES MY CAR. WELL! I MUSTN'T MISS IT, SO ME DO A HOTFOOT FOR IT. I HATE RUN LIKE THIS BUT IT MEANS BIG MONEY IF I GET TO WALL STREET-
OH! HAAA I-AH GOT IT. WHEO! I'M TIRED. OH! WHAT A RUN. WHEE I'M WARM AND PERSPIRING TOO. OH! OH!
WELL I NEVER BEFORE HAVE PERSPIRED LIKE THIS. I MUST GET TO WALL STREET AT ONCE OR LOSE A FORTUNE OTHERWISE I SHOULD NEVER HAVE RUN LIKE THAT OH! BUT IT'S HOT.
THIS IS GETTING A LITTLE TOO MUCH OF A GOOD THING. OH! MY! I'M SIMPLY DRENCHED IN PERSPIRATION. OH!
OH! WHAT AILS ME? I'M SUFFOCATING. BUT I MUST GET TO THE CITY. OH! THEY'RE LEAVING THE CAR
THAT FAT GUY IS FLOODING THIS CAR. I'LL SUE THIS ROAD IT'S FIERCE
WE'LL DO OUR BEST BUT YOU WILL HAVE TO-
GET ME TO THE CITY. I MUST GET THERE. I'VE PAID MY FARE YOU'VE GOT TO HAUL ME. NEVER MIND THOSE KICKERS
WHAT NEXT WILL HAPPEN?
I CAN ONLY DO MY BEST. THIS CAR CAN GO ONLY JUST SO-
GET ME TO THE CITY AND I'LL MAKE YOU A PRESENT OF A THOUSAND DOLLARS. IF YOU DONT WE'LL ALL DROWN AND-
WE MUST ABANDON THIS CAR THE MOTORS WONT WORK
STOP PERSPIRING AND WE'LL PROCEED BUT THIS LAKE IS GETTING TOO DEEP. HIRE THAT BOAT OR SWIM WE CAN'T HAUL YOU-
OH! HOOO! WHEO! HOW HOT IT— OH! I WAS DREAMING. THAT RAREBIT DONE THAT. OH! WHY DO I EAT THOSE THINGS ANYWAY? WHEO! THAT WAS A TERROR! OHHO!
SILAS

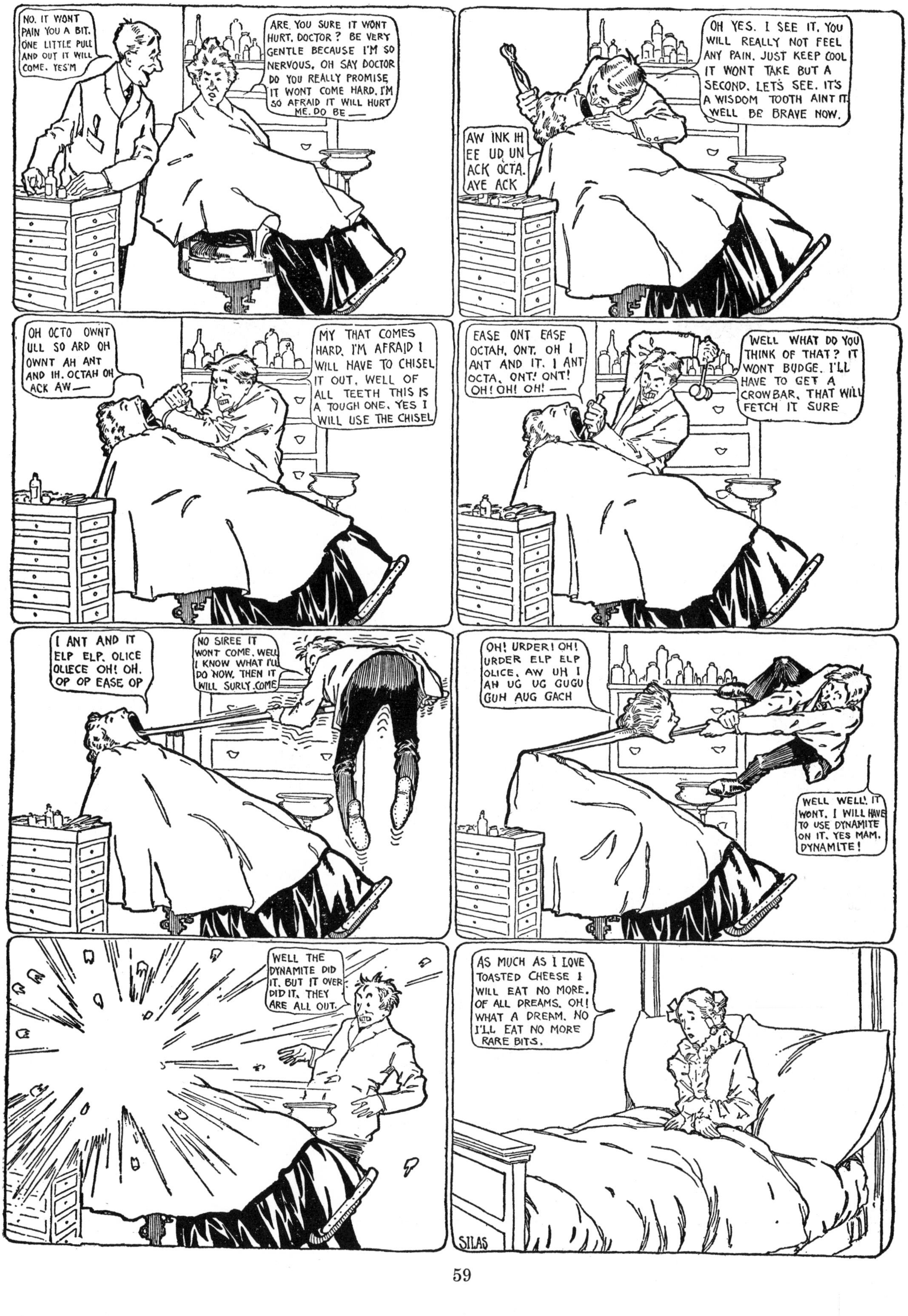
NO. IT WONT PAIN YOU A BIT. ONE LITTLE PULL AND OUT IT WILL COME. YES'M
ARE. YOU SURE IT WONT HURT, DOCTOR? BE VERY GENTLE BECAUSE I'M SO NERVOUS, OH SAY DOCTOR DO YOU REALLY PROMISE IT WONT COME HARD. I'M SO AFRAID IT WILL HURT ME. DO BE —
OH YES. I SEE IT. YOU WILL REALLY NOT FEEL ANY PAIN. JUST KEEP COOL IT WONT TAKE BUT A SECOND. LETS SEE. IT'S A WISDOM TOOTH AINT IT. WELL BE BRAVE NOW.
AW INK IH EE UD UN ACK OCTA. AYE ACK
OH OCTO OWNT ULL SO ARD OH OWNT AH ANT AND IH. OCTAH OH ACK AW —
MY THAT COMES HARD. I'M AFRAID I WILL HAVE TO CHISEL IT OUT. WELL OF ALL TEETH THIS IS A TOUGH ONE. YES I WILL USE THE CHISEL
EASE ONT EASE OCTAH. ONT. OH I ANT AND IT. I ANT OCTA. ONT! ONT! OH! OH! OH! —
WELL WHAT DO YOU THINK OF THAT? IT WONT BUDGE. I'LL HAVE TO GET A CROWBAR. THAT WILL FETCH IT SURE
I ANT AND IT ELP ELP. OLICE OLIECE OH! OH. OP OP EASE OP
NO SIREE IT WONT COME. WELL I KNOW WHAT I'LL DO NOW. THEN IT WILL SURLY COME
OH! URDER! OH! URDER ELP ELP OLICE. AW UH I AH UG UG GUGU GUH AUG GACH
WELL WELL! IT WONT. I WILL HAVE TO USE DYNAMITE ON IT. YES MAM. DYNAMITE!
WELL THE DYNAMITE DID IT. BUT IT OVER DID IT. THEY ARE ALL OUT.
AS MUCH AS I LOVE TOASTED CHEESE I WILL EAT NO MORE. OF ALL DREAMS. OH! WHAT A DREAM. NO I'LL EAT NO MORE RARE BITS.
SILAS

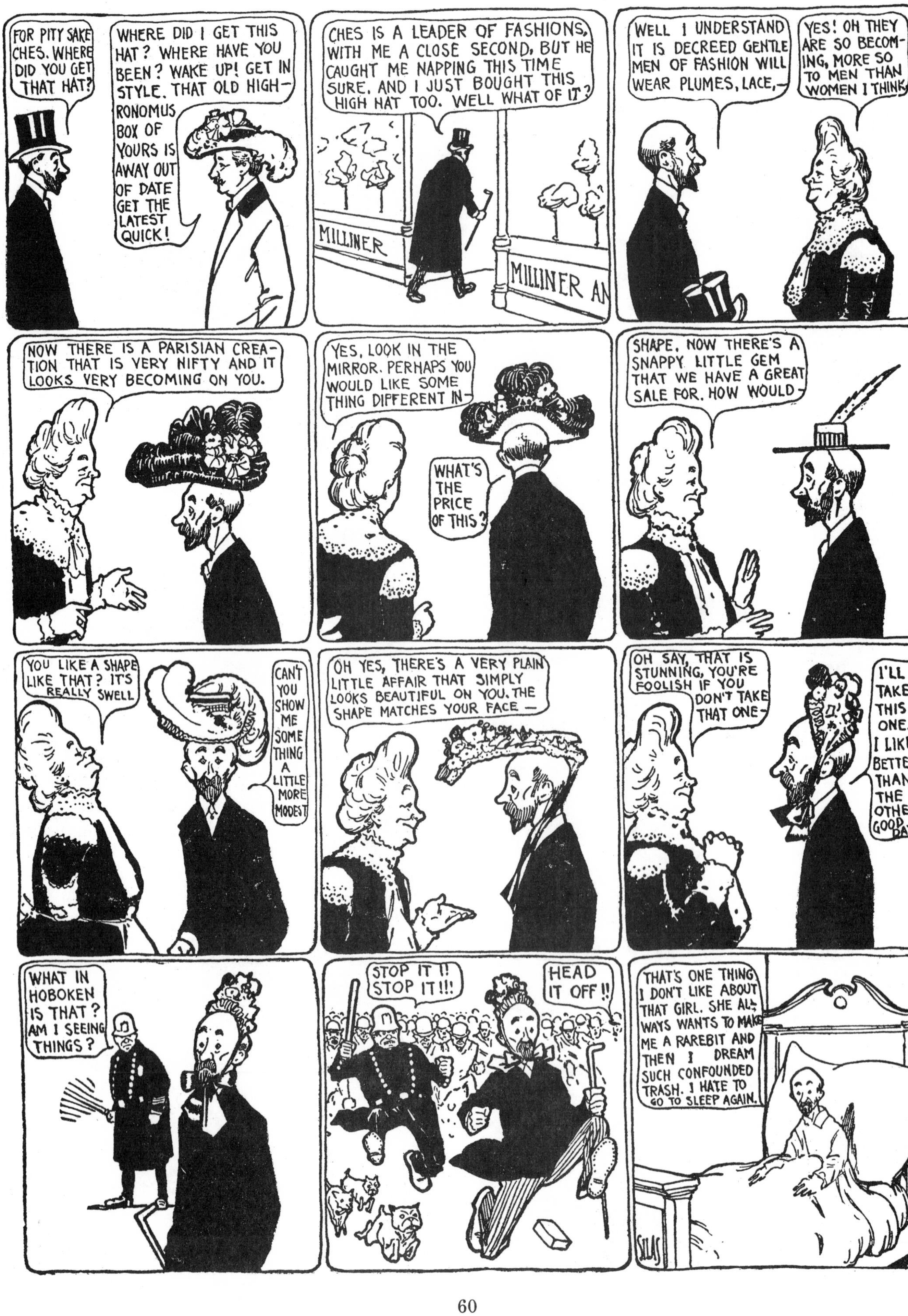

FOR PITY SAKE CHES. WHERE DID YOU GET THAT HAT?
WHERE DID I GET THIS HAT? WHERE HAVE YOU BEEN? WAKE UP! GET IN STYLE. THAT OLD HIGH-RONOMUS BOX OF YOURS IS AWAY OUT OF DATE GET THE LATEST QUICK!
CHES IS A LEADER OF FASHIONS, WITH ME A CLOSE SECOND, BUT HE CAUGHT ME NAPPING THIS TIME SURE. AND I JUST BOUGHT THIS HIGH HAT TOO. WELL WHAT OF IT?
MILLINER
MILLINER AN
WELL I UNDERSTAND IT IS DECREED GENTLEMEN OF FASHION WILL WEAR PLUMES, LACE,—
YES! OH THEY ARE SO BECOMING, MORE SO TO MEN THAN WOMEN I THINK
NOW THERE IS A PARISIAN CREATION THAT IS VERY NIFTY AND IT LOOKS VERY BECOMING ON YOU.
YES, LOOK IN THE MIRROR. PERHAPS YOU WOULD LIKE SOME THING DIFFERENT IN-
WHAT'S THE PRICE OF THIS?
SHAPE. NOW THERE'S A SNAPPY LITTLE GEM THAT WE HAVE A GREAT SALE FOR. HOW WOULD-
YOU LIKE A SHAPE LIKE THAT? IT'S REALLY SWELL
CAN'T YOU SHOW ME SOME THING A LITTLE MORE MODEST
OH YES, THERE'S A VERY PLAIN LITTLE AFFAIR THAT SIMPLY LOOKS BEAUTIFUL ON YOU. THE SHAPE MATCHES YOUR FACE—
OH SAY, THAT IS STUNNING, YOU'RE FOOLISH IF YOU DON'T TAKE THAT ONE-
I'LL TAKE THIS ONE. I LIKE IT BETTER THAN THE OTHERS GOOD DAY
WHAT IN HOBOKEN IS THAT? AM I SEEING THINGS?
STOP IT!! STOP IT!!!
HEAD IT OFF!!
THAT'S ONE THING I DON'T LIKE ABOUT THAT GIRL. SHE ALL-WAYS WANTS TO MAKE ME A RAREBIT AND THEN I DREAM SUCH CONFOUNDED TRASH. I HATE TO GO TO SLEEP AGAIN.
SILAS

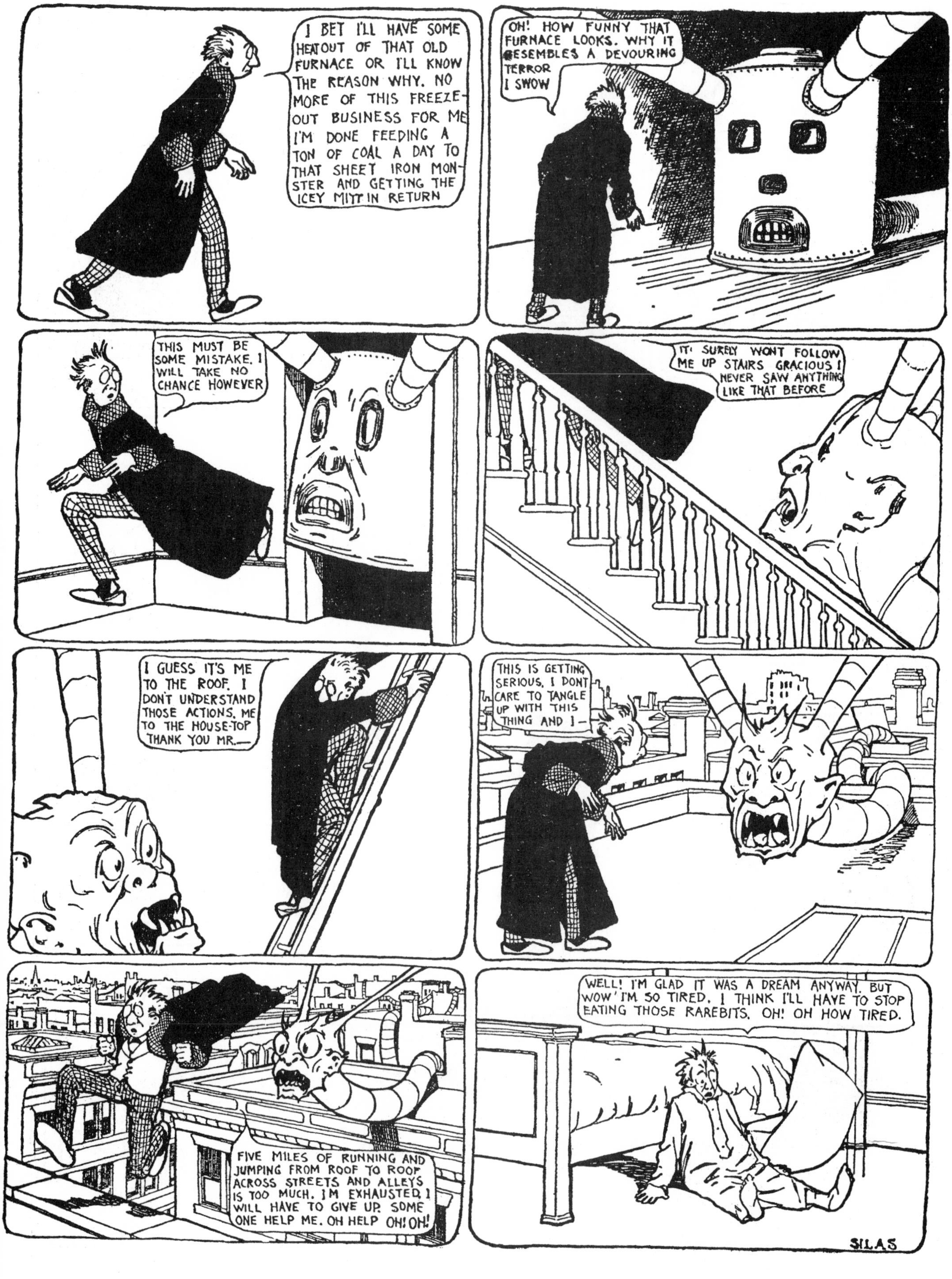
I BET I'LL HAVE SOME HEATOUT OF THAT OLD FURNACE OR I'LL KNOW THE REASON WHY. NO MORE OF THIS FREEZE-OUT BUSINESS FOR ME I'M DONE FEEDING A TON OF COAL A DAY TO THAT SHEET IRON MONSTER AND GETTING THE ICEY MITT IN RETURN
OH! HOW FUNNY THAT FURNACE LOOKS. WHY IT RESEMBLES A DEVOURING TERROR I SWOW
THIS MUST BE SOME MISTAKE. I WILL TAKE NO CHANCE HOWEVER
IT SURELY WONT FOLLOW ME UP STAIRS GRACIOUS I NEVER SAW ANYTHING LIKE THAT BEFORE
I GUESS IT'S ME TO THE ROOF. I DON'T UNDERSTAND THOSE ACTIONS. ME TO THE HOUSE-TOP THANK YOU MR.—
THIS IS GETTING SERIOUS. I DONT CARE TO TANGLE UP WITH THIS THING AND I—
FIVE MILES OF RUNNING AND JUMPING FROM ROOF TO ROOF ACROSS STREETS AND ALLEYS IS TOO MUCH. I'M EXHAUSTED I WILL HAVE TO GIVE UP. SOME ONE HELP ME. OH HELP OH! OH!
WELL! I'M GLAD IT WAS A DREAM ANYWAY. BUT WOW' I'M SO TIRED. I THINK I'LL HAVE TO STOP EATING THOSE RAREBITS. OH! OH HOW TIRED.
SILAS

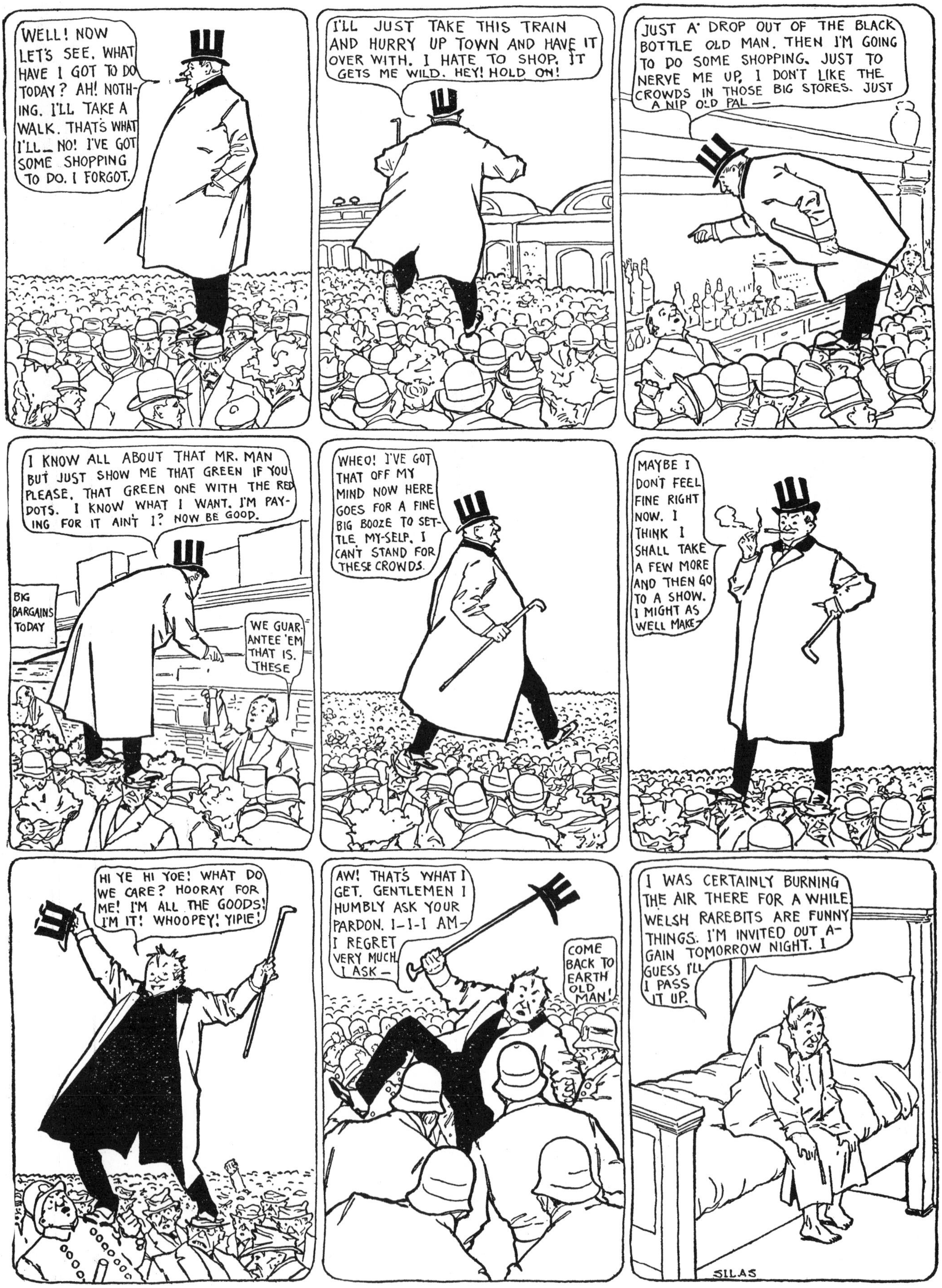
WELL! NOW LET'S SEE. WHAT HAVE I GOT TO DO TODAY? AH! NOTHING. I'LL TAKE A WALK. THAT'S WHAT I'LL_ NO! I'VE GOT SOME SHOPPING TO DO. I FORGOT.
I'LL JUST TAKE THIS TRAIN AND HURRY UP TOWN AND HAVE IT OVER WITH. I HATE TO SHOP. IT GETS ME WILD. HEY! HOLD ON!
JUST A' DROP OUT OF THE BLACK BOTTLE OLD MAN. THEN I'M GOING TO DO SOME SHOPPING. JUST TO NERVE ME UP. I DON'T LIKE THE CROWDS IN THOSE BIG STORES. JUST A NIP OLD PAL —
I KNOW ALL ABOUT THAT MR. MAN BUT JUST SHOW ME THAT GREEN IF YOU PLEASE. THAT GREEN ONE WITH THE RED DOTS. I KNOW WHAT I WANT. I'M PAYING FOR IT AIN'T I? NOW BE GOOD.
BIG BARGAINS TODAY
WE GUARANTEE 'EM THAT IS. THESE
WHEO! I'VE GOT THAT OFF MY MIND NOW HERE GOES FOR A FINE BIG BOOZE TO SETTLE MY-SELF. I CAN'T STAND FOR THESE CROWDS.
MAYBE I DON'T FEEL FINE RIGHT NOW. I THINK I SHALL TAKE A FEW MORE AND THEN GO TO A SHOW. I MIGHT AS WELL MAKE—
HI YE HI YOE! WHAT DO WE CARE? HOORAY FOR ME! I'M ALL THE GOODS! I'M IT! WHOOPEY! YIPIE!
AW! THAT'S WHAT I GET. GENTLEMEN I HUMBLY ASK YOUR PARDON. I-I-I AM- I REGRET VERY MUCH. I ASK—
COME BACK TO EARTH OLD MAN!
I WAS CERTAINLY BURNING THE AIR THERE FOR A WHILE. WELSH RAREBITS ARE FUNNY THINGS. I'M INVITED OUT AGAIN TOMORROW NIGHT. I GUESS I'LL I PASS IT UP.
SILAS